The Story of

J. Breckenridge Ellis

Alpha Editions

This edition published in 2024

ISBN : 9789362926562

Design and Setting By
Alpha Editions
www.alphaedis.com
Email - info@alphaedis.com

As per information held with us this book is in Public Domain.
This book is a reproduction of an important historical work. Alpha Editions uses the best technology to reproduce historical work in the same manner it was first published to preserve its original nature. Any marks or number seen are left intentionally to preserve its true form.

Contents

INTRODUCTION. ....- 1 -

CHAPTER I. ....- 2 -

A KENTUCKY GIRL ....- 2 -

CHAPTER II. ....- 9 -

IDEALS. ....- 9 -

CHAPTER III. ....- 16 -

A KENTUCKY BOY. ....- 16 -

CHAPTER IV. ....- 26 -

A SCHOOL GIRL'S NOTE BOOK. ....- 26 -

CHAPTER V. ....- 33 -

A UNIVERSITY STUDENT. ....- 33 -

CHAPTER VI. ....- 43 -

LOVE AND SACRIFICE. ....- 43 -

CHAPTER VII. ....- 61 -

"I WILL GO." ....- 61 -

CHAPTER VIII. ....- 66 -

AN ENGLISH PRIMROSE.	- 66 -
CHAPTER IX.	- 73 -
THE LONG VOYAGE.	- 73 -
CHAPTER X.	- 79 -
LIFE IN MELBOURNE.	- 79 -
CHAPTER XI.	- 105 -
BUSY YEARS IN AUSTRALIA.	- 105 -
CHAPTER XII.	- 122 -
EXPERIENCES IN TASMANIA.	- 122 -
CHAPTER XIII.	- 129 -
TRAVELS IN THE ORIENT.	- 129 -
CHAPTER XIV.	- 138 -
WORK IN KENTUCKY AND MISSOURI.	- 138 -
CHAPTER XV	- 150 -
LADY PRINCIPAL OF THE UNIVERSITY OF MISSOURI.	- 150 -
CHAPTER XVI.	- 159 -
PURSUING ONE'S IDEAL.	- 159 -
CHAPTER XVII.	- 175 -
ACHIEVING ONE'S IDEAL.	- 175 -

CHAPTER XVIII .... - 190 -

APPENDIX. .... - 197 -

By O. A. Carr. .... - 197 -

FOOTNOTES: .... - 207 -

INTRODUCTION.

The story of any life, if fully portrayed, should be more interesting than the story of a dream-phantom of fiction. In hearing of one who really lived, there is with us the feeling that the sunshine which greets our eyes, the rain which dashes against our window, in brief, the joys and sorrows which like flowers and thistles grow everywhere, were all known to that real character in the world's drama. Therefore, since, in a measure, our experience and his are in common, his life, inasmuch as it touches us at so many points, should lead us into new fields of interest and instruction, as it goes on its way alone.This is true of any life, if we could know it in its entirety. But how much more strikingly true it is found, when the life selected is one that leads from the twilight dawn of infancy to the twilight close of life, in one straight line of definite desire and inspiring achievement. It is the purpose of this book to trace such a life, from the little bed in the nursery, a bed of weakness and tears, to thehuge pile of brick and stone which stands as a monument to that life as if to show what may be accomplished in spite of tears and weakness.In the story of this life will be found stirring scenes and distant travels; romance will not be lacking; here and there the faces of famous men and women will, for a moment, appear; across the bloom of youth and hope will fall the shadows of war. All these realities will be presented in the colors of truth. But something deeper than an interest in connected links of a story is here to be found; it shall be our endeavor to discover the causes that lead to wider activities.In endeavoring to divine, and clearly reveal, the motives that prompt action, we shall try to hold ourselves detached from the subject, finding no fault, and indulging in no encomium, defining beliefs and ambitions, not because they are ours, but because they were those of Mattie Myers, and, to understand her, one must understand them.It will not be sufficient to consider her work, and the opinions of those who knew her, in order to reach the desired result. As far aspossible, she shall speak out herself, out of her old diaries and the abundance of her letters. As her biographer, I would be but the setting to uphold the gem, that it may shine by its own light. And yet, there is no life whose story may be fully understood, unless a knowledge is gained of those other lives with which it comes in contact. In the present story, this truth is of wider significance than one finds in the lives of the majority. Here will be painted scenes as widely separated as Kentucky, Missouri, Texas, Australia, England, and the Levant.

CHAPTER I.

A KENTUCKY GIRL

"I don't believe she's going to live long," said the black nurse, mournfully shaking her head. "She's so thin and weak, and she cries nearly every night!"

The nurse was speaking of little Mattie Myers, who lived in the old Kentucky town of Stanford. The child was seldom to be seen engaged in those sports natural to children. She was grave, quiet, thoughtful. Her one amusement was found in her family of dolls; she was always their teacher, and they were daily going to school to her. For companions, she chose those who were much older than herself, and she would sit by the hour, soberly listening to theological discussion, weighing, in her infant mind, the arguments of learned men.

Her mother was dead, but Mattie could recall her sympathetic touch, and tender smile. It seemed to her that out of the shadow of death her life had emerged, to be clouded by new losses. One after the other, her two sisters were taken from her. Then the brother, who was her only intimate companion, went to another town to teach school. Mattie found herself the only young person in the large house of her wealthy father.

Of course she received all care; her slightest wishes were granted; the love of her widowed father was doubly hers, because of his bereavements. But the little girl was very lonely. When the flowers sent forth their perfume on the warm Kentucky breezes, she was reminded of three graves; and when the sunshine gilded the level pike leading toward Lancaster, she felt as if her brother Joe were calling her to come and nestle against his loving breast.

At every turn, the big house in Stanford reminded her of her mother's footsteps, her sisters' voices forever hushed, and that beloved brother from whom, for the first time, she found herself separated. Is it a wonder that the nights often witnessed her tears? Is it strange that there should have grown up within her, the intense desire to go to her brother? She made this wish known to her father, and her brother seconded her in the plan. Why not stay with Joe during the school year? Then they could spend the vacations at home, together.

Henry Myers, the wealthy and influential father, considered this proposition. He was an ambitious man. He had spared no expense in giving his son a thorough education. He was pleased, now, to find that little Mattie should show a disposition for learning. She was only eight years old, and yet he felt that, in the companionship of her brother, she would find ample protection. Moreover, while a child of eight is usually no fit inmate of a boarding-school, and while it is not best to send one so young, to dwell among strangers, Mattie was no ordinary child.

Nor was her mother an ordinary woman. Mary Burdette possessed a cultured and original mind, related in sympathies to that of her cousin who is known to the world, in the familiarity of affection, as "Bob Burdette." When Mrs. Mary Burdette Myers died, it was supposed that Mattie was too young to appreciate her loss. She could not, of course, appraise that loss at its full value, but its shadow rested upon her girlhood. This death, and that of her sisters, had rendered her serious, had brought enforced reflections upon death and immortality. The letters that she wrote, almost to the days of maturity, are found inclosed in faded little envelopes, which show the black band of mourning.

No, there was no danger in sending Mattie to Lancaster where brother Joe would be her protector. Her father consented.

The ambition to teach school, entertained by one who was a man of means, was a rare thing in the South before the Civil War; or, at any rate, it was rare in Kentucky. Yet that was the ambition of Joe Myers, and to this ambition he devoted his life. He was a natural teacher, and Mattie, who admired him above all others, imitated him in all things. What he liked, she liked, and what he wanted to do, she meant to do. The young man was very fond of music—so was his little sister. He opened up an academy at Lancaster—Mattie established her first school, as we have seen—a college of dolls.

When at last it was decided that Mattie should go to Joe, great was her joy. Some of those few golden hours of childhood, which she afterward recalled, came to her then. She went—the pike had not called in vain—but she did not leave her dolls at home. She boarded with her brother Joe Myers, and her education began in earnest.

"I was only eight," she afterwards said, "when I entered a boarding school; my whole family of dolls matriculated with me."

Lancaster and Stanford were not far apart, though in different counties. It was a short journey to go home Friday evening, and visit there until Monday morning. But of course these visits were not of weekly occurrence.

There was Joe to stay with, and these two never tired of each other's companionship. In the twilight-hours, the young teacher would play his flute, and the little girl would sit listening with all her soul, translating his music into definite resolves. Just as he had given his life to teaching, so would she. She declared her purpose at that age of eight. She would teach a school—a school for girls. It was a purpose she never changed.

Thus the years passed by, in sweet companionship with her brother during the school months, and with the reunited family every summer. Mattie did not grow strong. The black nurse still shook her head. "We never thought she would live!" she often declared, in after years.

In the meantime, Mattie still associated with those who were much older than herself, still found pleasure in discussion of religious differences. We shall find her, at the age of eighteen, saying that most of her friends are married or dead, thus showing that no intimacies existed between herself and girls of her own age.

At twelve, a change came into her life. So thoroughly had she pursued her studies at Lancaster, that it was determined to send her away to college. At that time, the strongest college for girls of her father's faith, was at Harrodsburg, Kentucky. The name of it was "Daughters' College." Mattie's brother and father, justly proud of her attainments, and still resolved to encourage her in her desire to become thoroughly educated, sent her to Harrodsburg to be instructed by John Augustus Williams, the President of "Daughters' College."

Boarding among strangers, now far from home, Mattie found accentuated both her spirit of self-reliance, and her attitude of reserve toward others, two traits always shown in her childhood. The six years at Harrodsburg served to strengthen and deepen her already-preconceived ideals. John Augustus Williams carried on the work that Joe Myers had begun. The Harrodsburg President was as devoted to learning as the Lancaster professor; and he had farther penetrated its depths. He was, indeed, a remarkable man, one who magnified the dignity of his calling, always conscious that the better he succeeded as a teacher, the greater would prove his blessing to the lives of others.

On Sunday we may follow the college girls to church. There goes Mattie Myers, in her solid-green woolen dress, her wonderful suit of hair arranged as plainly as such a wealth of heavy brown will permit. We see the neat and unpretentious hat from under which appear the serious brow, and the eyes always bright and intelligent. We note her reliant step; her form, too thin; her face a little weary from over-hard studying.

Shall we not enter this church on Main street, and watch the young ladies as they seat themselves in a bright oblong of femininity, if not of beauty?

We shall certainly do so, if we are young ministerial students, attending the University! Unfortunately, young Oliver Carr cannot enter with us, for he is still over yonder at May's Lick; but never mind—he will presently be coming down to find out what Latin is like! What happy fortune has brought the University for young men into the same town that affords a college for young ladies? That, too, we shall presently understand.

At any rate, here sits Mattie Myers, decorously listening, it would appear—we hope she is not thinking about her studies—while Dr. Robert Richardson, or Robert Graham, or Robert Milligan—all teachers at the University (among whom "Robert" seems a favorite name)—preaches and preaches. About what? Why, about what we must do to be saved, to be sure. And Mattie listening eagerly—for of course she listens—finds that these distinguished men agree entirely with her father, that what we must do to be saved is very much like what Peter declared we must do—nay, is exactly what Peter declared, to the very words. Far, indeed, is it from the mind of this thin, erect girl in the dress of solid-green, and under the hair whose splendor refuses to be concealed—far is it from her mind that any young man of the Kentucky "froglands" is ever to enter her life as an integral part!

Pres. Jno. Aug. Williams. Daughters College. Harrodsburg Ky

Little time is there for day dreams for this child!—Little time, and no inclination. Study—ever deeper and more persistent study for her; late hours after the lamps are out, sitting in the window with long hair streaming, borrowing favor from the moon—that means spectacles in no very short time! Study—ever more absorbed, and absorbing study, at noon-recess, in early morning, on holidays—till the form grows thinner, the face paler; and, indeed, she had better have a care, or all this will come to an end, with pain and disappointment!

The sermon is nearly ended. Are you sorry you missed it? An hour and a quarter, already! Do the school girls move uneasily in the straight-backed benches? Let us hope they are entertained by this searching examination of sectarian "positions." How new that church building seems to them! Why, it was finished only a few years ago—that is to say, in 1850. There was a time when two bodies of believers met in Harrodsburg; one organized by the followers of Barton Stone, who called themselves "Christians", another the "disciples" who had followed John Smith and John T. Johnson out of the Baptist church. The Christians met from house to house; the "disciples" in the old frame building at the corner of South Main and Depot streets, nearly opposite the public square. Each body was suspicious of the other till, one day, they found out that they taught the same things, believed the same truths, were, in short, blood-brothers of faith and practice. So they came together and formed the church which Mattie is attending. She comes every Sunday; and every Sunday you will find, if you examine her closely, that she is a little paler, a little weaker. Working too hard! The end must come if this is kept up, year after year.

We find the girl subject to an unappeasable hunger for facts. Is she not to devote her life to teaching her sex? Now is the time to store the mind. John Augustus Williams spurs her on, leads her into untold scientific difficulties; lets her realize how little is her strength; then aids by teaching her to help herself. One thing he does not help her do—that is to husband her physical forces. As he stands before his "daughters" in chapel he hammers away at this idea:

"Teaching is woman's profession and her natural vocation. No lady can claim to be well educated, therefore, or trained for her proper sphere in life, until she has learned to teach, and to govern the young. The learning which prepares her for the school-room, prepares her at the same time for the highest social and domestic position. No time is lost by such a training, even should the student never become a professional teacher."

It is no wonder that the enunciation of these ideas strengthened the girl's resolutions. Here was the most learned man she had ever met in daily life, a polished speaker, a graceful author, a correct translator; one who reads the pages of his manuscript, "The Life of John Smith," that his class may parse it;[1] a preacher, too, who pointed the way back to Pentecost. Wisdom flowed from his lips, and his lips proclaimed teaching the "natural vocation" of woman.

And the way in which this teaching was to be done—in a word, his conception of what an education means—that justified his dictum. He said over and over again:

"You have an infallible criterion by which you may determine the success of your own and your teacher's labors. If you feel in your heart a greater susceptibility to truth, a livelier appreciation of the purely beautiful, a profounder regard for virtue, a warmer affection for the good, and sublimer devotion to God, esteem your labors as eminently successful; but if your attainments, varied and extensive as they may be, are to render you less amiable in disposition, or less pure in thought—less charitable to your fellows, or less devoted to God, then have we labored in vain, and your learning, also, has been in vain."

To such a teacher as this, every year is a book written full of sweet influences,—books far deeper and more permanent than any work of the pen. The girl understood this; that is why her determination to be a teacher grew and ripened; not to impart facts but, by means of facts, to inculcate the love of learning and of truth. She wanted to come into touch with the world, and to send the ripple of her personal influence far out into those magic circles of infinite distance, which the casting of an idea forms on the sea of thought. She wanted girls, many girls, countless girls,—to receive a higher view of life by having known her; to enter more fully into the inheritance of their estate through her ministration. No other relation than that of teacher and pupil, could connect this circuit of spiritual influence.

Teachers—the world was full of them in those days, just such as they are now; teachers who bend beneath their burden, who seek in their business but a means of livelihood, and who are ready to lay aside the textbook and close the desk, when fortune smiles: who see their day's end at four o'clock, and their happiness, at the dawn of vacation. But there have always been, of teachers, a few who regarded their work as Williams regarded his, and who, as in Mattie's case, with no spur of necessity, selected it from all careers the future had to offer.

But we do not mean that these highest ambitions of a teacher's sovereign realm took definite shape in the girl's mind in her twelfth year; for see! She is no longer twelve, but thirteen—fourteen— fifteen—how fast she is getting her education!—sixteen—

And then the blow fell—we said it would!—hours too late, and thought too intense, and eyes too severely taxed! Has it been for nothing, after all? She must flutter back home, now, like a disabled bird; high ideas all lost in a maze, definite purposes fused white-hot in a raging fever.

Not only so, but in her sudden breakdown of vital force, there is no one to understand the despair over her own weakness, except, indeed, that brother Joe who alone understands her. Mother and father are both dead, now; and the sisters who are proud of her attainments—for she had finished in the Junior Year at Daughters' College,—wonder that she is not satisfied. Is it not enough? Already she is "educated."

And she is sixteen; and her inheritance assures her of future freedom from necessity. It will be a long time, the doctors say, before she can resume her studies—a year, at least; maybe two. But does that matter? In two years she will be of age, and rich, or nearly so, in her own right.

"And then," said brother Joe, "I will find her a rich husband, and see her handsomely established for life!"

Not that Joe had himself married; he was too busy teaching school, and too absorbed in his beloved work; but he felt the responsibility of his guardianship. Mattie was too ill, too broken in spirit, to combat his plans or to form any of her own. She could only lie silent and, suffering, uncertain of the outcome.

Leaving her thus, as we found her at the beginning, in suffering and tears, let us make a journey to Mason County, in search of that possible husband. He may not prove so rich as brother Joe could desire. We shall see.

CHAPTER II.

IDEALS.

But no, the biographer, on second thought, will not go up to May's Lick in the present chapter. Let that expedition be reserved for Chapter Third. And let those who care for the story of lives merely for events, not for motive-springs of action, skip the present chapter, if they will. It will be to their loss, if they do so; for what life is to be understood, without an understanding of the principles that direct its course?

In the life we are seeking to trace, there were three great principles that shaped events. The first has already been amplified—the resolve to become a teacher of girls. The other two must be defined—one's thought of country, and one's religious faith.

In those days, a man who had no opinion on the "slavery question," or on the "current reformation," was no true Kentuckian. If one has slaves, his children are not only disposed to regard slavery as right, but as highly fortunate and desirable. Also, when one's religion is being placed on trial at every crossroad's log-schoolhouse, the smallest girls in the household have some opinions on the Gospel Restored, on Election, on Baptism.

"Studying too Hard."

"Brother Joe."

In the veins of Mattie Myers flowed Southern blood, and it was with the South that she sympathized with all that fire of young enthusiasm that characterized Southern adherents in those days. As for her religion, that calls for more particular description, because it is indistinguishably blended with all her emotions and purposes. It was no more Mattie's intention to become a teacher of girls, than it was to spread a knowledge of the Gospel as she herself understood it.

In portraying the belief of this child—a belief that time served only to strengthen—it is far from our thought to influence the particular faith of the reader. That biographer is unworthy of his task who allows his own opinions to color his narrative. What I believe has no more to do with the life of Mattie Myers, than has the belief of the reader; and this is the story of a life, not a controversy in disguise.

But at the same time, it is not only due the reader, but the object of the biography, that the faith of Mattie should be presented so clearly and so fairly that no one can fail to understand what it was. I shall do my utmost to make it plain. It occupied too great a part of the girl's life and the woman's life, to be ignored. As she sat at her father's knee in Stanford, as she rested with her brother on the porch of the boarding-house in Lancaster, as she made her stage-journeys, in short, where-ever she was, she heard religion discussed in all its phases. And that phase which appealed to her was the same that Walter Scott—kinsman of the illustrious novelist—had proclaimed from state to state.

One peculiarity of this faith was, that whoever accepted it with zeal, became more or less antagonistic, combative. It was not because it despised peace, although peace, in later years has sometimes proved fatal to it; but it was because every hand seemed turned against it. Had it asked for peace in 1850, that petition would doubtless have been derided.

And why? Because an acceptance of this faith meant an end to all creeds, to all sects, to all denominational barriers. Therefore all denominations felt that the faith of Mattie Myers had raised its hand against them. When Walter Scott and his co-workers prayed the Savior's prayer that all might be one, what—if that prayer be granted—was to become of the *many*?

It may be true, in the Twentieth Century, that one need only have enough money to hire a hall, in order to start a new religion; that Society has but to smile upon the dancing of Dervishes to popularize Orientalism; that a woman, by the writing of a book, can convince intelligent thousands that diseases are but delusions of their mortal minds—perhaps instincts would be a better word, since unimaginative quadrupeds sometimes "think" themselves sick. But whether this is true or not, it is certain that, in the first half of the Nineteenth Century, it required much more than money, and more than the writing of many books, this endeavor to re-establish the old religion of Pentecost. It called for courage, firmness and ability; it invited persecution and misrepresentation.

"I would rather," an aunt of Oliver Carr once declared—herself a stern soldier of the Cross—"see you go to your grave, than have you join the Campbellite Church!"

What was this "Campbellite Church" of which some spoke thus disparagingly? And why "Campbellite"? And why did the denominations regard the people they thus designated much as, at a later day, the Mormons were regarded? Before we enter into details, it is enough at this point to emphasize the fact of general intolerance. To worship God in your own way is the right of all; and no man disputes that inborn right, so long as you agree with him in your religious belief. The Puritans were ready to sacrifice their lives to preserve religious freedom, and to take the lives of those who desired a separate freedom.

In the first half of the Nineteenth Century, more especially in the first quarter, the jangling and wrangling among different sects was almost inconceivable. It would appear that often where differences of tenets were but slight, the fight was the more determined, as if the possibility of preserving a denominational integrity, depended largely upon keeping alive a spirit of hostility to all other denominations. Happily that spirit of antagonism has largely died out, and men are not so ready to take each other by the throat because they are seeking to gain Heaven by different ways. This tendency to minimize differences of speculative opinions, and to draw close to each other on the fundamental truths as they are revealed in the life, death and resurrection of Jesus Christ, is doubtless in a large measure due to the pioneers of that faith which Mattie Myers had accepted, and which, at the time of her acceptance, was the object of so much bitterness and ridicule.

Thirty years had already passed since Walter Scott and Alexander Campbell first proclaimed their views in the "Christian Baptist." The distracted state of the religious world had grieved many a pious and erudite soul before 1819. In looking for a solution to the amazing perplexities that baffled the seeker after God, in trying to avoid the anomalous condition of changing a gospel of love to a gospel of interminable disputation, the solution proposed by Thomas Campbell was a return to the practices and faith of the early disciples. This solution was urged by Walter Scott and Alexander Campbell. What more simple? Everybody should be willing to accept the Bible; everybody should be willing to discard everything else!

In brief, then, that was the work of the "current reformation." It would call for a sacrifice of individual opinions, of sectarian names and dogmas, of that poetic atmosphere which time bestows upon any organization, of those intimate human associations derived from a commingling with relatives and friends whom a common rule of practice holds together. As a recompense for this sacrifice, was offered the privilege of returning to the Apostolic faith and manner of worship, the sense of security that should spring from following closely in the footsteps of the earliest disciples, and the privilege of performing one's part in the realization of the prayer of the Savior of mankind.

Alexander Campbell's life was given to this fundamental idea—that the world should go back, in its religious beliefs and practices, nineteen hundred years, to learn again the conditions of its salvation from the lips of Christ's apostles. Campbell himself, was but a voice calling in the wilderness. He seemed always to be crying, "Look back! Behold the Lamb of God!" As for himself, he would have been but the medium through which an enlightened vision might see that glorious spectacle of God in man. "Do not regard me," he seemed to say, "For I am nothing. I am but a voice—a voice proclaiming no new doctrine, only the old; asking you not to originate a new faith, but to remember the old. Look back! Behold the Lamb of God!"

But the world did not wish to look back. It exclaimed that these people who pretended to do away with all sects, were themselves the narrowest sect of all. These preachers who proclaimed that there was but one church, were accused of "wanting to get us into their church." The result was endless debates. We have seen that the denominations were at war with one another; but all of them became more or less cohesive, in their attack upon these people who claimed to be no denomination.

If Campbell and his friends urged that baptism should be administered as in the days of the Apostles, the cry was immediately raised that "These men believe in nothing but baptism." If their editors asked for an instance of infant baptism between the lids of the Bible, it was retorted that "They have only a head religion—they don't believe in a change of heart." If a preacher said no more about baptism than did Peter on Pentecost, his listeners went away observing that "he believed water would save him." If nothing was said about baptism, if on the contrary, the discourse were concentrated upon the idea that all Christians should follow the same rule and practice, should dwell together in one great homogeneous body, it was charged, "That is really another way of saying that immersion is the only mode of baptism." If, by dint of innumerable repetitions, Herculean efforts at self-restraint, monotonous insistence, these "reformers" succeeded in convincing the antagonist of the fact that nobody believed water would save him, and every Christian believes in a change of heart, all this laborious and indefatigable endeavor went for nothing.

"Well, maybe you do believe in a change of heart," it would at last be conceded, "but your church don't." Or "Maybe *you* don't believe water will save you, but your church does."

Such as the views of the disciples of Christ really were, Mattie Myers had received them at first hand. Her father was one of the "new faith." His home had from her earliest recollections, been a rallying point for the sturdy pioneers of the "Old Jerusalem Gospel." In that home, "Raccoon" John Smith and Barton W. Stone had held her upon their knees. She had seen Walter Scott and Alexander Campbell in childhood, and had heard L. L. Pinkerton's eloquence, and Robert Milligan's logic. She knew the matters debated, the arguments that sustained each side in its opinion,—and she could point out the verse of scripture that seemed to substantiate every claim of her friends, and to confound those of the enemy. And she knew how families had become divided; how bitterness crept in between life-long friends; how misunderstanding led to misrepresentation, and argument to vilification, and disapproval to hatred.

Whatever else the plea of the disciples accomplished, it led to a closer study of the scriptures; and to a fuller admission of their authority. This was inevitable because the adherents of what was disparagingly called the "new religion," based all their positions upon the Word of God. Even farther than that they went, in declaring that they entertained no doctrine not fully presented in the New Testament; they were willing to relinquish any belief, no matter how dear, on being shown that it was not divinely authorized.

It was futile to meet such claims by references to any other book than that of the inspired writers, unless those books were lexicons and dictionaries devoted to an explanation of biblical terms. To the lexicons, the friends and enemies of the "reformation" did indeed go. There were times when, if Polycarp, or Chrysostum, or even Sophocles, or Plato, could have stepped into the debating-room, he might have fancied himself just awakened from his long sleep, to hear confused murmurs in his native tongue.

Under this awful weight of learning, the brain sometimes staggered. To the imprudent, to the rash, to the over-zealous, vital truths might, at times, be half-obscured, in showing the eunuch as he went down into the water—*eis*, into; ah! shall we ever forget that *eis* with its suggestion of the cooling tide?—Into the water, then, the eunuch descended; and good care was taken that he should not be left there. The jailer, too,—was there no water in the courtyard? And Lydia's household—what right has one to presume her mistress over a nursery? At these debates, even the eloquent Henry Clay may act as moderator, generously appreciative of the eloquence of A. Campbell. So, as we have said, the theme may at times grow obscured with a sort of Greek mist; but out of this mist there rises, at last, a face of meekness and suffering beneath its crown of thorns—a crown of thorns, dear reader, which the Son of God wore that you and I might wear crowns of glory.

It is interesting to note that here is a religion which its opponents refused to take at its face value. Its adherents wished to be called only by Bible names, such as Christians, or disciples of Christ. Their opponents called them "Campbellites." These disciples claimed that they had gone back to the days of the beginning of the church, to find there the true standard of faith and practice. Their opponents said they had started a new religion, and that it dated from the days of Alexander Campbell. The disciples said that they added nothing to the Word of God, took from it nothing; that where the Bible was silent they were silent, that where it spoke they spoke; that, in matters of opinion, everyone might think what he pleased, but that, in matters of essentials, there should be unity. The opponents said that as a matter of fact, the religion of the reformers was a religion of the head, and that its central idea was baptism.

"You do not believe that baptism is necessary to salvation," the disciples said; "then why do you baptize?"

"Aha!" the old cry was raised, "you think water will save you!" And then the begrudged concession, "Well, if *you* don't believe it, your church does!"

In a word, then, the individual adherents of the religion were allowed to hold opinions contrary to what the adherents as a whole, were supposed to believe; while, at the same time, not one adherent of the religion could be found who professed to hold the views that the opponents of the religion ascribed to all the brotherhood! This was not from a willful determination to misrepresent, but rather from a sense of generous good-will. It was the only way to rescue one's kindred and friends from the inevitable hell that awaits the adherents of heretical doctrines.

"Tom is a good man," said a devout adherent of the established order of things, referring to minister Thomas Arnold of the Kentucky disciples, "but he preaches a lie and will be damned for it!" And the way to save one's beloved from this damnation was to believe that they did not really hold the views of these Ishmaelites of the "new religion," but were "Baptists at heart"—or Pedobaptists, according to one's point of view.

Thomas Campbell's "Declaration and Address" appeared in 1809; but it was not until September, 1832 that the first general meeting of the disciples of Christ was held, in Lexington, Kentucky. Everyone understood that such an assemblage had no authority over local organizations. Christian soldiers came together to talk over their victories and defeats, and to plan for fresh campaigns. As time passed by, such men as John T. Johnson and John I. Rogers were appointed state evangelists; but they were supported by several churches combining to furnish the funds.

At the time Mattie Carr was boarding at her brother's school, there was no general board behind missionary enterprises. But later a convention met at Harrodsburg and employed four evangelists; that was in 1857. The next year sixteen were employed, and in a year they won 1,936 converts to the church. The year following, twenty evangelists added to the faith 2,020. The "new religion" was growing at an unheard of rate, and the more it grew the hotter raged the noise of battle and the clash of arms.

It is in such circumstances as these that one learns to weigh one's own opinion, to use it, if need be, as a battering-ram against the opinions of other folk; that one learns to realize the importance of self-reliance, self-defense, self-assertion. Before Mattie Myers was twelve years old, the leading purposes of her after-life were already crystalized in thought and determination. It will be interesting to watch how she adhered to these principles, and whither they brought her at last. As we have said, they were three in number, more or less commingled in her girlhood's plans of life; an unwavering devotion to the South; a fixed resolve to become a teacher of girls; and a conviction that the plea of the disciples of Christ was the need of the world.

CHAPTER III.

A KENTUCKY BOY.

It was while the black nurse was doubtfully shaking her head over the prospect of a long life for Mattie Myers, that two boys presented themselves at the village schoolhouse of May's Lick, Kentucky. They were two brothers who resembled each other so closely, and were so inseparable, that they were often thought to be twins. Oliver Carr, however, was two years younger than Owen[2]. They had come up from the country in the old family barouche, and the fact that they were from the country, was shown in their movements and their dress.

Their father, while still on the farm in Lewis County, had declared, "I will educate my children, if I don't leave them a cent when I die." That is why he sold his farm to invest the proceeds in town property at May's Lick; and that is why Owen and Oliver are presenting themselves at the door of May's Lick Academy. The family that had just moved to town, consisted of William Carr and his wife, and their four sons and three daughters. Of the children, the only one essential to this narrative is he who gave his name to the teacher as Oliver A. Carr—better known in his family and among his young companions as "Ollie."

The year was 1857. Of all the proud towns of Kentucky—proud of blood and wealth—no city was prouder than May's Lick. Not even Lexington, five counties to the southwest, thought more of her high birth, her fine horses, her opulence, than did this little May's Lick of Mason County. The schoolmates of the Carrs were the children of the wealthy. The boys came to school in red-topped boots, riding prancing ponies, and were waited upon by their black bodyguards. The girls were, petted, and spoiled, clad in dainty apparel, born to refinement and a nicety of taste, intolerant of whatever appeared to their sensitive minds as "common." Nor was this superiority of manner merely superficial. Beneath the gleam of showy beauty, there was the gold of culture.

Naturally enough, these children of the rich, whether on the play-ground, or in the school-room, stood aloof from Owen and Oliver,—or as they were called "Bud and Ollie." In the first place, they were newcomers; again, they were awkward and their clothes were made from the same piece of their mother's weaving; and their father had purchased one of the two hotels in town. "He works, himself!" it was said, with pity, or contempt.

And the sentiment against William Carr because his work was not done by slaves, was reflected against his seven children.

But William Carr, rugged and unyielding, firm in his belief that education would place his boys and girls on a footing with the best, conducted the hotel, while his wife, patient and tireless, sewed long after the hours of the day's inevitable work were ended. To clothe and educate seven children while all the time one's cashier is stealing systematically—that is the problem!

It is a problem that little concerns the lads of the red-topped boots and prancing ponies, or the girls of fine laces,—still less the fathers of these; for all their spare time is spent in reminiscences of Henry Clay, and in defining differences between the North and South—for this is 1857, as we have said, and in a few years something may happen.

But it is not given to every boy to wear red-tops, nor to every girl, real lace. Of course there were other families falling under the supercilious classification of "those who do their own work." At such times as the Carrs were not studying, or reciting to L. P. Streater, or helping at home, companions were to be found, to bear a hand at a game of marbles. Oliver had the genius of making friends; and, when no artificial barriers interposed, his gentle nature thawed the ice in natures most reserved.

Sometimes it happened that, as Oliver and his friends were engaged in sports along the roadside, they would see a venerable man drawing near, smooth faced, broad browed, stately in bearing, kindly in expression. If it chanced to be a time of heated altercation, the warning would go round—

"Hush! hush! There comes Brother Walter Scott."

The old man would pause with, "Well, dears, how do you do, this nice morning? Are you on your way to school?"

Then he would pat one on the head, and say a pleasant word to all. In his presence ill-humor melted away, and evil purposes were corrected. It was not only so with the school boys, but with their fathers. His very presence seemed a rebuke to wrong-doing and wrong-thinking. Sometimes he came to the Academy and addressed the pupils. Oliver stood at the head of the class in mathematics. One day after reciting geometry, "Elder" Scott, as he was called—or "Brother" Scott—said, with that gracious smile which lent the aspect of perennial youth to his wrinkled face,

"Young gentlemen, you have made good progress in Euclid." It was the first time Oliver had ever heard of Euclid, but he knew the enunciation of every proposition in the first five Books, and had drawn the figures with elaborate care on his father's barn door! But he had not studied Latin.

"That language," said his practical father, "is dead!"

The almost daily meeting with Walter Scott was one of those formative influences, unperceived at the time, which help to shape one's ideals. Let us look for a moment at this benign figure with his gentle smile, his keen, penetrating glance, and his still almost raven-black locks. He had brought to the Kentucky village an atmosphere of the great outside world, for he was a man who had not only come in touch with the great and illustrious, but who had himself participated in great affairs.

It meant much to the young mathematician at May's Lick Academy, this daily intercourse with such a man. It inevitably raised his mind above the daily toil, the unstimulating routine of a small town; it gave him a certain outlook upon a wider life, suggesting higher things than had hitherto entered his experience.

This venerable Walter Scott—he who had held little Mattie Myers upon his knee—was a man in whose veins flowed the blood of Wat, of Hardin—most illustrious of Scottish heroes. He was kin to the creator of *Ivanhoe* and *Rebecca*; a man who had graduated from the University of Edinburg; who had sailed the seas and traveled in many distant scenes; whose music instructor had been the friend of Sir Ralph Abercrombie; who had been by turn teacher, preacher, editor, author; who had traversed the circular avenues of poplars and pines leading to the mansion-house of Henry Clay, trees "which made me fancy myself once more in Scotia",—and who had sat in Clay's parlor in charming intercourse with the statesman while the portrait of Washington looked down, and the elegant simplicity of the apartments presented nothing "to make poor men afraid, or rich men ashamed;" who had ridden on the steamboat with the distinguished companionship of General Schuyler's daughter, the widow of Alexander Hamilton, then in her eighty-fourth year; who had visited the home of Colonel Richard M. Johnson; and who, finally, had come to May's Lick to pass the remainder of his days.

It was natural enough that the very sight of this man should suggest to the studious youth, thoughts of greatness and of travel. His kinship to Sir Walter Scott and his familiarity with the lands beyond the seas, no doubt lent him a sort of halo, to the imagination of boyhood. But it must have done more than this; it must have suggested that one need not remain poor and unknown; and that, as Walter Scott, when a poor young man had lifted himself above his condition by means of his education, so might Oliver Carr.

The postoffice was in William Carr's hotel. William was the postmaster, and during vacation, or at intervals, Oliver served as deputy. After the arrival of the mail, the distinguished scholar, Walter Scott, would appear at the counter with his benignant smile, and his "Dear—" he called all young people thus—"Dear, is there anything for me, this morning?"

And Oliver was as pleased as he, when there was a *Louisville Courier* to hand his friend, or a letter from Ohio, or Pittsburg, or New York.

There remains a word to be said as to what this Walter Scott was; for, after all, where one has traveled, or whom one has met, speaks little of the inner self; and it was this personal value of the man that counted most with those he met.

It was in 1819 that Walter Scott landed in New York, and began teaching Latin in Long Island—diverting himself with his flute at the close of the day. But he soon felt the call of the West, and obeyed it afoot. It brought him to Pittsburg, where he found himself drawn into school work again. He became an assistant in the Academy conducted by Mr. Forrester, a fellow-countryman. Scott had been reared in the Presbyterian faith, and his soul had been perfectly satisfied in those religious grounds staked off by his denomination's creed. He had not associated long with Forrester before he found to his amazement that the latter, though apparently of sincere piety, did not subscribe to all the articles; but, instead of seeking to attack the Confession with the Discipline or the Prayer Book, had recourse to the Bible. Not only so, but Forrester professed himself ready to give up any article of faith that did not appear fully warranted by the Scriptures; or, in other words, he had resolved to be guided in religious matters by the Bible alone.

It is difficult for one of the present day to realize how radical, unheard of, and unorthodox, such a determination as Forrester's appeared in the year 1819. It is true that men here and there, in places far removed from one another, were beginning to weary of the burden of the creeds; they were reaching out to grasp something that might pull their feet from the shackles of doubt or predetermined damnation, and in desperate blindness they seized upon the Word of God as likely to prove of most avail. It was, indeed, heresy; for if all had deserted creeds for the Bible, what would have become of the creeds? In Luther's day it had been heretical to decry Indulgences; if a Baptist, it was heretical not to believe "in the peculiar and eternal election of men and angels to glory," and "in a particular redemption of a definite number of persons to eternal life," and "the final perseverance of the saints in grace to the end."

Walter Scott felt no hesitation in joining Forrester in his studies of the New Testament, secure in the belief that nothing could be found there, inconsistent with his creed; henceforth, we find him sitting far into the night, no longer solacing himself with the music of his flute, but studying the Bible with ever greater and greater perplexity; studying it as diligently as ever he had studied the Confession; studying it with increasing uneasiness, as it seemed to lead him from the faith of his fathers.

There was, at that time, no body of associated men who had agreed to surrender all creeds, and take the Bible as their only guide. There were isolated examples of such men. Alexander Campbell, of whom Walter Scott had never heard, had been forced by his convictions from the Presbyterian church into the Baptist association. Not long after the beginning of Scott's explorations into this dimly-known field of original research, he and the celebrated scholar met; but neither had a thought of breaking away from the accepted religious bodies; the only question was to find the one nearest approximating the truth, and to seek reformation within that body.

The result of that effort to bring back the primitive church upon earth, is seen today in the church of the disciples of Christ. This is not the place to argue the feasibility of the plea, or to adduce arguments against it. But what that plea was, should be presented clearly and dispassionately. It is not the office of the biographer to point out the right or wrong of his subject's dominating ideas, so much as it is to show how the life was influenced by those motive-springs of thought.

Walter Scott, as an evangelist, pastor, author and editor, had come into contact with tens of thousands, and had influenced countless lives. His followers were called by the unsympathetic, "Scottites," just as those of Alexander Campbell were nicknamed "Campbellites." Thomas and Alexander Campbell and Walter Scott, the triumvirate of the dawning "Reformation," did not come, however, to found denominations, but, so far as they could, to do away with them.

They believed that it was possible for the church of New Testament days to exist in the modern world, just as it had existed then. They believed that the means of entering the church now, are what they were then; that Christ's conditions were in their very nature of divinity, unalterable. As Peter preached on the day of Pentecost, so Walter Scott preached in the Nineteenth Century. As Cornelius and the jailer and the eunuch and Lydia and all other recorded instances of sinners converted in olden times, so man today, in turning to God, must turn as they turned, come as they came, obey as they obeyed.

And if the old order should be restored, there would be but one order in the earth; but one Faith, one Lord and one Baptism. The saints would sit down to one table from which no saint would be excluded; they would join their hymns of undenominational ecstasy, and, if they did not see every subject exactly alike, they would at least agree in their contemplation of essentials. After all, the important matter seemed to be, to get safely into the church, and to stay in it; and if all entered in the same way, the way the apostles had taught, and then dwelt in harmony, not as Presbyterians and Baptists and Episcopals and Methodists, whose very names appeared to draw lines, whether the lines were definitely understood or not—this ideal body would be simply disciples of Christ, or Christians, as they had been eighteen hundred years ago. Then indeed would a shout of thanksgiving go up from the earth, that the prayer of Jesus had been answered; not only his apostles but all those who now believed on his name, had become one; one in thought and love and life; one as he and the Father were one, eternal, indivisible.

Whether or not the reader believes such a union possible, or desirable, it will surely call for no great task of the imagination upon his part, to enter somewhat into the thrilling rapture this picture presented to the hearts of the early "reformers." One feels his heart leap with a sympathetic throb when men who had dreamed of such a return to the old paths, but who had dreamed of it in solitude, not knowing it had found a voice in the earth—suddenly heard it pronounced from the pulpit. Men who had brooded in seclusion over their Bibles, finding there, as it appeared to them, sublime statements antagonistic to sectarianism, were suddenly transfixed by hearing the words of old, "Believe on the Lord Jesus Christ, and thou shalt be saved!" It seemed to them that the "Old Gospel" was once more sounding in the land. On a visit to Missouri, Walter Scott met an eminent preacher, Moses E. Lard.

"You do not know me," said Lard, as he threw his arm about the other; "but you are the man who first taught me the Gospel."

"How so!" the other inquired.

"It was reading your book—'The Gospel Restored,'" was the answer.

That is how this movement appeared to those who came under its influence,—the Gospel must be restored. The preachers proclaimed and debated from the rostrum, and pulpit, and on horseback. The laymen talked about it on the street, and in the field, ready at any moment to draw the Bible from their pockets to show just what the "Old Jerusalem Gospel" had to say for itself. The women discussed regeneration and baptism over their sewing and knitting. The children taunted each other at school and at play, and the swaggering bully might say to the despised "Campbellite," "*We* believe in a change of heart!" or "*You* believe water will save you!"

Such taunts, however, did not assail the young Carrs, for their parents belonged to no church, and their grandparents and numerous relations were Presbyterians and Methodists. Oliver's teacher, L. P. Streator, was a disciple of Christ; his life, as well as that of Walter Scott, were arguments, in their way, for the "new religion"; but after all, Oliver had thought little of religion during his first years at the Academy. Martin Streator, his teacher's son, persuaded him to attend the Sunday-school at the Christian church; he went once or twice, and then tried the Baptist Sunday-school to find out what "they did over there". The teacher of the Baptist class devoted his hour to an explanation of the Holy Ghost, which proved so baffling to the young mathematician, that for some time thereafter he discharged no religious duties.

Across the street from Carr's Hotel, was a blacksmith shop. The smith was an Englishman, Eneas Myall. Fifteen years before William Carr drove from Lewis County in the old barouche, Myall had come over from England, and had stood on dry dock with only twenty-five cents in his pocket. He walked twelve miles to find work; needless to say, he found it. He earned the passage-money from England for his father, two brothers, and cousin. All worked together; the cousin was a wagon-maker, and under the newly made wagon-wheels, as they rested upon their trestles, were the shavings that had curled up at the making. In the cold dark mornings, when young Oliver came down stairs to make his fires, the flames leaped up from these very shavings, which he had carried over the evening before. They liked him at the shop, and Eneas, in particular, believed he read an expression in the thin face of the ambitious student, that promised something better than a hotel life.

Eneas was a Christian; [3]he and his two brothers and his cousin had all heard the Gospel preached by R. C. Ricketts, as they had never heard it in the old country. Over there, to escape the formalism of the Church of England, they had listened to the Dissenters; they had watched sinners hovering on the Anxious-seat of the Presbyterians, and the Mourning-bench of the Methodists. Such ante-rooms to Grace were held indispensable. As the eminent Congregationalist, Dr. Finney explained, so nearly all believed: "The church has always felt it necessary to have something of this kind. In the days of the apostles baptism answered this purpose. The Gospel was preached to the people and all who were willing to be on Christ's side were called on to be baptized. It held the precise place that the anxious seat does now, as a public manifestation of their determination to be Christians."

But Eneas and his relatives had been called upon by the preacher, not to come to something which served the same purpose as an institution of old, but to the institution itself. "Repent and be baptized every one of you in the name of Jesus Christ for the remission of sins, and you shall receive the gift of the Holy Spirit!" This was the trumpet call of R. C. Ricketts. To the simple blacksmith, it sounded like a voice long silent, issuing from the sacred past. He had never heard it proclaimed before. He and his obeyed the call. Having entered upon the Christian life, this blacksmith felt an inexhaustible enthusiasm for the cause. He had been made so happy by his acceptance of what opponents called the "new religion" that he wanted all his friends to partake of his happiness. When W. T. Moore came to May's Lick to raise funds for Bethany College, the first college of the disciples,— Eneas took his old rusty pen and wrote "$100."

Moore, in surprise, looked at the stalwart form in its rude garb, and then at the homely scene in which it seemed in keeping. "This is more than you ought to give!" he exclaimed. "How do you make it?"

"Oh," said the blacksmith, casting the pen aside, and lifting his hammer, "I beat it out of this iron! It is such a good cause, I'm sure I can give $100.00."

That was when Oliver was fifteen. W. T. Moore was holding a meeting at the church, working up the college endowment during the day. One evening, when Oliver entered the shop, as he did daily, seeking his kindling, Ed Myall looked up from his work, and said, "Ollie, isn't it time for you to be a Christian?" He would have said more, but his voice failed him. The boy, without a word, turned and went away. It was the first time anyone had ever spoken to him about being a Christian. He had dropped out of the Sunday school; he rarely attended church.

His sister Minnie was the first of the family to become a Christian. She repented; she confessed her faith; she was baptized; and then she became a missionary, thus: She met Oliver in the hall, as by accident—such matters come hard to the young and inexperienced—and said, "Ol, I want you to be a good boy!"

That was all; but he knew what she meant. The opportunity to go to church was not wanting, for Mr. and Mrs. Carr were always ready to take the work in hand for that purpose. They wanted the children to go to church, though, to be sure, they would have preferred the churches of their fathers. So on Sunday, Oliver went to church and heard W. T. Moore preach the first sermon he had ever understood. The same points were preached over and over, "What must I do to be saved?" And after that, when Oliver was driving passengers to and fro, or hauling wheat to market, he was thinking incessantly over what he had heard, that question of old,—"What must I do to be saved?" and then of the answer, as it had come from the lips of Peter and Silas and Paul. And he made the resolution, "Next Sunday, I will do what I think right!"

He asked his father's permission to "join the church." "If you know what you are doing," said William Carr, "go ahead."

Oliver thought he knew. The next Sunday he did up his morning's work, then walked to the Christian Church, where he made his confession of faith. It was a joyous occasion, and few eyes were dry, as the lad stood up to make known the new born desire of his heart. There were no looks cast at him askance, no chill of social cast. All felt one in Christ Jesus, and there was nothing but love for the lad from Lewis County.

And his mother who was by inheritance a Methodist, said, "The Campbellites have got Ollie!" He was baptized; of all his family, only Minnie was present.

One afternoon Oliver, now sixteen, came home for the last time from May's Lick Academy. He had finished the course. He carried his report proudly. "Seven" was the highest mark according to the teacher's system. Oliver's card was sprinkled all over with "7's." As he drew near the tavern, he saw his father in his chair, which had been brought outside.

He examined the report of his son with laudable pride, then said, "Well, Ollie, you will have to finish for yourself, now. I'm not able to send you to school any longer."

Of course, there was plenty of hard work. There was the wheat for him to haul across the county to Maysville, and the loads of coal to be brought home from the river; and there were the passengers to be carried to and fro; and, always, the home tasks.

But this life of crushed ambitions was not long to continue. Soon after Oliver's admission into the church, Eneas Myall, the blacksmith, walked into Carr's Hotel, accompanied by a prominent member of the church. Oliver happened to be in the hall when they began speaking to his father. He heard a few words, and crept nearer the door, his heart leaping in wild tumult.

He heard the blacksmith's voice, that voice which had often cheered him as he went about his daily tasks. And now it was asking if William Carr would consent to Oliver's being sent to Kentucky University at Harrodsburg; saying that he and Dr. A. H. Wall would pledge themselves to furnish the money. Is it a wonder that to Oliver Carr, that voice "sounded like sweetest music?"

William expressed his sorrow at not being able to educate his children as he wished; he appreciated the offer now made. "But," he said, earnestly, "don't undertake this, unless you are sure you can go on with it; I don't want you to give him up!"

A few days later Eneas Myall came with his hard-earned money, and placed it in Oliver's hands, asking him to take it with the love of its donors. And so, at the age of sixteen, Oliver Carr went to the University at Harrodsburg, to study for the ministry.

So, this is what we have found, in our quest of a possible husband for Mattie Myers—this Oliver Carr, who, as it appears, is far from being a rich young man. Will brother Joe be satisfied? Nay, will he ever consent? At any rate, they must be brought together. Let us return to the overworked pupil of John Augustus Williams, she who parsed, in class, too much of that MS. of his "Life of John Smith" for her health. We shall find her still upon her sick-bed, hovering between life and death.

CHAPTER IV.

A SCHOOL GIRL'S NOTE BOOK.

Of course she recovered, else there need be no biography of Mattie Myers, except to teach young girls not to study too hard—a lesson seldom needed. But the life we are following is to teach a quite different lesson. She emerges from the sickroom with a constitution shattered; not altogether broken, but much out of repair every way; mentally, in particular; for the mind has developed enormous energy in proportion as the body has wasted away; and all the nerves that are controlled from the general office are sent tingling at the least noise—even at the tread of a great thought.

The girl of sixteen is bewildered with herself. That grasp of the will which had held her to her tasks, to the outraging of her physical self, has suddenly slipped—it cannot be tightened up to the proper tension, at least not now. This inability to sleep that has come upon her, is to continue throughout her life; this nervous excitement of vital forces, this disproportion of mind and matter, this thinness of form, this determination to carry self to the end marked out, shown in the firm mouth—we are to find all these unchanged in after years.

In the meantime, her resolution to carry on her education has not faltered. She cannot go back to Daughters' College—Professor Williams does not know how to bear lightly upon the mind, and the girl has not even yet learned to spare herself. But there is a certain convent, the St. Catherine de Sienna's—Joe will send her there for a year. The very name is restful. The course is such that a young girl may carry it with one hand. Mattie will attend a year; that will graduate her from the St. Catherine de Sienna's. If, by that time, her strength has come back, she may finish at Harrodsburg. The convent will be so quiet—no levees, no marching to church in solid-green, no receptions in the parlors—nothing but trees and birds and silent-footed sisters, and cool gray walls, and a little French, a little ancient history, and such portions of the Old Testament history as have not become Protestantized.

Joe and Mattie discuss these plans at the close of Joe's school-day, as they sit on his piazza, his flute for the time silent. If they ever considered her ability to go back to John Augustus Williams instead of seeking the tutelage of the saint, an event took place that rendered such a course impossible. It was an event that grew out of other events, all of which had been preparing for many years.

To young Oliver Carr, far to the north in Mason County, the beginning had been announced by his old friend Walter Scott. It had come about in this way:

One evening the almost-raven locks and the keen but always kindly eyes, of Walter Scott appeared at Carr's hotel, which is for the nonce, the post office.

"Dear," he said to the youth who, for the time, is deputy post master, "have you anything for me this evening?"

Oliver, feeling that pleasure he always experienced when this question could be affirmed by a paper or letter, handed out the *Louisville Courier*. The old man opened it, and caught sight of words in large black letters that stared from the top of the page. At the door he read the line aloud:

"FIRING ON FORT SUMPTER!"

The reader burst into tears, and sank down upon the sidewalk. His friends hastened up, thinking he was ill, but Walter Scott could only say, as he pointed at the page,—"Oh, my country is ruined!" They carried him to his home, to that bed from which he was never to rise. That was in April, 1861. On the 21st he whispered his dying message to his friend L. P. Streator, Oliver's teacher,—

"It has been my privilege to develop the kingdom of God. I have been greatly honored". On the 23rd, he was no more, for God took him.

The war broke in all its fury upon "neutral" Kentucky. It brought the mountain guerrillas down on May's Lick with all their cruelty, all their wanton destruction. Woe to the goodly stores in William Carr's larder, the furniture of the hotel, the splendid horses in the stables, when they come shouting and cursing at his door! John Augustus Williams is obliged to close his Daughters' College and save his learning for another day. The young ladies have laid aside metaphysics and rhetoric to make clothes for the boys fighting in the Carolinas. For a time it seems not so important to classify the metonymies as to make peas or dandelion taste like coffee.

But gentle St. Catherine de Sienna raises its voice in pious song, and tolls its beads, and murmurs in pensive recitivo "*Je suis, tu es, il est, elle est*"—and hears not the echo of Perryville cannon, as one hears in Harrodsburg; or, if hearing, puts it to the account of the flesh and the devil, and chants *Te deum laudamus*.

Mattie's year in the convent is of all things the one needful. She rests and learns. At the end of the year she knows what St. Catherine de Sienna had to teach, and her strength is no worse from the acquisition. But as for any influence upon her mind or heart by this year's experience, we seek in vain for a trace. It may be that the beliefs she took behind the convent walls were made firmer to resist soft influences; or it may be that her faith was so impregnable at the beginning of this gentle eclipse, that it had nothing to fear.

The girl of seventeen bade farewell to St. Catherine's with the warm affection of the girl, and the serene self-poise of the woman. It left her just where it had found her, except that she knew a little more about the light graces of learning, and—the main thing, after all,—that she was now able to go on with serious study. It is often the case, when a Protestant so young as Mattie, graduates from the convent, that she carries through life a little cloistered chamber in her heart, where thoughts slip in the quiet hour to count their beads, and whisper "Ave Maria".

The next year Mattie returned to Daughters' College, where she graduated with honors, in 1865. There is an old gray-mottled composition-book written through in different inks, the prevailing color suggesting iron-rust, the pages showing the shadows of half a century, and the oft-repeated contact of a school-girl's hand. We find on the title page, "Miss Mattie Forbes Myers," written by her own hand—that was when she was thirteen. Later—for this book was used during her college days—we find "Mattie F. Myers"—no use now, for her to prefix the "Miss;" that is done by others.

This book is filled with notes taken at lectures, with poems, some original and some copied or memorized, with essays, with school notes; and here alone, save in a few essays on separate sheets, are we given a glimpse into the girl's mind, by the girl herself. Here we may find what she thought of life and death and immortality—but nothing of her daily life.

The book is interesting because of its omissions. There are no straggling lines such as one naturally writes in one's school-days when it is raining, for instance; or when one feels dull or impatient for the closing hour. There are no pyramids of schoolmates' names, no idle pictures that might be faces or geometrical figures, no allusions to Harrodsburg, or Lancaster, or Stanford, or any place or person more concrete than Moses crossing the Red Sea, or Hannibal crossing the Alps. Above all, in whatever disquisition upon the "Atonement" or "The Johnsonian Era," there is no flash of humor. One cannot avoid the impression in turning over these 209 closely written pages that here was a girl who, from year to year—that is, from twelve to twenty,—was serious, was intent upon a definite plan, was adhering closely to a central theme, unmindful of aught that detracts or turns the mind aside, though that digression be but the pleasant recreation of a smile.

It is true that all these pages do not present "solid reading matter." There is poetry here which shows a deeper love of poetry than of a poetic gift. One sees that this love of poetry was no superficial acquirement; it was not that nice taste for forms that contents the modern reader of magazines with a four-line stanza about any subject that can be put into four lines. Mattie read Mrs. Browning because she loved her. Of all books in English literature, she seems to have cared most for "Aurora Leigh." We find her in after years advising her friends to read Mrs. Browning, if they would taste the purest literary joys. A serious business, indeed, was life to that great-souled English poet with the slender hand up-propping the heavy head—this life so full of song and gaiety to most of us, before we stop laughing—also it meant serious business to Mattie Myers. And as Elizabeth Barrett found in later years a great love upon which she could always rest her weary heart, even so was Mattie Myers to find a love resourceful and deathless? We shall see, by-and-by.

The first writing in the book—written somewhere in her thirteenth year, is this: "A forehead royal with the truth"—*Elizabeth Barrett Browning*. Then we find, "As stars differ from one another in glory, so shall it be in the resurrection morn." Later comes, "Heaven is fair, earth pitiless; why is life so dear?" And, "He who has most of heart has most of sword." Then, "Oh life, is all thy song, Endure and die?" These are interesting as showing what sort of sentiments interested the little girl at the boarding-school. They are all like these, her written selections, grave to solemnity. Her original poetry is like it:

"In this narrow vale of life,Amid its scoldings and its strife,Amid its darkness and its gloom,Loving children, welcome, come."

Nor was this that seriousness which many an author confines to his writings, living a life far different from one's tragic numbers. Mattie was not an author, she had no desire to be one, and what she wrote was not apart from her life, but a part of it.

The style she developed was the oratorical. Her sentences were balanced, and her thoughts enforced by repetition. What she wrote after her graduation was, in the main, written to be delivered in public address. Her college theses represent the highest development of her style. Even as one reads them, he feels that they should be proclaimed. They are suited to the public platform. If the girl who wrote these does not, in time, become a popular lecturer, we shall be much mistaken! Moreover, apart from the embellishment which she loved to give her sentences, we find that whatever subject she undertakes, she treats with a whole-souled enthusiasm, as if it were a matter of immediate, vital importance, and as if she were an eyewitness of the event. Hear her:

"But when Aurora with her rosy fingers lifted the veil of night and robed the earth in sparkling gems, the predominant trait of his character again swayed his being, and again his solemn oath was violated. Infatuated man!

Think you that because the stream now flows smoothly, and the thunder of the cataract has transiently ceased, that you are far removed from danger? Already you are within the rapids." Who is this man that is in such terrible danger? None other than our old friend Pharaoh. In such thrilling words is his doom presently presented, that we feel that while he got no worse than he deserved, still it was enough. This was written at St. Catherine's. She is just as intimate with, just as keenly alive to, the sorrows of Spenser:

"Though the ashes of Spenser repose at Westminister, yet he still lives in the hearts of every lover of the beautiful and the good. The casket has decayed, but the jewel is firmly set in the coronet of Literature. There it will shine in undimmed splendor and beauty until the Empire of Genius shall fall. Even in our school-girl heart he has found a place, and memory of his woes and his joys, of his poverty and his unsearchable riches, will be with us forever."

The same spirit of bringing heart and soul into the theme, is shown in her treatment of her favorites of the Elizabethan era, the time of Queen Anne, or the Fall of Carthage. One does not feel that these essays are "pieces" so much as they are fragments of a sincere and enthusiastic mind. That which rouses her to greatest exaltation is the description of a soul encountering supreme difficulties; and we find her standing by Hannibal with a trumpet call to duty and heroism, when all his own have deserted him. Here is her hero of history, to none other does she so freely pour forth the unstinted admiration of her girl's heart.

Two other qualities should be mentioned in this connection. One is the intellectual force shown in these really remarkable productions, the ability to take the accepted positions of critics and clothe them in new and pulsing words. No need to ask for help in writing these compositions! who indeed could have done so well? In a few instances we find where the pencil of John Augustus Williams has culled out superlative phrases, or where he has inquired (for instance, after such a phrase as "we weep for him") if this is not rather "strong?" But on the whole, he leaves her articles unchanged, doubtless taking keen delight in the ability that has produced them. A young girl who can write thus at fifteen and seventeen, might do great things as an author; but as we have seen, her plans were formed for other fields.

The last quality of her writings which we have reserved, is one that permeates everything she wrote. No matter what the subject—whether the "Vail of Wyoming," or the general title, "Logic"—religion comes in; we do not say it creeps in; it walks in with head erect. It quite often overflows and submerges the point under consideration. One feels at times that the subject has been a means of getting at more vital matters. All through the composition-book we find pieces of sermons, and quotations of moral reflections, and verses from the Bible. Here and there are penciled little prayers such as a school girl might make who has deep purposes. There are pages of reflections on the Holy Spirit, side by side with French lessons. The religious nature of man; Christ as Prophet; Christ as Law-giver; God and Justice; Faith—these are discussed at length between sections of Botany notes and Geology and Civil Government classifications. The last word of all is given, not to a remark about some seatmate, or teacher, but to John the Baptist—what she thought of *his* life and purpose.

In this schoolbook, closed so long ago, there is a page almost filled with a discussion of Lady Macbeth; then, inverted lines, penciled as if to stow it away from conspicuous sight—and, indeed, against the background of iron-rusted ink, it is hardly discernible—are these lines without a subject heading: "God grant that I may never find enjoyment in the foolish pleasures of the world; but that my soul may soar far above its ephemeral joys unto the unsearchable riches of Christ Jesus my Lord."

That was the prayer of her young days; it explains what she has written—the pages we have been examining. By the light of this prayer, we may follow her from the schoolroom to her active service in the outer world. We see her attentive upon the worship of God; not only going, but leading; not only listening, but ministering. She finds her work in the songs of the church. At Mount Carmel lives her married sister, Mrs. Kate O'Bannon, a devoted member of the Church of Christ. During her latter summer vacations, Mattie stays with her; at church, she leads the singing.

In the early mornings, Mattie delighted in her walk along the ridge-road, from which the woods could be heard speaking in the myriad voices of bird-happiness. And she loved the little church, fresh from her school-duties, loved each greeting at the sunny door, and down the quiet aisles, coming as voices from long voyages apart. She led the singing with all her heart, and the congregation sang with all theirs; and when a protracted meeting was to be held, there was pleasurable excitement among the singers, over what to sing, and how to sing it.

One day, excitement is rife among church-members; one hears that a strange preacher is coming to hold a meeting—a young man Mattie has never seen. Who can it be? Surely not the boy from May's Lick? Surely not the Oliver Carr who was startled one evening with an armful of shavings, poised for bearing home, at hearing the wagon-maker say—"Ollie, isn't it time for you to be a Christian?"

Certainly, it would be strange if Oliver Carr should come to preach in the church where Mattie Myers leads the singing! The hard-earned money of Eneas Myall and his friend would not have been spent in vain, should such be the case! Let us return to May's Lick at the time of Oliver's starting to college, and find how, by any means, we can bring him to Mount Carmel to hold this very meeting, for which "Miss Mattie" is making ready.

CHAPTER V.

A UNIVERSITY STUDENT.

That was a wonderful day for the boy Oliver when, with the farewells of his parents, brothers and sisters, friends and benefactors, ringing in his ears, he started to college. As the stage coach rushed across the corner of Fleming County, and plunged through Nicholas and wound its way among the bluegrass pasture lands of Bourbon, he felt that he was seeing the world, at last; and not only seeing the world, but had the means to take an honored place in it; for to this youth of sixteen, there seemed no honor greater than that of preaching the Gospel.

It was so plain to him, this plea of the disciples of Christ; it appeared so evidently the truth of the whole matter; he was anxious to tell others about it, imagining in his inexperienced zeal, that others would be as glad to hear as he had been. But before he could preach, the collegiate fortresses of wisdom must be stormed and captured. Head of his class in mathematics at the academy—that is the best we can say for him now, and souls are not won from sin and error by the demonstrations of Euclid.

Here we are in Fayette County, and the train stops at Lexington. Here Oliver pauses, but does not stop, for the University is wanting several years of reaching this point. We must hold on our course—down through Jessamine County to Mercer. And now indeed, our blood thrills as if needles were pricking our veins, for we are near our destination,—near Harrodsburg the goal of our boyhood's ambition.

There are other boys in the stage coach going to the University, and we talk about the history of that institution, and of its professors, and of what we will do when we stop at the station, and where we will go,—all strangers as we are, and all young, in this year, 1861.

Some one tells how Bacon College was established by the disciples of Christ in Georgetown twenty-five years ago, and how its first president was Walter Scott—a name sufficient to bring up May's Lick before Oliver's mind, with a far-away suggestion of homesickness.

And another tells (or should tell for the refreshing of the reader's memory) of ten years of college life under James Shannon, until Bacon College went to sleep, or underwent suspended animation, and had to be brought to Harrodsburg by J. B. Bowman, to try what a new climate and a new name could do for it. So Bacon College became Kentucky University in 1858—just three years ago.

Then another—for there were four of these[4] boys, and being boys they talked a great deal, and, as we see, very much to our purpose—congratulates all upon the fortunate circumstances that have provided the University with the first teachers of the land—a fortunate circumstance for Harrodsburg, he means; of course a fortunate circumstance for anybody has a curious way of being unfortunate so far as somebody else is concerned.

Bethany College had been reduced to ashes; and although new walls were starting up from the gray ruins, such men of learning and piety as Bethany College boasted could not sit idly by, while brick was laid upon brick; they, too, might be building, and, by happy fortune, something more durable than stone. So Robert Milligan leaves his chair of mathematics at Bethany, to assume the presidency of our reawakened or newborn institution—old Bacon College, or new Kentucky University—one hardly knows if the author was Bacon or Shakespeare!—and Dr. Robt. Richardson entrusts his chair of Physical Science at Bethany to Dr. H. Christopher, and becomes vice-president at Harrodsburg. So now we know—by listening to the chatter of these prospective students—how it came about that Mattie Myers was treated to the preaching of these giants. She is over yonder at Daughters' College even now a girl of fourteen. Even then, she says, she "had given her life to serious study and preparation for her chosen life-work."

And what of Bethany College? How can it survive the loss of those illustrious men? Perhaps with its Alexander Campbell for president, it can weather the gale!

But certainly those of us who are Kentuckians and who have been attending the College in Virginia, because we had none of our own, now feel unbounded elation over our newly-captured prize! For in those days, says S. W. Crutcher, who was just such a student, "We had somehow gotten into the habit of spelling Kentucky with a big 'K' and the United States in small letters."

It was Crutcher who, then in Virginia, went with the other Kentuckians to "Hybernia" to congratulate Professor Milligan on being chosen president of Kentucky University. The Professor—who had already grown cautious about standing in draughts—expressed his resolution to spend the remainder of his life in the service of the University; and Mrs. Milligan, with thoughts for the present life, led the young men into the dining-room. Belle is in short dresses; for, as we have said, this was three years ago; and it is only last year that Robt. Graham left Harrodsburg for Arkansas.

We were speaking of S. W. Crutcher; and by a queer coincidence, there he is in the middle of the street as the stage coach brings Oliver Carr to Harrodsburg. We are here at last. Crutcher takes Oliver and his three traveling-companions to a boarding-house which proves an undesirable place, and President Milligan takes Oliver into his own home; there he finds Belle's dress three years nearer the floor than when Sam Crutcher told her farewell in Bethany; and Oliver is, of course, very much afraid of her; for was there ever a boy more awkward or more conscious of his tallness and thinness, than this youth from Lewis and Mason County?

Perhaps not. But he is much at ease with the president, himself, for the president is a man—and Oliver has dealt thus far principally with men—and not only so, but with a prince of men. If Eneas Myall, the blacksmith, could have had the choosing of Oliver's companions, knowing in his practical English head that his protege was in the danger-zone of youth, when companionship counts most—he could have selected with no greater care than Providence seemed to have done.

First of all, there was the Milligan household with its atmosphere as unlike that of the village hotel, as if it had been of another world. Then there was the man with whom Oliver used to walk home from school, with whom he loved to stroll in the twilight—the Professor of English, who examined the youth's fitness for his junior year by having him analyze and parse a hymn. Between this man and boy grew a liking that was soon ardent love. "My boy"—that is what L. L. Pinkerton called Oliver. And Oliver, as he walked with his favorite teacher, and heard him quote poetry—poetry in the balmy evenings of autumn, poetry in the crisp winter afternoon, poetry wherever Pinkerton was, whether that of others, or that of his own joyous temperament—here was another formative influence for the boy from the froglands.

When we, of another day, look back upon that time, and watch this sweet association, it is hard to understand the bitterness—we must not say hatred—that used to be roused at the mention of the Professor of English. Let us take a closer look at this man from Baltimore County, Maryland; a brief look, necessarily, but one which will seek to envelope his main attributes. In so doing, we have not forgotten that our central aim is to present the life of Mattie Myers over yonder in Daughters' College—where she has scarcely heard of Oliver Carr, though she knows Pinkerton by sight.

To begin at the beginning of L. L. Pinkerton's life—which was in his eighteenth year—we find him building a post-and-rail fence in West Virginia not far from Bethany; "black locust posts, black walnut rails," he remembers, "all taken from the stump, and fence set, for twenty-five cents per panel of eight feet." Not that the quality of wood or price of wages matters—at least now; what does matter is that one morning, before going to work, he found a paper on the table, edited by Alexander Campbell. The *Millennial Harbinger* was its name. Lewis picked up the paper casually, and was soon reading with strange intentness—reading and re-reading. Strange reading-matter to absorb the attention of a fence-builder of eighteen—it was all about Truth! Presently he went to Bethany to hear more about it, and at the close of a sermon by A. Campbell, was baptized—he rode home that night four miles in dripping garments. It was so wonderful to him, this plea of the disciples of Christ—one name for all Christendom, one rule of faith and practice, and that rule the Bible alone—he could not but believe that it would be eagerly accepted by a sect-divided world! He began preaching.

From Lexington he went to Midway, where he established the Orphan School of the Christian church. For sixteen years he labored in raising funds, and in teaching, for this exponent of practical Christianity. The same enthusiasm which had marked his acceptance of the "reformed religion" carried him over innumerable obstacles, whether of miserliness, poverty, or cold discouragement. Now the Midway Orphan School was firmly established, and the year before Oliver came to the University, Pinkerton accepted the English professorship.

But, unfortunately for his peace of mind, however fortunate for truth in the abstract and concrete, poetry was not the only thing that L. L. Pinkerton talked, outside of school hours. When we seek to pierce the clouds of misunderstanding and accusation that darken the atmosphere of those days, the charges of heresy, and the retorts of sectarianism, above all, the trumpet call that one or the other was not "sound,"—which opprobrious epithet, indeed, sounds above all the other jarring cries,—we cannot believe that this resolution to "down Pinkerton" came from the sole desire to exalt the Christ. No doubt his opposers believed such to be the case, but they were mistaken. It was all the war, the spirit of the times. Though the heavens fall, Pinkerton must proclaim his conviction that slavery was of the devil, must lecture about it, must do everything that lay in his power to convince others, must declare his satisfaction when Lincoln's Proclamation—that one proclamation that calls for no explanatory data to remind one *what* proclamation—outraged those who did not believe slavery to be of the devil; far otherwise, indeed.

For the war has burst upon us, now in all its fury, and though we, as a state, are "neutral," everybody knows what that means, and suspects his neighbor accordingly. In Midway, Pinkerton in building up the church, established and nurtured a church for the black folk—preached for it until out of African darkness was evolved a light to shine for itself. He believed these slaves had souls, and somehow, he looked upon his labors for their salvation as a part of the practical good-doing that flowered in the Orphan School. If he could only believe these things to himself, and not say anything! But in that case, he would not have been Pinkerton. And so, after the year 1862—the year in which Oliver Carr preached his first sermon—no church-door was opened that L. L. Pinkerton might preach therein—never again was he to be thought "sound" enough.

Oliver heard much of "soundness" in those days, just as we do now. But happily for his peace of mind, he was not disturbed by the continuous jarring and clashing of orthodox and heretical opinions. He was too busy—too busy, almost to eat; there is no recreation for him save as he trudges to and fro between school and lodgings, with, or without, the poetical friend. For he is most irregular in his classes; mathematics—fine; Latin and Greek—nothing!—"Dead," his father had objected. Dead indeed, and buried so deep, that the boy must dig hard and late, to unearth the skeletons. The result of which exhausting excavation we hear announced in the language of Dr. Richardson: "If you don't improve in health I do not see how you can continue your studies—" And, a little later: "You had better go home!"

Dark days—a weary struggle for health—a conviction that this is consumption—a last futile fight for victory—back home goes the broken invalid, just as Mattie Myers had been forced to quit the field.

But there is a difference, since Oliver is obliged to stop in the midst of everything—and since he can ill afford a rest. He has had his chance and it seems all in vain. For three months he stays with his sister drinking mineral-water, filled with torturing regrets and inextinguishable hope. His sister—it is Mary—has married; we are to hear of her again. Three months—and he realizes that if he goes back, it will mean as severe a regime as before. The ground is hardly broken above those dead languages, and he has not the strength he had thought he possessed. However, if we could, later on, take a peep at the young men about the grounds, we would find Oliver Carr holding his own with Surber, Keith and Mountjoy and Albert Myles. For six years we find him studying—"as hard as anybody," in his opinion; but not again is ill-health to drive him home, though always hovering at his elbow. Let us take glimpses, here and there, at these years, with the happy privilege of the reader, of attending the school of his hero without being compelled to study his hero's lessons.

At the close of his full year he goes back to May's Lick. To rest? Yes, if to do what lies closest to the heart is rest. He borrows a horse, gets his saddlebags, arms himself with Bible and hymn-book, and starts out for Carter county where Henry Pangburn and Thomas Munnell have "started a meeting." He informs the girl who keeps the tollgate that he is a preacher;

no doubt in this boy's mind as to what he is! He loses his way in the mountain trails—"Babe" will go to show him the school-house, if he will catch her old white horse with burrs in its tail; "Babe" is a young lady of two hundred pounds—what matter her other name? On they go, in and out among the hills—Babe's girth breaks and Oliver gives up his horse to her.

"Hello Babe!" thus the father of Frank Kibbey from his doorway, "who's that you have with you?"

"Oh, a little rebel I picked up on the way!"—a laughing matter to Babe, but not to Oliver, for he sees her drawn aside, and hears the whispered demand, "*Is* he a rebel?"—and wonders if he will be hung.

But they are all rebels together. Thomas Munnell says "Ollie, you must preach tonight!" And Oliver knows off-hand what he will preach, because he has only one sermon! So the benches are brought into the home of "Bro. Kibbey"—for in the morning the preaching had been in the woods,—and Oliver stood in a corner, the preacher's point of vantage in those days, and preached. "And some old women bragged on me," he said afterward.

These fledgling students—Kibbey and Carr—sent an appointment to preach in the mountains. As they rode along, talking about their faith,—for that is what these boys loved to talk about—they saw a beautiful pool sparkling among lordly oaks, and they said, "Here is where we will baptize!" Why not? Not a word had been preached, nor had they ever looked upon the faces of their prospective auditors; but did they not have the truth? So they preached to the mountaineers; and presently came back to the pool among the oaks, where they baptized four young men and four young women.

Another picture, brief, almost brusque in its bold coloring: the young man is called into the office of the Professor of Mathematics, Henry H. White. The teacher abruptly extends his hand, "This is for you; take it."

It is fifty dollars. Oliver, the tears springing to his eyes, would falter his thanks. "That will do sir!" says the Professor with mathematical dryness. "That will do sir! you're dismissed,"—so sharply, so conclusively, that nothing is to be done but go. There are two such scenes, precisely alike; fifty dollars each time, and, "That will do sir!" as an end to the incident.

Never were such kindnesses more gratefully received, or more sorely needed. For men have come down from the mountains, seizing upon the property of Southern sympathizers, and none too particular about your sympathies, if they can get away with horses and money. William Carr sees his hard-earned savings disappear in a night. The horses from his stables are spirited away; his hotel is looted; nor is there wanting the suspicion that some of his neighbors have pointed out the spoils to the enemy. To his sudden necessity is added the bitterness against injustice and ingratitude. Farther into the night his wife must sew, earlier in the morning they must rise; for though one son is away at college, and one daughter is married, there is little left to support the other five children. So here at May's Lick is a battle for daily bread, while Oliver, at Harrodsburg, battles for daily Latin and Greek.

Nor is this time of stress without its element of heroism. One might pause in the narrative to show the young University student in danger of his life, on the occasion of one of his home-comings. A drunken soldier, having robbed William Carr of his horse, is about to shoot the hotel-keeper because he is a "Southerner." Oliver leaps between, fastens his gaze upon the infuriated face, holds out his defenceless arms, and saves his father's life.

This is Oliver's experience of the war, this crushing blow upon his parents; this, and the booming of cannon at Perryville, and the long line of stragglers coming back from a beaten field; and then the wounded and the dead. Harrodsburg is taxed to the utmost in giving shelter to the fallen heroes. Daughters' College from which, as we have seen, the young ladies have been banished, is opened up as a hospital.

L. L. Pinkerton is no longer teaching; he has resigned to become surgeon in the Eleventh Kentucky Cavalry; just as he marched to the defense of orphan girls and negroes groping in spiritual darkness, so now he sallies forth for his country; leading the soldiers in prayer every evening, dressing the wounds of the blue or gray, and singing Northern battle hymns. And just as he always worked too hard for Midway Orphan School, or for the disciples' plea, or whatever he worked at—never resting till failing resources made him rest,—so now, he toils at regimental prayer-meeting and midnight diagnoses and presently finds himself bedfast. Too feeble to stand, he lies praying that the South may be conquered; and, so praying, he is carried to the home of an old friend, a Captain Carr, who is a Southerner to the core.

For weeks the friend of Lincoln lies at the point of death, cared for with all tenderness by the friend of Jefferson Davis. Then J. B. Bowman, he who turned Bacon College into Kentucky University, came up from Harrodsburg to Louisville; here the Professor of English lay, and, taking him in his strong arms, Bowman carried him out to the carriage and rode away with him. So, we have him back at Harrodsburg at last, where he may walk with Oliver again, and quote poetry. Of course he tells Oliver about his kind treatment in the home of Captain Carr, and speaks of the tender and faithful ministrations of Southern nurses. And then, quickly, lest he be misunderstood, he asserts his unalterable faith in the justice of the Union cause; he will have no doubts as to where he stands.

"I could scatter flowers over the graves of the Confederate dead," he says, "and even bedew them with my tears; but I must still say, if forced to it, 'These poor, brave young men fell in an unrighteous war against a beneficent government!'" He must still say it, later on, to the destruction of his peace of mind; to the dissolution of many a friendly tie; must still say it, if forced to it; and must say it, whether forced or not, such being the impetuosity of his character, which consumes prudence and policy in one blaze of enthusiasm.

In the meantime, Oliver is at war in his own way. That the South should prove its right to self-government appeared to him self-evident, but it did not rouse his fighting blood. Souls to be saved from sin and error—that is his ever-pressing consideration. That all religious bodies should take the name of Christian, and worship according to the Scriptures—could anything be simpler? That the six or seven denominations in small tows, instead of utilizing half their vitality in keeping themselves going, should all combine in one glorious purpose to exalt the Christ—could anything be more like Heaven on Earth? Oliver thought thus. He believed it might come to pass; and he was eager to do his part in bringing it about. So every summer he left the University halls to carry his message into the hills and valleys of Kentucky; and such was his youthful ardor, his enthusiastic conviction of success, that people for a time stopped talking about John Morgan and friends in Canada, and went to hear the boy from the village tavern.

The time came when he resolved to carry the war into his own country. So he packed his saddlebags and rode into the land of his youth. There was no building of the disciples of Christ, but Oliver was offered the Methodist meeting house.

When it was noised abroad that Oliver Carr was going to preach, hearts were stirred and the farmers, many miles away, began catching up their horses to take the family to meeting. Men who had not been to church for years expressed themselves to this effect: "Ol going to preach? Yes, I'll go to hear *him*."

The meeting began Thursday night; on Saturday he baptized fourteen. Sunday morning the church building was locked; an agitated congregation hovered in the yard. "Oliver has opened the doors of the church!" complained his aunt—meaning the spiritual church; she had taken care that the church of pine boards should be more closely guarded. Across the street from the inhospitable meeting house stood the school house. The audience moved thither. The women went within; the men remained outside. Oliver stood in the door, and preached on "Christian Union".

Mrs. O'Bannon was there, she and her school-girl sister, Mattie Myers. And Mattie led the singing, and listened to the young University student with unqualified approval. In after days she was to hear him preach many a sermon, and in many lands; "But that was the best sermon he ever preached!" she declared. For they were both so young, then, and both so fired with zeal for the same cause which to them seemed the supreme cause of earth and heaven. And they were both so confident that this cause must triumph—perhaps in their own lifetime!

Oliver went to Orangeburg to preach in another Methodist church, and people came from May's Lick to hear the boy, his father among the number. Very seldom, if ever, had Oliver seen William Carr at church before; here he baptized fourteen—but alas! his father was not one of them. Then ten days at Sardis, and forty baptized—but we need not follow the youth from point to point; it was everywhere the same indestructible faith, and many converts, and the beginnings of church life.

Daniel Carr, Oliver's grandfather, sent for him to come up to Lewis county and preach in his home. Daniel was a prominent class-leader of the Methodist church, 76 years old. Oliver responded gladly, entered the county of his birth, where his uncles and aunts all lived, faithful Methodists. His grandfather brought benches and chairs into his house, and called in neighbors and kinsfolk. Oliver saw before him the boys and girls with whom he had gone to school in the country before his father's removal to May's Lick. Here were Old-School Baptists and Presbyterians, come to hear what the "Campbellite" had to tell them. But they did not come in hostility; far from that. It was with wonder, rather, that they looked upon this young man and thought of his past—the hard work on the farm, the harder work in his father's hotel. They knew how he had been obliged to leave the University on account of ill-health, and how, since then, he had taxed his strength to the utmost in evangelistic campaigns among the hills. And now he had come to them, his old neighbors, to tell them about Christ!

His grandfather knelt down to open the meeting with prayer, but suddenly the wonder and the joy of it came upon him, and they heard nothing but his sobs. When he was able to utter words, they burst from a heart that throbbed with heavenly thanksgiving.

Then Oliver rose. At last, at last! the privilege was his to speak to these dear people, words of eternal life. As he looked into their kindly faces, he too, was overcome by emotion. Minute after minute passed by, and he could but weep, while the faces of his audience, bathed in tears, told him that the yearning of his heart was understood. It seems wonderful when a celebrated man rises to address an audience, and, for ten minutes, stands dumb before tireless applause. But what shall we say of this boy who stands ten minutes unable to speak for tears of joy, while his friends wait, unable to hear for weeping?

This we must say; that we have found here a youth who has given himself with all his soul to an idea; an idea that grips at the roots of emotions and desires and life itself. Will not he who weeps with joy at the opportunity to deliver his message, also fight for it? But though fighting, will not his valor be tempered with the tenderness of tears?

CHAPTER VI.

LOVE AND SACRIFICE.

So they have met at last, the preacher and the singer. They might have finished their education there at Harrodsburg, Oliver Carr at the University and Mattie Myers at Daughters' College—if the meeting had not brought them together—who knows! But, being brought together in that way, and being the grave and purposeful characters we have found them to be, it is easy enough to comprehend the friendship that came into being; a friendship sanctified, as it were, by the sound of hymn and the fervor of prayer.

After the services we find Oliver going home with Mrs. O'Bannon, in whose parlor he meets the school-girl sister. Serious enough is their talk—you might have thought them staid Christians of middle life! She finds him awkward and embarrassed, except when the talk runs religiously. He finds her, to his thinking, highly educated, and feels due awe for her superior advantages. Behold him, now, driving up with a spring-wagon to take Mattie and her friends on an excursion to the mineral springs—"Æsculapia", it is called—certainly an appropriate spot for these two health-needing students! Drink of that mineral-water as deeply as you may and let us hope Old Æsculapius himself will infuse strength into the sparkling drops!

After this pleasant companionship, Oliver and Mattie were never again to be strangers. Now he knows one girl at Daughters' College who leads singing in the church—and she knows one young man at the University whose very soul is wrapped up in the things nearest her own heart. He comes to the college to see her; and John Augustus Williams sits with them in the parlor to complete the triangle,—very properly; are not triangles the least-sided figures known in the halls of learning? And when President Milligan gives a levee, who comes for Mattie to escort her thither? Ask if you choose; I shall not answer!

We have seen how Kentucky University emerged from Bacon College, but we have not witnessed the closing scene of the transformation. Out of Georgetown came Bacon College to Harrodsburg; and out of Danville came Transylvania Seminary to Lexington; here the Seminary found Kentucky Academy, and these two were fused into Transylvania University. For sixty-six years Transylvania University flourished and then declined. Then fire destroyed the college building at Harrodsburg, and Milligan came to Lexington, and Kentucky University was amalgamated with old Transylvania, and these two were one. Which takes Oliver away from Harrodsburg, and that means letters; letters between him and Mattie Myers.

It was in 1865 that Kentucky University gave its last exercises in Harrodsburg. The "Franklin Literary and Philosophical Society" gave its "exhibit," June 21st. From his "speeches" written out and now among the relics it appears that Oliver was usually chosen to represent the "Franklins." One subject discussed was, "Should we in the administration of law, be influenced by Justice alone?" J. T. Spillman of Harrodsburg affirms; O. A. Carr of May's Lick denies. And the speech that O. A. Carr delivers is sent on eight pages, the words liberally italicised, to "Miss Mattie." "I do this to gratify my friend," he adds at the end of the poetry that closes the debate, "and I hope that she will not forget her promise—I will expect those notes on President Williams' lecture soon." Thus begins the correspondence: a debate from him, lecture notes from her.

Mattie Myers is only eighteen, now, and she speaks with all that age-wisdom one finds in the sober-minded young: "I have been living over all the delights of the past," she writes to a friend, "and when the bright dream passed away before the storm actualities of the present, my heart has wept that the golden hours of childhood shall never, never return. True, my childhood was not all joyous; yet there is a luxury in remembering even the grief that tore my young heart. Many changes have taken place since then. The death-angel has taken from our circle two dear sisters. Is it not hard for the human heart, so full of pride, to pass submissive under the rod? Yet in each affliction there is a blessing. There is a holy, purifying influence that the children of God must feel in order to be made fit for His inheritance,— an influence that even mighty truth, alone, cannot bring; an influence that only trial can exert upon the proud heart. This will make the weakest strong; God accepts no sacrifice without salt or without fire. Trial gives us our Christian character, brings us into closer communion with our God. With it our hearts may be made fair and pure as the snow that encircles the mountain-crest. It was a bright-winged messenger that took from us our sisters, though with the eye of flesh we could not see the brightness of His glory."[5]

"Many of the old friends are married," she continues, "and many are sleeping. One hardly recognizes the old Kentucky Home. Dearest friends have moved away. The home of one's youth seems strange. But of one I must tell you, one dearer to me than all others—*my brother*. God grant that I may not love him too well lest I forget Him who gave me one so dear!"

This year brought the war to a close. We find Oliver Carr once more on an evangelistic tour, followed, we may be sure, by best wishes from Mattie

Myers for his success. He is accompanied by John W. Mountjoy. They borrow horses at May's Lick, load their saddle-pockets, and start for the mountains. Let us take a look at them, July 14, 1865,—"A bright, beautiful morning," says Mountjoy, writing joyously in his pocket-diary; "we rose with the sun, welcomed by the song of birds and the gayety of nature."

It is interesting to note just what preaching means, and what it includes for these young University students. "We led George and Davy to water, fed them and rubbed them off." (Davy is Oliver's colt, so named for David Armstrong, and George is John's colt, so called after George Ranck, who trudged on foot with Oliver to hear his first sermon at a school house on the Perryville road three miles from Harrodsburg, and afterward became the Lexington historian.) "Went to the house, had prayers, and then breakfast. Left immediately on our journey for Vanceburg,—rode slowly on account of the lameness of Ol's 'Davy.' Singing joyously"—this beautiful morning—"we reached rows of cabins humbly situated by the roadside—the little children, the old grand-mother with her white cap—an old man mowing by the wayside. I would gladly have helped him, could I have stopped. * * * We are now at the blacksmith shop, having 'Davy' shod—sixteen miles yet to ride before we reach Vanceburg."

Presently they pass the little school-house where Oliver learned his first lesson, his a b c's the first day; the second day it was a-b ab, and the University student sees himself, barefoot and tiny, trudging up to the doorway that looked so large to him then. It is hard for him to believe that little boy himself. The years at May's Lick Academy have come since then, and the years at Harrodsburg, and now the prospect of years at Lexington. He is already so removed from that little boy, and all the world of that little boy, so removed in life-purposes, in eternal desires! and yet there is something of the little child in his tall awkwardform—or in his heart, rather—something always childlike.

"The school-house where Ol. learned his first lesson," says Mountjoy—"I could not enter into half the joys of his sweet remembrances of happier days." Could not, truly; but why "happier" days? Is it not because they are past, those days of youth, never to be ours again; surely it is not because they were in reality happier!

We pass through Clarksburg about 12, we reach Vicksburg about one, and now we—or I should say, "I," am sitting on the bank of the Ohio,—Oliver is doubtless resting from his experiences with "Davy." For, "While riding along about halfway between Mount Carmel and Vanceburg, talking of Geo. Ranck and Davy Armstrong, Ol. took a notion that his beast was becoming insensible to the spur on his right foot, and concluded he would make a change. He raised his left leg over the shoulder of Davy"—and then we are treated to a bit of Greek in the diary-narrative, the spirit, if not the letter, of which may be gleaned from a line further on—"I thought Ol. would surely be killed."

Away goes Davy, free of any spur, scattering saddle-pockets and hymn-books to right and left. A quarter of a mile away he stops, and looks back at the other borrowed horse as if to say, "George, throw John Mountjoy off and let's go back to old man Chancellor!"—the old man, evidently from whom they were borrowed. At which, George's spirit begins to rage, and Mountjoy has all he can do to keep *in statu quo*. And his thought—if one can afterwards remember what his thought was at such a crisis—ran thus; "Ol. is killed or half-dead; I suppose I will have all the preaching to do!" Preaching he has to do, but only his share, but no funeral, for Ol. staggers up and mounts and clings. And now we find Mountjoy alone on the river bank, wishing that the music of the waves could inspire him to do justice to the thrilling scene just closed.

But after all, Oliver is not resting up from his dethronement, for we are presently to discover him in a situation none too heroic, by the canons of genteel fiction. We have come down to the landing to see the steamer "Telegraph." We are now down the river a little way. "While I have been writing, Ol. has been washing his boots, with sand for soap. The boat has just passed down the river and the waves are lashing the shore, making melody. Ol. will preach tonight in the little school-house."

And somewhat further down we find in another handwriting—"All sitting together tonight, and Johnnie proposes that each of us write something in his diary and sign his name.

O. A. CARR."

So the day, bright and beautiful, is at a close; the waves of the Ohio no longer sparkle with diamonds as the steamboat plows its way southward; and the jolts of the journey—let us hope—are eased; and the sermon has been preached; and if we smile at the thought of the sand-scouring of the boots, is it not with the smile of sympathy? For we, too, find beautiful the feet of those who bring tidings of great joy! So, as we say, gone is that bright day of July, so many years ago; and every little movement in the river one saw that day has, for many years, lapsed into stillness, to give place to the movements of other times. But the words spoken then, the sermon preached, the hymns sung, the prayers offered,—who shall say there is not in the world to-day a greater love for humanity, a deeper adoration of the Christ, because of them?

This same year Mattie Myers wrote,

"The leafy bowers their shadows cast, and on the grass so cool, We lay our burning brows and weep the fleeting joys of school"—

For her school-days are at last ended.

Four years of instruction under her brother's surveillance, six more at St. Catherine de Sienna's and Daughters' College—ten years of lingering at the founts of knowledge! And now that they have slipped away, and the young girl faces the graver problem of life itself, the school-girl breaks into swan-song, and dies to her youth, as she immerges into womanhood:

"We leave thee, Alma Mater, dear, with all the bitter grief That farewell brings to loving hearts, yet with a sweet relief,— A hope to tread thy walks again, to breathe thy fragrant air,— A hope to hear again thy voice, thy holy truth to share."

To her mind, education was not only acquirement of truth, but of holy truth; such an acquisition as called for its inevitable reward:

"When from the dust the good shall rise When glory's streaming from the skies; The hand of love a wreath will twine, Eternal, glorious, divine."

"Miss Mattie: Dear Sister—" What is this? Nothing less than a Kentucky University student, writing from "Social Hall," on the 12th of January, 1866. "Don't be surprised to find the name of your friend Ollie at the conclusion of these lines," he goes on, "though I admit it is enough to surprise you." But not us! He was disappointed, he says, because she did not come to Mount Carmel during his last meeting, "for I had *all* the preaching to do myself—" signifying that there was no young girl fresh from college to lead the singing. The letter is all about his evangelistic work. "Uncle Gilbert, who had not been within a church for twenty years, was constantly in his seat before me, looking and listening with intent interest."

And then he mourns because his sister Mary did not "purify her soul by obeying the truth through the spirit." Privately, she tells her preacher-brother that she believes; but she will wait awhile before confessing her belief, will wait for the husband to come. But he does not come. "I left that dear good sister sitting on the stile, watching to catch the last glimpse of me, departing perhaps forever." But that vacation was not spent in vain. "During two months I reported 133 additions, organized four Sunday schools and two churches. Oh, how happy I would be tonight, if all my dear relations were among those who have obeyed!" Then he gives us an insight into the sort of things he and "Miss Mattie" conversed about at social gatherings. "Although my summer was indeed a happy one, yet when I returned to where all are so worldly, my heart seemed almost broken. I will always remember the remark you made at President Milligan's reception, in regard to the conversion of my parents; and of your faith in prayer."

Serious, indeed, but sweet in its strong helpfulness, is this correspondence, now springing up. We have but one side of it, but it reveals the other. His next letter: "I will never forget your good advice, nor will I cease to thank you for it. Mattie, I regard you as my most wholesome counselor. I seldom find a young lady who will give me advice; and none ever gave me more consolation than you. I have just read your letter, and I feel stronger spiritually. How cheering to the poor boy, are these words from a sister in Christ. You ask me what message you shall bear to Mary"—the sister we left gazing sadly from the stile, waiting, but unready. "If you have an opportunity, please encourage her to become a Christian. I took tea with President Williams last night. He says if he returns to Harrodsburg next year, he will have you as his assistant teacher. I hope you will sufficiently recover your health to be able to take up that employment next to the Christian ministry in point of usefulness, that you may labor for God and humanity."

School Days Ended.

He writes in March: "I have been on a visit to my sister, Minnie Fox, to attend an exhibition given by her husband's school. From there I went to Winchester to preach, and have just returned. My roommate"—here he pauses to take futile revenge—"Dr. Sweeny, is amusing himself with his flute and vexing me no little with his discordant notes. Of course *good natured Ol.* bears it all in good part, hoping however, that the doctor's serenade will soon conclude!"—a side-remark which we might have made ourselves. Then to the more serious matters: "I admire more than ever the kind, easy and natural manner breathed in your letters. Your style portrays a good heart. I love *talking* letters, and such talk, too, that expresses spontaneous emotions. How happy I am under the conviction that you feel solicitations about my welfare, and offer up prayers in my behalf. Mattie, I often think of your remark to me last June, stating what you thought could be done through faith."

He has two regular appointments now, for preaching; at Macedonia[6] and Providence. He touches upon the latest news: "I suppose you have heard of Brother A. Campbell's death. How sad to think that one so great and good must lose his power and fade away! 'He had fought a good fight,' and now goes away to wear the crown. President Williams will go back to Harrodsburg. He prefers teaching young ladies to boys. Mattie! I am trying to compose an oration on the 'True and Good in Man,' and would be very much obliged if you will give a few suggestions. (Bad luck to that pen for dropping the ink! please excuse the blot.) I will be very glad to hear from you soon on the True and Good in Man. Good night! May the choicest blessings of heaven be yours, in time and eternity."

Mattie Myers is still seeking to regain her strength—for health has fled after the closing days at Daughters' College; and as she rests, she reads the "Quarterly,"—no light reading, one would think, for a girl of eighteen—and "Aurora Leigh," always her favorite,—and at night—these beautiful nights in May, she goes to the meeting held at Stanford by Moses E. Lard. Oliver has no such excuses, he writes her, for delaying his answer, but he has others just as good. "I have yet those five studies this hot weather," he says; "besides, I go to the country to preach nearly every Lord's day." However, we would not have her think his preaching excuses any dereliction of duty. "I have had occasion to pronounce my love for the ministry, and I need only say that it is still my chief delight."

And then he comes to deal with the man about whom the storm-clouds had gathered, the favorite professor who used to walk with the boy Oliver when friends were few and the University was at Harrodsburg: "Last Friday night Dr. Pinkerton addressed our society—the Philothean,—to encourage us in our undertaking—about twenty-five of us are studying for the ministry. His subject was 'True Greatness.' All were entertained with the originality of his conceptions, and his peculiarly terse, pointed and feeling manner. It just seemed a picture of the man revealing his noble heart, and showing his fervent religious sentiments. Perhaps you have been prejudiced against the doctor, owing to his political proclivities. But Mattie, allow me to say that although he acted as a Christian should not act, while overwhelmed in excitement, and had his all in the 'Negro Bureau,' still, I cannot but believe he was sincere. *Yes!* he was so deeply convinced of the correctness of his position that he would have been a miserable man, a vile hypocrite, had he acted otherwise. He is ready to sacrifice popularity and friends; yes, I verily believe life itself, for what his conscience tells him is right. For this I admire him. For his sympathy, I esteem him; and because he is a good man, I *love* him. I know many lips have hissed stern anathemas against poor, passionate Dr. Pinkerton; but his goodness will compare favorably with that of any of his accusers. I hope the brethren will labor to restore him to his proper orbit, where he will shine among the brightest stars of the Reformation."

So this generous young defender goes on and on, till he reaches a blaze of eloquence of which we are duly suspicious, knowing not what element of actuality (which is seldom eloquent) may have been consumed in the heat of chivalrous ardor. It is enough to know that we have found a voice to speak for the man "who had his all in the Negro Bureau," nor was it a light thing to speak thus to Mattie Myers, whose schoolbook is written close with Southern songs. She loves to sing—else she would not have taken the pains to write it down so carefully—

"Oh, yes, I am a Southern girl, and glory in the name, And boast it with far greater pride than glittering wealth or fame. I envy not the Northern girl her robes of beauty rare Though diamonds grace her snowy neck, and pearls bedeck her hair.

"Hurrah, hurrah, for the Sunny South so dear! Three cheers for the homespun dress The Southern ladies wear."

After the exalted strain of the first part of this letter, we confess to a great satisfaction in the latter part, which seems to come so much closer to the ground on which most of us live: "I delivered your message to Miss Shaw Turner. She expressed an ardent desire to see you, and gave evidence to a strong attachment to you,—*which* I suppose you will allow me to do." (Observe the artfulness of that "*which*") "I am very much obliged to you for the invitation to the railroad picnic, and I think it would be altogether proper for the *Car* to beat the railroad, ric, tic." (A pun! what next?) "Well, I have heard Brother Lard preach lately; no wonder I can't write to you! We are anticipating a happy time in June at our society exhibitions. Please come! But before you come, oblige me by writing some of your thoughts on this subject: 'The Tears of History and the Smiles of Prophecy.' This is my subject and I have not written a word. Jas. C. Keith, Albert Myles and myself are to represent the University on the 28th June—a distinguished honor, indeed. I am also elected to represent the Philothean society, and I have not prepared *that* speech. Oh, what a fix I'm in! Please, Mattie, help me! Next summer, let us visit Mount Carmel again, and go to Æsculapia for our health." (Only for our health?) "Brother Myles sends his kindest regards, and says he doesn't think near so much of Miss Ada as of you! Mattie, please write soon."

Next month comes the "exhibits," and in July—this from Oliver,—"I know you will be surprised at the caption of this letter—Ghent, Carroll County, Kentucky." It does, indeed, surprise her, for after a year's absence, one would have supposed the student anxious to go back to his parents, kindred and friends. But "I have sacrificed the pleasure of meeting my loved ones, and given up all, for the good of this people." His roommate, Albert Myles, has urged him to this course, for Albert, who has been assisted in College by Mrs. Drusie Tandy Ellis of Ghent, is called there to hold the meeting. "College days were over June 28th," he continues. "I underwent six critical, trying examinations, and prepared my two speeches—and was then so sick I could hardly walk. The doctor brought me out of a weakening disease so that I could stand on the stage while I spoke; but that was about all. When the boys parted for their homes, they left me in extreme agony. My poor frame was racked and tortured by unmerciful disease. Many I did not get to bid goodby—dear boys! God be with you, and may we meet again next October. My roommate, Brother Myles, remained with me. When I recovered, he plead so affectionately for his 'chum Ol.' to go with him to Ghent, that I could not refuse."

And so they go to Covington, and at Cincinnati take the "Joe Anderson" for the river town. But in about two weeks, Oliver will be at Mount Carmel where Mattie is now—he urges her to stay till he comes—and he will bring her a book by one of his favorite professors—McGarvey's "Commentary"—solid food for the young lady, one would think.

Back in the University next fall—let us hope in better health than when he left it!—we find Oliver again pen in hand: "James Keith, Albert Myles and myself will finish the course this year by hard study, having about twenty-five recitations each week—and I am in wretchedly poor condition. I'm fearful of my health's giving way under the great burden. I hope and pray for strength of mind and body to prepare for a long service. I sometimes think it is almost a sin for us young men who are preparing for the ministry, to stay here conning over dull lessons in mathematics, Latin and Greek. Like a caged bird, I long to be free of the College-wall cage. I am anxious to go into the world and preach the Gospel. I have been telling my friend of how you and I preach together, and what a good, assistant preacher you are. How I would like to be with you and your sister tonight. Dear me! What a contrast this dull monotony presents to that blissful happy meeting—to do such noble work as that in which we were engaged! Never can I forget that meeting, nor our trips to Orangeburg! neither can I forget you who cling so tenaciously to 'that good part.' You and Sister O'Bannon both impressed me as being God's dear children. Remember your mission to speak to my sister Mary about becoming a Christian. I suppose you heard of my good meeting at Sardis. Forty-five were added—four of my cousins among the number. Don't fail to send that sermon. Mattie, I send the promised photograph, please send me yours. Write to me soon, and tell me what you are doing. I know you are not hearing Brother Lard *now*. I think you might write poor Ol. a long letter very soon!"

"Poor Ol." received the letter; for we find him answering in a short time—from his letter we may gain an insight into hers: "You speak of your benevolent scheme in progress for the 'poor wanderers of New York.' I do not know your exact meaning, but ever since I formed your acquaintance, I have believed you a chosen instrument of God to accomplish great good for poor mortals. Now you are making the step. Dear me! How I wish such a spirit of Christianity infused itself through the purposes of the ten thousand accomplished and efficient young ladies of Kentucky! How much good might be done by womanhood, if they would devote their time, means and energy to alleviating suffering. Perhaps it would be a better plan to look nearer home. I am glad to know that you whom God has blessed with a mind and heart able to conceive, plan and feel, are breathing a prayer for the distressed. Mattie, it speaks well for you, and makes me rejoice. A young friend of mine insists on my preaching at Mount Sterling that he may obey the Gospel. I can't refuse to go. I know I will lose time, and distract my attention from my studies, but what is that in comparison to saving a soul? I don't hesitate to go, but will be off soon. Encourage the building of the church at Mount Carmel all you can. They will receive $50.00 from me next summer for that purpose. Excuse bad writing. You know I can do better."

In Oliver's next letter—December—we find him in a rather sensitive mood. Mattie has accused him of "Some egotism clearly manifested in a parenthesis" he appears to have stowed away in his last epistle. "Dear me!" says Oliver, wounded and perplexed, "What can it be?" After trying to recall anything that may have prompted her "sarcasm," and after an eloquent outburst against the meanness of egotism wherever found, he is obliged to give it up. After relieving his feelings he falls back on "Brother Lard," who appears as a convenient stalking-horse for both sides. "If you think my writing home a poor excuse for not writing to you, I have a very good one at hand. Brother Lard is preaching here every night. That, as you know (having offered it yourself) is a valid excuse! I have just returned from a visit to President Williams who is in high spirits. He has just been giving me a lecture on my returning here for still another year. He is a dear good man, and often gives me good advice; but I don't think it would be right, after taking a diploma in the Bible College and another in the College of Arts, to remain another year. Now, Mattie, I have always paid much attention to your advice; what do you think on the subject? You know my deficiences; but you also know my burning desire to be at work. Like you, I admire Geo. D. Prentice's 'Closing Year' extravagantly. He has immortalized himself with that inimitable production. What a pity that such a man is not a Christian! The world is presenting a sad picture. The people are beginning to lose confidence even in the clergy. I am convinced that, as a Christian body, we are more in need of deep-toned piety than of anything else. We have more learning than we put to good use. We need exemplary conduct in young men and women. I am going to start out in the New Year to live a holier, better and consequently a happier life. Please remember me in your prayers."

Our next letter to "Miss Mattie," dated December 25th, is not from Oliver Carr, but from another University student, who signs himself by his initials. Poor young gentleman, we seek not to know his name, as he pours out his love of near half a century gone. Her "very welcome favor," it appears, had nipped his sweetest hopes in the bud, but he was "glad to receive it." He goes to the point: "You say that no more intimate relationship can exist between us than that of friendship. Miss Mattie, why not? I do not presume to ask for details, whether your heart is prepossessed in favor of another or whether * * *" But no, this was very real to the "D.," of those days, let us not listen to his heart-beats, but hope rather that "D." now sixty-odd, if he is a day, has long since forgotten all about it. He is introduced here merely to cast one tiny ray upon the character-development of the young lady addressed: "In the mean time, you will allow me to thank you very sincerely for the candor with which you have dealt with me, not only in this correspondence, but ever since our acquaintanceship." And then, remembering that it is the 25th, he adds with a stout heart, "Just while I think of it, I will take your 'Christmas Gift!'"

He gives a flash-light of those vacation days: "Most of the students have gone to their homes. Egg-nog is flowing freely here. The landlady has it in abundance, today. Some of the company partook largely; among them I noticed two young ladies. By the way, a little news afloat: Miss Jennie Lard is to be married to a very interesting youth" (Note the bitterness of our rejected lover!) "of fifty and odd summers: This lovely lad is Woodson, a lawyer of St. Louis, who is very promising for a mere beginner in this up-hill business of life. In the exuberance of his youthful feelings he has presented her with a gold watch, rings infinite, and earbobs not a few." (Oh, the bitterness of it!)

Then, in this incidental fashion, we find introduced a subject which is presently to deepen until it envelops all other thoughts of Mattie Myers: "Alex. Milligan received a letter of twelve pages from Brother Gore, dated Liverpool. He and Surber intend to start for Australia on the 21st"—two young friends of Oliver Carr and Mattie Myers, going forth as missionaries. "They have visited Spurgeon's tabernacle, Crystal Palace, etc. They describe the English manner of worship, different from ours. They have no preaching Lord's Day morning; that part of the day is spent in taking the Lord's Supper, Scripture reading, etc. Preaching at night." And then "D." enters upon the subject of Conscience, in which it seems Mattie is greatly interested; but our own will not permit us to follow him into those intricate depths.

Three months pass by, but Oliver has not forgotten Mattie's thrust: "I do wish you had gratified me by sending the sentence in quotation in which I expressed *egotism*. I have been much troubled about it and I would like to know exactly what it was." Then after several pages of severe self-inspection, to find the contamination, he urges her to see again his sister Mary and his other relatives who are out of the church, and continue with zest, in finding a delightful means of prolonging this correspondence: "You say that the affirmative of the question, 'Will Christ's Second Coming be Premillenial?' is Scriptural. Well, we will have a debate, if you say so. You must make the first speech; I'm simply to reply. But as suggestive of the arguments, I wish you "to prove to me, First * * *"

And so they debate; and spring blooms in Kentucky, and summer comes with its hard work and balmy airs. Mattie Myers is not as strong as she might be, but she has had a long rest, and can rest no longer; for that active spirit calls her to her chosen work. She has already done some teaching, but in the autumn of 1867, she purchases Franklin College at Lancaster, and starts definitely upon her career. She is the president, of course; and she feels as she walks the familiar streets,—no longer a little girl under her brother Joe's tutelage, but a grave young teacher—a girl of twenty now, surrounded by other girls—that her life-work has, indeed, begun. Her first school! It does not, indeed, promise that wide field she has so long coveted; the conditions are straight, the capabilities rather narrow; but after all, it will serve for a time. Why it served so short a time—but one school term, in all,—may be gleaned from the continuation of the correspondence:

"I confide in you," Oliver writes in September, "as I do in my own kin. The plain truth is that you seem much nearer to me than some of my kindred who are ever opposing my humble work. I am thankful that I ever met you, and that we have learned to sympathize with each other. I made a flying visit to Mount Carmel, and cannot say how sad I felt at not seeing you there. I preached at Orangeburg, and had the pleasure of receiving among others, my little cousin Rachel. I have long been praying for her conversion. I baptized her and her husband both at the same time.

"From there I went to the State Meeting at Lexington, and a happy time I had. It was said by old men that they had never known one so *good*. During the meeting, a letter was received and read before the convention by

Brother J. W. McGarvey. It was from Brother Surber. He stated very touchingly the need of more preachers in Australia, and urged Brother Myles and me to come. He expressly stated that the Australian brethren had—under the recommendation of himself and Gore—selected *us*, and wanted no others. Brother Surber wrote to me, and gave a description of Melbourne, where he wants me to preach. His description made me wonder at the degree of refinement there. The city is beautifully adorned with flower-gardens; 140,000 inhabitants. He imagines I'm there, walking with him through the city. He says, 'Come, Ollie, it is just as near Heaven from this country as from Kentucky.' He says we will be to the Cause there what Walter Scott and Barton Stone were here, etc. The brethren there are almost wild for an evangelist from Kentucky; have sent $800.00 in gold to bear expenses of Brother Myles and myself. Above all considerations, the good I might do is the grandest—to preach to people who are not tired of hearing! I know my relatives will oppose my going, and that it will almost break my heart to leave them; but I cannot consult flesh and blood. I have prayed and wept over this, but I cannot escape the conviction that it is my duty to go. All the brethren except Dr. Pinkerton advised me to go. President Milligan just wept like a child. I've not let the folks at home know anything about it; there is great excitement here. Mattie, what do you think of my going? Would you go with me? *I'm in earnest.* Brother Keith and I are holding a meeting at Millersburg. I wish I had you as an assistant preacher, as I did last summer. I hear that people are well educated in Australia. Please write immediately."

We have broken the news to the reader, just as it was broken to Mattie Myers; but there is a difference; for in those days, knowledge of Australia was very superficial in Kentucky. It was immensely farther away then than now, and in proportion as it took so long to go there, to that degree did it appear wild and barbarous, semi-civilized at best. To Carr, Myles and Keith, the senior class of 1867,—the three young preachers and roommates, who were called "the Trio,"—the Australians were a mixture of exported English convicts and bush-men with bristling hair. To their imagination, an Australian was hardly to be classified with any of the recognized races of mankind; he was a mongrel, a mystery. And even if they could have received the enthusiastic laudations of young Surber and Gore, the perils of months upon the deep which rendered passage full of dangers, and a speedy return impossible, must still have appalled the fancy. To go to Australia, then, was to cut away from the old life with all its ties of love, of laughter and of tears, and to find what consolation one might in the thought that the distance from there to heaven was as short as from a Kentucky haven!

The next month, Oliver writes to Mattie Myers: "Your touching letter gave me more encouragement in my expected trip to Australia than any I have received, leaving my heart literally steeped in faith, hope and love. I hated to tell you my plan, for you are always holding up to my view the amount of work to be done in Kentucky. This is the hardest question I was ever called on to decide. It came to me something like the question of my soul's salvation. At the State Meeting, old and young advised me to go—all except Dr. Pinkerton, whose counsel was always very weighty with me. His argument was that the people of Northeast Kentucky need my labor too badly, and that their souls are just as precious as those in Australia. But you know that in Lewis County I have not the opportunities to labor that I'd have in Australia. Life is too short—we must use every advantage. There are others to take my place in this country.

"I wept all the way from Lexington. And then I placed in the scales, home with all the meaning of HOME—father, mother, sisters, brothers, and friends—and no one has dearer friends than I, and God knows I love them dearly,—and on the other side I placed the salvation of perhaps thousands of souls, the love of Jesus and his Cause. I looked at the balance with tearful eyes, and resolved to tell parents, kindred and friends adieu. The scale turned. My love for all dear to me on earth, cannot deter me from going with glad tidings to the weary and heavy-laden. And yet how sad to leave you and all others so dear. I declare, it almost breaks my heart. Yet go I must! I wrote home and told all about it. Oh, I hated to let my poor mother know anything about it. I am to stay three or five years. I will have an audience of 1,000 every Sunday. The salary will be $1,000 in gold. Some of this I will send home to my poor parents; and some to my brother Dick whom I am going to educate; and some to the young man I am already educating for the ministry. I am going to make one more strong appeal to my parents to obey the Gospel. How shall I be able to tell them goodby, if I am to go away with no hope of meeting them in heaven? I am glad you have such a good school. Oh, you are doing a noble work! Just think of training 90 or 100 little hearts and leading them to Jesus!"

December comes, and the stress of resolution grows harder to bear: "I have come home at last, but not to rejoice in the association of friends. I am chilled by translation from a fervid spiritual labor and fellowship of the saints, into a fellowship of worldly affairs where every effort is to get something to eat, drink and wear, with scarcely a thought of the hereafter. Brother Dick is dangerously ill. The dear fellow suffers the most excruciating pain. As I gaze upon his tender form, I wonder if I am ever to realize that thought—my brother, a preacher! Added to this sorrow is the sympathy I have for my poor mother, who weeps whenever Australia is mentioned. It is very distressing. All charge me with not loving them. My dear father rests his heavy head upon his hand, and weeps to think of the future. His frail body is tottering as he descends the hill of life. I fear I shall never see him again, after I say farewell. It well nigh breaks my heart to hear them chide me for resolving to go on that long, long voyage. I close this sad picture by throwing myself into my only refuge—faithful prayer, and immortal hope." The next part of the letter shows that Oliver was "in earnest" when he asked Mattie Myers to go with him:

"In Lexington I met Brother McGarvey on the street" (his teacher with whom he lodged during his last year at the University.) "He urged me to tell him all that happened during my brief visit to you at Lancaster" (where she is teaching her first school.) "In confidence, I told him your objections and difficulties. When I had finished, he said,—

"'I admire her consideration. It is a serious question, I admit. With regard to her health, and the dangers of the voyage, you and she are on a common footing. She need not be deterred by the supposition that you die and leave her in that distant land; the brethren here would, in that case, have her safely returned home.' He urged our marriage, and trip to Australia. He was delighted with the idea of having you there as a teacher. We talked of the sacrifice of your school at Lancaster, and he argued that it would be far better for the cause of Christianity and education to have some one take your place in Lancaster, and have you occupy a higher sphere of usefulness. I wish you had been present to hear him talk; he is a dear, good fellow. With his strong clear brain, he adjusts his plans; with an eye of faith, he views the future. I pray you, weigh his opinions in your well-balanced judgment before you conclude. I talked with President Williams; I fear he will not advise you to go. Brother McGarvey says it will depend upon the mood in which you find him. Then *do* cheer him up, and prepare him for a happy answer!"

The letter concludes with urging the marriage, cautioning her against giving heed to the advice of others—as in the case of John Augustus Williams— but the wisdom of *sometimes* heeding the counsel of others—for instance, that of John W. McGarvey.

"Though a stranger to you in person—" What is this? A letter written to Mattie Myers by this very J. W. McGarvey! "By request of Brother Carr," he says. One would not expect a passionate, enthusiastic burst of eloquence from the author of the "Commentary on Acts." What is said here, emanates from a "strong, clear brain." As the Bible instructor sees it, the situation stands thus: "After all, your own heart must decide whether you go or stay. One thing seems certain, that *he* will go. It is for you to endure his long absence, and risk the uncertainties of his return, or share the voyage with him, and help the noble cause to which he consecrates his all."

This same month, Oliver returns to the charge: "I waited a week with the keenest anxiety, hoping each night to get an answer from you. It has come at last. Mattie! I anticipated what it would be, from reading President Williams' letter. I know he has tried to mould your life for teaching, alone. He is true and noble and I doubt not he gave you, as you say, 'his wisest judgment and the fullest expression of his good heart on the subject.' I believe he meant to point to our highest good; but I cannot follow his advice. I have pondered both your and his reasons for wishing delay. Both of you urge a year's preparation. Well, what kind of preparation? You are already prepared to teach those in Australia; and I know I can tell them what to do to be saved. I know I am weak; but Northeast Kentucky is not the place for me to get strong. You say I 'need to know assuredly that I can meet stern realities victoriously.' I do not think I will know more about that than I do now, till I meet them. Of course a year's experience would increase my usefulness, but why not acquire it where the brethren want me? I don't know what especial point you had in view by saying you would like a year's hard study under President Williams. What were you going to study? You have taken his full course, I presume. We have simply the story of the Cross to tell and I believe that we can do it *now*."

So the letter goes on for eight closely-written pages, showing the fervor of eloquence quite lacking in the concise review by McGarvey; but, then, it was not McGarvey who was in love. Oliver is in love, doubly so; first and always first, with his Cause; and then always with Mattie. It is a terrible struggle for the young girl, for she too, is in love; but her affections have always associated teaching with the Cause. She must know in her heart that this missionary enterprise is a divergence from her central idea, however much more good it may accomplish. Here is her college, bought and paid for, and here are her 90 or 100 girls for training. She may hope for different blessings beyond the seas, but not of this sort.

Prof. J. B. Myers

"Considering His Letter."

And here is her brother Joe bitterly opposed to the plan, as one's brother Joe may very naturally be. It is well enough for McGarvey, who thinks first of the dissemination of the Gospel, to smile upon her going; and how could Williams, whose ideal for woman is the vocation of teaching, say otherwise than wait? It is well enough for Oliver to see but one course before him; he never entertained himself with dreams of teaching school. He always meant to preach, and Australia means more of it, with wider good to hope for. But it is no simple problem for Mattie Myers.

A one-sided correspondence, we have been treated to, which, though one-sided, has nevertheless given us as good an insight into the one addressed as if she had done all the writing; better perhaps; for now we are to hear her voice, which in its agitation and perplexity, does not, it may be, reveal her as she is:

"I have stretched forth my hands and nailed my heart to the Cross. You may cast it from you, but conscience nailed it there. For awhile I cheated myself with the belief that its voice mingled with the voice of my heart, 'You are already prepared; go with him.' But it was only the echo of my heart's happy song. I feel that I would be an incumbrance, rather than your co-worker. However mournfully my heart may cry, however beseechingly, *I cannot go with you.* Conscience, my guide, beckons me, and fervently I follow, though my heart is torn asunder. Ah, the bloodless battles that are fought in our world! You have said, 'Although I love you as I love no one else on earth, still, if you deny me, I must go alone.' I say in reply, that though I love you with that love of which only a Christian woman is susceptible, I cannot go with you. Your capabilities fit you for one field of labor, mine fit me for another. We have all to build an altar. I have built mine, and laid thereon my tenderest feelings, the yearning desire of the woman-nature to be loved. I know that this mysterious yearning which God has planted with his own hand in woman's heart will, if left unsatisfied, cast a shadow over her life; that however strong, however self-reliant a woman may be, her heart reaches out for something to complete her happiness. But the giant will can strengthen the trembling, faltering heart.

"And it is well to nail the heart to the Cross that raises it nearer to God. He will give it strength to suffer. And his love can never fail. Do not think that I am staggering under complaint. Like a cheerful traveler I will take up my life-burden, and continue the journey, with a song in my mouth, keeping time to the voice of conscience and my God. Do not think for a moment, Ollie, that I would dissuade you from entering upon your grand mission. What I said to you before I knew you loved me, I say to you now, though it wrings my heart with an anguish that I sometimes think cannot be borne. Sometimes I feel that my heart must break, but it is sustained by the love of God. If conscience bids you go, then you must go. But I cannot conceive how conscience would say to you to leave a field in which laborers are few, for one which may cost you your life. I am impressed that going is a matter of inclination rather than of conscience. Nevertheless, if conscience does tell you so, then I urge you with all the earnestness of my soul, to go. Go; and the burdens of my prayers will be for him so far away, and yet so very near."

Alas! how great a mountain is our own conscience, and how small a molehill that of our neighbor! Mattie, who has been pointing out that all her future misery is to come from obeying her own, pauses to doubt if Oliver's conscience is a conscience at all! On such provocation as that, who can blame Oliver for having doubts about Mattie's conscience? That he did have doubts, and that he did his utmost to cause her to agree with him, no one can doubt with the following letter before him:

"Dear Mattie:—Yours received. I heartily agree to March 26th as *our wedding day*. I will write to tell sister Mary and Matt to come down to May's Lick on the 27th. Saturday I will deliver my farewell address here. We will go to Maysville en route for Cincinnati. Horace came from Flemingsburg yesterday to find out something about it. Matt, Bud and Mollie are coming.

"Mattie, I have the best kind of news to tell you. Hold your breath while you read. Father came forward at church yesterday, and made the good confession. 'Bless the Lord, O my soul and all that is within me, bless his holy name!' I recognized in that, the answer to many a prayer. And now if my mother would obey the gospel I would believe your prophecy uttered at President Milligan's reception was fulfilled. Do you remember what it was?—'Brother Ollie, I believe God will make you instrumental in bringing your family into the fold.' Oh, will that ever be? Mother won't go to church. She has never heard me preach but twice; but I will pray on, and hope on."

CHAPTER VII.

"I WILL GO."

It was September, 1867 that Oliver Carr asked Mattie Myers to go with him to Australia. For six months she hesitated, refused, wavered. It was not a question of devotion to each other, but of loyalty to the life-ideal of each. Going to Australia meant three or five or seven years away from Mattie's chosen vocation. She weighed at its full value the argument that she could teach in Melbourne; of course, she could teach; but teaching must necessarily be subordinate to missionary work. Mattie did not undervalue the importance of missionary labors; but neither did she undervalue the importance of touching girls' lives in the school room.

In the struggle, McGarvey and Williams, as we have seen, took opposite sides; McGarvey was for his pupil, Oliver; Williams was for his pupil, Mattie. Each looked at the question from his point of view. To the President of the Bible College, what was more important than carrying the Bible across the sea? To the President of Daughters' College, teaching was the exalted vocation of woman—Let O. A. Carr do his man's work, he argued; and let Mattie Myers do her woman's work.

And there was brother Joe, who had done so much for Mattie—the brother whom she feared she might love too well—pleading, arguing, exhorting. "Let Oliver go to Australia," he insisted, "and when he comes back—at the end of his five or seven years, then, if you and he think as much of each other as you do now, why—" But the proposition seemed quite safe, so he added with a stout heart, "then you can get married!" But on this side of the five years, No! Never! And when words fail him, and arguments need to be rested, each having done service so often for want of new ones—Joe gets his flute and sits on the piazza with Mattie, these balmy spring evenings of 1868, and plays and plays—plays always the old familiar melodies, the airs that are wrapped up with her most sacred memories—"Old Kentucky Home," and "Home, Sweet Home," and—we fear—"Bonnie Blue Flag" that carries up the bars and would sweep the stars from the Heaven of Union blue.

"I Will Go."

All this is too much for Mattie; her own conscience, the advice of Williams, "that prince of instructors," as she calls him, and beloved Joe; all cry out against Australia. She writes to Oliver—

"I pray that the love of God may strengthen you to accomplish your holy mission, and bring you back to waiting hearts in your own Kentucky land. I may regret the decision that prevents me from going with you. I may, after you are gone, regret that my hand is not to help you; I weep to labor with you. I do not know. But I have tried to enlighten my conscience, and it must not be disregarded. Go, and give to the weary rest, and to those that thirst, of the well of living water. Though I must suffer, there is a morn and land beyond it all. Go, and work for God."

In these days when evangelistic work would permit Oliver to come to Lancaster, he visited Mattie Myers as her accepted suitor. After her day's work in the schoolroom, she listened to his reading of "Lady of Lyons," and after the "Lady of Lyons" had had her say, talk would drift to Australia. It was at the conclusion of such a talk at Mt. Carmel—how earnest we may imagine—when Joe was not there—*that* we may take for granted—the young teacher rose with the solemnity of one who takes an irretrievable step, having counted all the costs—"I will go!"

Those are her words. And having spoken, the matter is settled. Let poor Joe play his flute-airs, and look mournfully into space; let Williams say what he will, or Pinkerton, or anybody else. Mattie has spoken. That means a wedding-day on March the twenty-sixth.

Not that Joe understands how unalterable is her mind. Indeed, he is in no condition to bear the truth. That voyage seems to him a death, the going out from his life of the dearest object of his affections. He grows wild when she tries to make him understand her mind. When Oliver reasons with him, he no longer answers with arguments, but with mere incoherent passion, partly anger, partly despair. So this is what we will do; we will go to Mt.

Carmel without telling Joe,—yonder at the home of the sister, Mrs. O'Bannon, where we first met, whence we took that Spring-wagon excursion to the ineffective spring of Æsculapia. Mattie will take the stage that comes down to Maysville. Oliver will be standing upon the pike, out of sight of any kinsman's house. Mattie will order the stage to stop. He will get in—off we will go.

And so we might have made our trip without incident, without sorrow, but for the unforeseen, in this instance, embodied in brother Joe. He suddenly appears, wild and excited, having come in such nervous haste, that his hat is left at home. Hatless, but not breathless, he stops that stage and holds it while he delivers himself of all his arguments, seeking to bury Australia in an avalanche of spontaneous eloquence. But the word Mattie has spoken before the blazing hearth she speaks on the open pike: "I will go."

Why argue further? Clearly conscience nerves her to her purpose! Conscience—or love. Only one term of her first school so proudly begun—and she has put it in charge of another, and is starting forth to merge her life-work into that of another—and he, a stranger not long ago,—a mere lad gathering the shavings in the wagon-shop to start the tavern fires.

Events now come thick and fast. We are getting ready for the wedding now. Oliver rides in a buggy with a schoolmate from his home town, May's Lick, through Lexington to Lancaster, the home of Mattie Myers. Many times he stops on the way for farewells. The reception committee come forth in strength, but their spokesman bursts into tears, and Oliver is received with tears only. Albert Myles, his six-year schoolmate accompanies him to Lancaster. The wedding is to be at five in the morning. Bells ring. The village people, thinking there is a fire, are roused and come forth. Learning that it is a wedding, they troop to the church. The spectators look on through their tears, thinking vaguely of the other side of the globe, whither the bridal pair is presently to set forth. Albert Myles performs the ceremony. It is a scene of early light and tears. "Mattie going away!" is the murmur—Mattie whom these folk have known from infancy—going away in early womanhood, perhaps never to return!

From Lancaster to Lexington in a carriage; and here J. B. Bowman, the University necromancer, gives the bride and groom a dinner in his home, once the home of Henry Clay,—Ashland, where we have seen Walter Scott admiring the picture of George Washington. Teachers and pupils of the University assemble, and there is another mournful farewell. In the afternoon, from Lexington to Stony point, and goodby to Mrs. Fox, that sister Minnie of the May's Lick days. At Millersburg, another wedding-dinner, given by Alex. McClintock, and then to May's Lick, thirty-six miles by carriage.

Before We Say Goodbye

Here they remain over Sunday—the last Sunday in the old May's Lick church, in which Eneas Myall is a deacon,—the blacksmith who said when first hearing the news, "I am sorry to see you go, Ollie, but it seems providential!" The elders of the church, the same who were elders when Walter Scott preached there, ordained Oliver on that last Sunday at home. He was surrounded by old friends, tearful but exultant in their sorrow. There was one who could not come because, "I can't tell him goodby," he said. That was Oliver's hard task now, to say goodby to all, hardest of all to those of his father's house. But he had nerved himself for the ordeal. "I could tell them all goodby," he says, "until I came to my mother."

They go, according to their plans, straight to Maysville, across the county, to take boat for Cincinnati. Not alone do Mattie and Oliver make that journey. His mother is with them. News runs before; the Australian missionaries are coming! The word is quickly passed back and forth, that there will be services at the church. When Oliver arrives he finds the appointment made. He rises to preach. It is his last night in Kentucky. Before his vision stretches a long vista of uncertain years in a strange land; years among strangers for this man who is blessed with so many friends. But that sorrow is swallowed up in the deeper joy of presenting Christ to the people, showing forth his loveliness for the last time in the land of his birth.

That sermon is not preserved, for which we are, we believe, sufficiently thankful. If love in its fulness cannot be spoken, much less can it be read. There is a simplicity and an inner earnestness, that is altogether baffling to the snare of leaded type. Whatever the subject of that sermon, Christ was in it, and we care nothing for its divisions and its order. We are thrilled with joy by that sermon—we who never heard it,—because we see the preacher's mother step forth—at last!—and stand before them all like a beautiful dream come true—or rather, like a spirit of love, whose enkindled face flashes into the son's eyes the answer to his prayers.

Not in vain, as we have seen, were her lonely vigils, sewing far toward midnight in the sleep-enwrapped tavern, that her children might be clothed, toiling before break of day, the pale candle guiding her hands to heroic labor that her loved ones might be fed. Much does Oliver owe her, and much is now repaid, on this last night in Kentucky. He baptized her; and as she came up out of the water, with his arm so tenderly passed about her, she looked at him through her wonderful, new-found happiness. "If all were as easy to obey as baptism," she murmured, "it would be easy enough!"

And so,—the boat to Cincinnati where W. T. Moore's father-in-law, he who is later to become Governor Bishop of Ohio,—entertains the bridal pair in his home, and other friends assemble for goodbys,—the goodbys at Macomb, Illinois. And then to New York to set forth for Australia, by way of England. On board at last—and under a sullen sky they stand on deck, watching their native land fade—fade—till nothing is to be seen but a world of angry waves.

CHAPTER VIII.

AN ENGLISH PRIMROSE.

The voyage, begun on a rough sea, was continued over angry waves. For seven days the ship was beaten by the winds. It was the first time Oliver and Mattie had been outside of Kentucky. Added to the distress of seasickness was the thought that, after this passage to England, another voyage of almost three months awaited them before they could set foot upon the strange land selected for their missionary labors. No wonder as the bride was borne farther and farther across the uneasy Atlantic, her thoughts went constantly back to Kentucky—"That far-off land," she writes, "my beautiful, sunny Southland."

Since the wedding-day, there have been a marvelous succession of strange scenes—the trip to New York, the hurried visits to points of interest in New York and Brooklyn, the mingling with the rush and roar of Broadway, and, stranger than all these, this helpless tossing in the cabin, as the ship throbs and lifts dizzily in air—lifts to sink down and down, as if never to ride the sea again.

"That Twenty-Sixth day of March!" she writes in pencil with shaking hand. "It dawned so bright and beautiful. In its soft morning twilight I knelt before an altar, and laid thereon not only the heart of a bride, but all that I had best known in childhood and in girlhood: Home with all its tender associations, friendship whose face shone as the face of an angel—the sweet brier that shed its fragrance beneath my window, the birds that sang for me, the dear old 'big spring' over whose cooling-ripples I have so often stooped to drink"—she remembers all these, as the ship bears her farther from that America she may never see again.

"Our blessed land of liberty," she says, "proud, beautiful, glorious America!" Truly, the war is over; and as she steams ever farther away from America, its states seem to melt magically into one another, and North and South blend, and become an indissoluble Union.

One day, less stormy than the rest, the young husband crept from his berth, hoping to find relief from days of nausea by greeting the keen wind. He went upon deck, and was presently engaged in conversation with a stranger.

He found that his companion was an Englishman who, for some time, had been in business in Chicago. He was much interested in the young man's missionary plans; the shrewd merchant read aright the intense zeal which shone upon the Kentuckian's face, and which trembled in his voice. "I have a brother living in London," he said; "when you go there, you must go to his house. I am on my way to visit him now, and I'll meet you there."

Oliver Carr had no intention of going to test the hospitality of a stranger, and, when he gave Mr. Murby his card, he supposed the incident closed. On the eighth day out the ship touched at Queenstown. Mr. and Mrs. Carr—we must no longer call them "Oliver" and "Mattie,"—took a ride on a Jaunting Car—in which one sits sidewise, while one's driver sparkles with Irish wit. A woman came to sell them fruit, and offered to toss pennies for the difference between what she wanted and they were willing to give. It was a jolly crowd that surrounded them, and every Irishman had a funny tale to tell the travelers. Before the ground ceased its semblance of rocking to and fro, they were again on board.

When they landed in Liverpool, everything seemed new and strange. They "found cabs instead of busses;" but doubtless the difference was most marked because they found Englishmen instead of Americans. At the hotel they were visited by G. Y. Tickle and other members of the church, and in the afternoon they crossed to Berkinhead to visit other Christians. On April 29th the train pulled out at 9 a. m. for London. Mrs. Carr took a few notes, as she looked upon Mrs. Browning's world—the world of "Aurora Leigh."

"Corn—undulating lands—rural improvements—daisies and primroses. Hedges—winding roads, and footpaths. Drains in the lowlands. Winding brooks and brooklets, through daisied meadows. Fir-clad hills."

Out of this primrose England, the car glides into the smoke and fog of London. London at last—how far away from the Lancaster and Stanford of one's girlhood! How far, indeed, even from the dreams of one's girlhood, this city that rises up, solidly real before the young woman's eyes! It seems pulsing with the thoughts of those who represent, to her mind, the highest peaks of literature; Dickens and Thackeray, George Eliot and Robert Browning, Bulwer Lytton and Macaulay and Carlyle and De Quincy—all are living; one might meet them any moment on Oxford or Regent streets, where "I took a promenade," she says; "I find they surpass Broadway in all but dress."

At 2:30, they are installed at the hotel; at three, they take luncheon and at four they have a visitor. It is the brother of the Chicago merchant. The merchant has written about the missionaries, and asked that they be looked up—doubtless, suspecting that the overtures must come from the English side. So this brother has come, a Mr. Murby of some distinction; for does he not edit the music department of the *Cornhill Magazine*?

He insists on the young bridal pair going to his own home; for O. A. Carr, in honor of the honeymoon, has selected a hotel of much pretention. "You must go with me," says Mr. Murby. "It is too expensive, staying at a hotel like this; you shall make your home in my house. My wife will take no refusal. She will entertain you as well as she can—we have one baby in the cradle, and another three years old. I've brought the wagon for the trunks."

All this from a man and woman one has never seen before, and never heard of, except from a chance fellow-passenger; a man and a woman who do not belong to one's church and has never heard of one's friends! But, after all, is it so strange? If one travels through the world with eyes open for primroses, and finds them growing along the wayside, why should not eyes that seek brotherly kindness, find it blooming in many a stranger's heart?

Away go the trunks, and the hotel knows our friends no more. Two weeks are to be spent in England, before sailing for the opposite side of the globe; and while they are in England, Mrs. Murby leaves the baby in the cradle, and acts as guide for the Americans. In their hurried visit, they could have seen little without her. She takes them to ride in the underground railroad, shows them the wonders of the waxworks, at the entrance of which stands George Washington with extended hand, and lingers with them in the British Museum.

Mrs. Carr's notes of her travels are meager in the extreme; she was too busy observing and studying, to write about what she saw; but the necessary enlargement of thought resulting from extended travel was to take its own part in developing her personality. "Chelsea Hospital for old soldiers—Buckingham Palace, the Queen's residence—Eaton Square—National school teachers trained for public schools—Duke of York's school—Geological exhibit—rock crystal—wood carving—Porcelain plate, 1585, Francesco de Medici—Venetian wine glass—Danish drinking-horn—Paul preaching at Athens—Christ changing the water into wine—Peter and John at the Beautiful Gate—Hogarth's Marriage a la Mode—Mrs. Siddons as Actress—Rosa Bonheur—Edwin Landseer—Hyde Park—House where the Duke of Wellington died—Parliament—Retiring Room—Her Majesty with Mercy and Justice in sculpture—Portrait of Kings and Queens—House of Lords—Throne—Queen's chair on the right—Prince of Wales on the left—The Prince Consort—Woolsack, seat for Lord Chancellor in front of Queen—Table on which are laid all petitions—books beneath—just behind the table, the bar—gallery for peeresses, above—Peers' Robing Room—Moses descending from the Mount—Lobby—Embarking of Pilgrim Fathers—Charles erecting Standard at Nottingham—Central Hall—Four windows—Lobby—Pictures—Square Hall—Commons Speaker's Chair—gallery—Each side of entrance, seats for liberals and tourists—St. Stephen's—Marble walls and floors—On each side, six stained glass windows, representing scenes in life of Stephen—On the Thames—Somerset House—Waterloo Bridge."

Thus we might follow her from spot to spot, as she hastily jots down the names of pictures, and of the illustrious dead, amidst a catalogue of wonders seen at the Crystal Palace, the India Museum, the National Gallery. "St. Paul—Whispering Gallery—Sculptor above—Scenes in the Life of Paul—Monument of Sir John Howard, Joshua Reynolds—geometrical stairway—Crypt—Newgate Prison for all offenders within the city's limits—Christ's Hospital, founded by Edward VI.—Boys' dress in the costume of that day—Yellow stockings, leather breeches—Former palace of Henry VIII. and Cardinal Wolsey—Post Office; just across the street, Returned Letter Office—Clock with two bells, one 'Time,' the other 'Death'—Publishing House belonging to the Religious Tract Society, built over the place where the martyrs suffered under Bloody Mary—Guild Hall—for public dinners—Grand dinner given to the Sultan—gold array—The Lord Mayor conducts trials—His Residence—Monument to Nelson.

"May 5th, the Tower—Gateway—Entrance, moats—Bell Tower—Bloody Tower, porte cullis--White Tower, 15 feet thick—Built, time William the Conqueror—Norman spear used by him—Dress of 1665—Gun taken by French at Malta and afterwards recaptured by English—Sir Walter Raleigh imprisoned 12 years—Lady Jane Grey—Queen Elizabeth on Horseback—Fire, 1841—Indian armor, 1750—Chamber from which Hastings was ordered to execution—Anne Boleyn's prison in the Tower—Beauchamp Tower." And so on, and on, from one spot of historic interest to another, the travelers absorbing all with thirsty minds, the hostess tireless, or at least uncomplaining—and at night the profound sleep of the sight-seer's utter exhaustion.

Mr. and Mrs. Murby took the stranger-guests to their hearts, and treated them like long-lost friends. The perfume of their gracious hospitality invested London with a tender aroma for these wanderers, to such a degree that whenever they afterward thought of England, they thought of disinterested kindliness. On one of Mrs. Carr's diary-pages, is to be seen a faint brownish stain, above which is written: "Found by Mrs. Murby on the streets of London—this primrose." The flower has long since slipped away and crumbled to dust, since it was placed there in the spring of 1868; I should like to think that it blooms again on my page, in honor of that quick and loving eye that discovered the primrose in the London streets, and the gold in the strangers' hearts.

Conway Castle, N. Wales

Beaumaris Castle, N. Wales

On Sunday, they went to hear Spurgeon preach. It was a very ordinary sermon; his statements had been made thousands of times before, and to none who listened, were they new. His manner was untheatrical, his flow of eloquence was not intense. Everything was the essence of simplicity. He began by holding up a rose. He said that on his way to the tabernacle, a woman had given it to him. He spoke of his happiness caused by this simple gift, then of the beauty of flowers, and of giving; and, as the audience of 3,000 listened, they were melted to tears. His subject was the Accessibility of Christ. It was the *tenderness* in his words and voice that wrought the charm. The singing was general; it seemed that each of the 3,000 took upon himself the responsibility of carrying the song through to its conclusion.

In Birmingham, the Carrs visited David King, editor of the *Harbinger*; he was the most prominent member of the Christian Church in England, of his day. It was his custom to question the preachers who passed through his country, to find out if they were "sound." It was from him that Mr. Carr discovered the British objection to the American custom of extending an invitation to the unsaved at the conclusion of the sermon. It was also Mr. King who went to the office to buy the Carrs their tickets up to London, fearing they would not get second-class ones. "Only fools and noblemen ride first-class in this country," was his dictum; "the second class is just as good and costs half as much."

The following brief notes show us that Mrs. Carr is in Scotland: "Holyrood—Rezzio's Slaughter—Residence of bygone monarchs—where Lord Murray held his Council—Residence of Mary Queen of Scots—where Her Majesty stops, when in Edinburg—Castle of Craigmillar—where Mary sometimes held her court—Lochleven Castle."

She was particularly interested in Wales: "Canarvon Castle, built by Edward I.—First Prince of Wales born here—April 25, 1284—Chamberlain Tower, occupied by the Lord Chamberlain—Eagle Tower, so called because of the Eagle Sculpture on its turret. Prisoner, or Dungeon Tower. It is supposed this castle was never completed. The banqueting hall, entirely destroyed— In this castle the present Prince and Princess of Wales were entertained during their visit to Canarvon, April 24. On this occasion, Wellington Tower was magnificently decorated.

"North Wales—across the straight of Angelsey; lodgings here. Ebb and flow of the tide—Hawthorne—a beautiful lodge, the entrance to a residence—Suspension bridge over the Menia Strait—Castle—Model village, Bethesda, near the slate quarries—20 galleries, each 60 feet high—the deeper the quarry, the better the slate—Tunnel and railways with round rails and grooved wheels, working with rope—Blasting signal, first a red flag, then the bugle. Each gallery one mile around the rail—1,200 feet from lowest gallery to top—300 men employed. Total wages per month, 1,200 pounds.—Penryln Castle, 16 years building, completed 30 years ago—Main entrance, heavy iron gate, swinging on massive pillars of stone, with imposing ivy-clad arch above; winding roads and bypaths; through rare shrubs and gorgeous flowers of innumerable species—Main entrance to Castle yard, a massive orchid gateway—Main entrance to Castle, massive cross-barred iron doors in base of tower—Four towers with the ivy, beautiful emblem of trust, clinging to them all—Interior; entrance hall, billiard room, innumerable lobbies with rare ceilings, main stairway, bedrooms with antique furniture, drawing-room, dining and breakfast rooms, library, chapel for family worship, minor stairways, etc.—Family of 10 children, two married and now in London—will return here in July. Culinary apartments; cook's sitting-room, where he writes the bill of fare."

All these sights, crowded as they are into a few days, delay the departure for Australia; moreover, the travelers have decided to take a sailship. They have sufficient knowledge of the deathly throb of the steamer, the quiver that sends unutterable faintness and nausea to those susceptible to seasickness. The sailship, they are told, skims the waves like a bird—one hardly knows he is afloat, or knowing, feels himself lightly carried through the air.

Mrs. Murby finds her new acquaintances have not left, and writes to Mrs. Carr at Liverpool, on May 15th, "I was very much pleased to receive your letter yesterday; I had supposed you would be far away from Old England by this time. I just wish you had stayed with us longer! There are lots of places besides the British Museum, I could have taken you to see. You say you are to leave on Saturday, the 19th, but the 19th is Tuesday, so we can hear from each other if we cannot meet. If I can find that church in Camden Town, for your sakes I will visit it. The few days we spent together will always be remembered by us with pleasure. I sincerely trust we may all be spared to meet again; you may rest assured of a hearty welcome. In the meantime we can correspond with each other. I went to sit for my portrait yesterday; it will be ready for me to-morrow, and I will send it to you before you leave Liverpool."

So writes the editor's wife—she who finds primroses in the streets of London; and her letter comes as a last voice of love to one about to embark upon a sea-voyage of more than a hundred days.

CHAPTER IX.

THE LONG VOYAGE.

The long voyage was made on the Oriental, Captain Myles. Mrs. Carr was the only lady who had taken first-class passage. There was a rich young man on board, who had been put under the care of a Scot of mature years; the young man was peculiarly susceptible to the temptation of strong drink, but the Captain reassured his sisters with the declaration that there would be no drinking aboard his vessel! The young man wished to visit Australia, one of the few countries he had never seen, and Duncan, the Scot, had undertaken his charge that he, too, might have the treat of foreign travel.

England had not faded from sight before the corks were flying.

Mrs. Carr found herself associated with a class of men who were far from corresponding to the degree of their tickets. She felt the need of woman's society, since her husband was the only man present who possessed that refinement and moral instinct which had been the breath of her life. She was unable to hide her disapproval of the drunken orgies which the officers of the crew shared, and it was particularly distressing to her to witness the deliberate ensnarement of the rich young man, the evident scheme to make him drink that he might be fleeced at the card-game.

She and her husband put their sentiments into words of remonstrance, which resulted in the Captain's making slighting remarks, as they sat at table. He took a spiteful pleasure in boasting in their presence that he wouldn't employ a "teetotaler on his ship."

The first Sunday out Mr. Carr was asked to conduct the religious services. He read the First Psalm and made remarks relative to the godly and ungodly. Captain Myles was enraged. "I supposed we would have the Church of England Service," he said at the conclusion; "we will have it after this; I will read it, myself." And so he did, when he was not too drunk; in that case, he had the ship's physician read it.

Mrs. Carr sought relief in the association of the other women on board, but this was peremptorily stopped. "If she wants to keep company with second-class people," said the Captain with a sneer, "let her buy a second-class ticket."

The ship had not been many days from the British Isles before the crew was almost completely demoralized. Drinking, gaming, coarse songs marked the hours of the night. The sailors were at the mercy of the winds.

The vessel drifted over to the coast of Africa. It was becalmed two weeks under the intolerable heat of the sun's vertical rays, while not a breath of air came to relieve the hot glare of the Equator.

One day the Captain exclaimed with the air of one who has made a terrible decision, "If we don't get wind to-morrow, I will jump overboard!" The morrow came, and there was no wind. Of course the threat of the Captain resulted in nothing more dangerous than a cooling bath in the peaceful waters, but the effect of his words, and of his sudden leap from the deck, were hard upon sensitive nerves.

Mrs. Carr being denied the companionship of women, found what relief from the monotony she might, in writing letters, and especially in writing in her commonplace-book many quotations from the poets. She beguiled the time, also, in composing poetry which deals rather with themes of home, than with those of distant scenes. The ship was wafted toward South Africa, but it did not weigh anchor. "The only view we had of South Africa consisted of some monkeys in the trees." When the Cape Verde Islands were sighted, Captain Myles was anxious to exhibit his skill by passing within a stone's throw of one on either side. Mrs. Carr, rejoicing at the sight of something more human and picturesque than monkeys in trees, took extensive notes:

"June 18. The Captain caught a large dolphin—change of color in dying. Breakfasted on flying fish.

"June 19. Sighted Antonio and St. Vincent islands—passing between them. Cape de Verde Islands, possessions of Portugese. Antonio with its innumerable rocky points, some losing themselves far above the clouds. The white haze peeping behind, lights up the acute angles of the points—the heights are dark, frowning and barren, with white bowlders at the feet. The gray terraces in the distance look like leaping waters, rushing onward to the ocean, to kiss the breakers. The shores are dotted with little villages whose houses are small and white, with red tiled roofs. Around these villages are spreading greens along the shore, and extending up the heights that, through the glass, are seemingly inaccessible. Yet these heights are laid out, far up, with hedges into green fields and waving orchards. The shore is indented with innumerable little bays, and the magnificent ravines to which they point, fill the soul with awe.

"St. Vincent is inhabited by the Portugese, yet there is not a spring, or well of fresh water, or a blade of grass in the whole island. There are the signs, far up the island, of the washing of the waves. What a glorious sight they would present in a storm! Here and there, far up the heights are solitary rocks and vast strata left bare by the washing of rains and waves, and blackened by the elements. Signals are hoisted opposite Porte Grande in order that the Oriental may be reported in Liverpool in 12 days. Two sailing ships are in the harbor. The Oriental passed between St. Vincent and Shell Island."

One day the discovery was made that there was a stowaway on board; it was a young man with a crippled arm, who had slipped into a hiding-place as the Oriental lay at the Liverpool dock. Captain Myles was all the more furious because he found himself helpless to rid himself of the unfortunate youth. He compelled the stowaway to do the meanest labor, and the hardest his crippled state would allow. When the sailors encountered him, they greeted him with oaths, if they greeted him at all. He was set to scour the decks, and it was a task that had no ending.

The Oriental drifted at last into the arms of the Trade Winds which sent it whirling around the Cape of Good Hope. A furious storm came on. The sea was lashed into mountain-peaks and was hurled in rushing torrents over the decks. Those sailors who were obliged to remain above, walked waist-deep in water. The man at the wheel was tied to his post—the Captain was up all night; but not, now, at cards and drink. The rumor spread among the passengers that the crew expressed their doubts of weathering the gale. The rumor was founded upon truth; the outcome was extremely doubtful. There was the usual scene preceding a probable capsizing; curses and prayers, the sudden scream of agonized fear, or of desperate appeal. "But we committed ourselves to the care of the All-wise and Almighty, and went to sleep."

Morning came to show under its dim light a battered ship, doors broken open, cabins inundated from the seas that had poured down the hatchways, and spars swept away. But suddenly the ocean grew calm, the wind became fair, and the vessel headed straight for Australia.

They were at table when the cry arose above, "Man overboard!" Captain Myers started up with an oath and went growling and storming to see into the matter. It was the stowaway, who had been cast dizzily from the life-boat he was trying to paint by a sudden lurch of the vessel. The Captain himself threw him a life-preserver and shouted, "Stop for him, he's too crippled to swim to it. Ship about! Man the life-boat!" In that boat brave sailors went down out of sight in the angry sea, then like a bird sat on the crest. Our ship "across sea" rolled fearfully and the Captain commanded the passengers to leave the deck. The sailors in the boat returned, but the poor crippled boy could not be found. And so the fair wind bore them on their way and the youth who had come from the unknown into our story, dropped back again into the unknown. Was there any one to care?[7]

One hundred and four days on the deep, during which period, land had been sighted only three times. Mrs. Carr continued to remember, and to write poetry. We find this, "Written on board the Oriental, South Atlantic, August, 1868:

Homeland, dearest, gentle homeland, Dearest now art thou to me— Dearest, for between us stretches, Dark and grim, the cruel sea.

I have left thee, home and homeland, I have bade thy joys adieu But, my heart, my heart is with thee, For I know thy heart is true.

Now I know how great thy soul is, Know its depths, so deep, so mild. Dear and tender home and homeland, Pray, pray for your wandering child.

So I smile—the Father's calling To a land beyond the sea, To the weary heavy-laden, Who are groaning to be free.

Yield I? Yes, I once was weary, Heavy-hearted and oppressed; Yield because Christ died to save me, Yield because he gave me rest.

With such glorious love to lead me Can my heart its thrilling tell? Home and homeland, I have left you; "Dear and tender, fare you well!"

Thus after her varied experiences, we find the young bride's poetic fancy slipping past the grandeur of the ocean life, its terrible storm and its terrible calm; she remembers not now the beautiful castle with its orchid gate, nor thinks of the family of ten who are to return to their peasantry in the stately rural life of Old England; nor of the wonders of the British Isles; it is Kentucky that claims her deepest love and sincerest tribute—And if her ears ring to the melody of "Old Kentucky Home," a voice seems to speak, breaking its way through the music with—"Go ye into all the world and preach the gospel to every creature."

At last, the Oriental casts anchor in Hobson's Bay. The voyage is ended, the experiences in a foreign land are to begin. The Carrs are urged by many of the second-class passengers to report the conduct of Captain Myles, but they let his insolence to them pass with the passing of unfavorable winds that have so long delayed the ship. At this entrance into a new life, they are saddened to discover that the Captain has persuaded the rich young man to go back with him—to refuse even to land. He has not yet been completely stripped at the gambling table, and he is so valuable and tractable a victim, that all arts are employed to feed his vanity and alienate him from his guardian. It is a fearful disappointment to the sturdy Scot, Duncan, to be deprived of his travels in Australia, but he will not leave his weak-minded charge; so he turns his back on the land to see which, he has endured contumely and abuse, and sails away to do all he can to save his ward from the Captain's rapacity—thus furnishing the Carrs with an example of fidelity to his promise made to the sisters of the unfortunate man, which they treasure in their hearts.

A hundred members of the church have come from Melbourne to Hobson's Bay, to welcome the missionaries. Among them, the happiest is Oliver's fellow-student at Harrodsburg, G. L. Surber.

"For many months we have been waiting to hear if some sacrificing ones would leave the United States for this country—" as he and Gore had left, a few years before. "Then at last," he writes, "we were rejoiced to hear that Brother O. A. Carr and wife had left Liverpool for Melbourne. Our anxiety was to see them in health. For a fortnight we read the daily papers eagerly, hoping to hear from them. At last our suspense was relieved by a telegram—the Oriental had entered the Head, which constitutes the entrance to the port of Melbourne, about 45 miles from the city. When I heard the news, I felt as I never felt before. Now, I thought, my long loneliness is to end, and the cause of Christ can be more fully met! I could not help weeping, but it was the weeping of a rejoicing soul. My brethren in America do not appreciate their blessings. What wonder that I, cast, as it were, upon a distant island, almost alone, should rejoice at the coming of a co-laborer!"

He continues: "After receiving the telegram, September 2nd, a number of brethren with myself went to the port, and took a skiff and went out to meet them. After rowing about till nearly sunset, we learned that the Oriental wouldn't cast anchor till the next day. So early the next morning we again made our way to the landing; by this time the brethren had begun to gather from all parts of the city and suburbs. At eight o'clock that spring morning, we went aboard—" It must be borne in mind that the Australian spring begins in September.

"Brother Carr didn't know I was there until I laid my hand upon his shoulder, and spoke to him. Picture that meeting, if you can! Here in this foreign land I grasped the hand of the dear companion of my school-days! What thrilling joy! Sister Carr was soon rejoicing with us. Blessed be our Heavenly Father, for bringing them safely across the seas!

"After a few moments their luggage was in our boat and we were rowing to the pier where we found a throng of brothers and sisters waving handkerchiefs, and praising God for his goodness. With what rejoicing the Christians grasped the hands of the missionaries, as they stepped on shore! There was no time for introductions, none waited for that; but such a shaking of hands, and welcoming of Brother and Sister Carr, was enough to move the angels to rejoice. In a few minutes they had taken the train for the city; then in a cab I took them to my residence, where they are now resting from their hardships, soothed by the climate, and delighting, after months upon the deep, in the bloom of peach and plum, and the blossoming of our spring gardens."

Thus G. L. Surber writes home that Benj. Franklin of the Christian Church may publish the letter; thus he writes, until he corrects and polishes up the sentences, changing his "We made our way to the landing" to—"we turned our faces," etc. and scratching out "waving handkerchiefs" for something about "open hearts." But we make nothing of his careful remoulding of ideas, nor give a snap for his "open heart." The handkerchiefs shall wave in this history—let them stream to the breeze, each a white fluttering banner of peace and love, raised above the heads of this vanguard of Christian soldiers, this beautiful spring morning of September 3rd, 1868.

CHAPTER X.

LIFE IN MELBOURNE.

The Carrs were formally welcomed to Melbourne, the evening of the day on which they landed, by a church tea meeting. We shall speak of it in detail, that a general notion may be gleaned of this popular Australian church social.

"Tea on the Tables at Half-past Six," is the way the invitation-cards read. We assemble in the basement. There are four tables, running the entire length of the Chapel (we are not to say "church" when speaking of a house.) Not alone is tea "on the tables." Here we find a bountiful repast, garnished forth with beautiful flowers fresh from our gardens.

After tea, we present the flowers to our guests of honor. By eight o'clock we have eaten, shaken hands, talked informally with every one, and are ready to adjourn to the auditorium. Here we listen to the Chairman's address, and the addresses of five others, including O. A. Carr and G. L. Surber. The congregation sings three hymns, the Singing Class renders another; we have, also, two anthems, and, after the benediction, feel that we have been to a Tea Meeting, indeed.

A few years ago, the Cause in Australia was very weak. Now the pressing need is laborers. The Melbourne Church is strong enough to divide; Surber will preach at the Chapel; a hall will be rented for $400 in gold, in which O. A. Carr will preach; thus forming a nucleus in two remote points in the great city. The speakers at the tea meeting are strong in their faith, and with good reason. Last year the church gave for home and foreign missions, and local expenses, $4000 in gold.

We have never had any trouble with expenses, because each of us does something—each one! that is our secret of success. Far away in Adelaide, Gore and Earl are laboring; here in Melbourne, Carr and Surber—four evangelists for Australia. But, as we shall see, all the preaching is not done by the evangelists. And what of Mrs. Carr? At this very first tea meeting we speak of a school for Sister Carr. "We expect in a few months to see her devoting all her time to the high calling of teaching."

Thus the new work is inaugurated. Not for the writer is the labor of seeking lodgings, or a house which will serve also as a school; not for the reader the weary days of forming an establishment, of settling down to the necessary routine of daily living, of forming grooves in which one may run automatically, the better to give the mind to higher things than food and a roof.

We are in a land where all is strange and new; but when we leave it, all shall have become familiar, and much of it dear. The reader need but glance along the peaks that rise out of the level plain of daily experiences—one tea meeting for him, to fifty for the Carrs; a few characters to be learned from among the thousands who cross the paths of the young missionaries.

One might crowd a large book with the people who come and go, never to return, people important in their own orbits, no doubt, but quite futile to ours. Happy would it be for us and ours, if all the time we scatter among the moving multitudes of life, we might concentrate upon the few who are to abide in our hearts and memory. But that is not to be while life is life; however, it may be reasonably accomplished in book-land.

So, of these hundreds and hundreds of letters before me, whose signatures are but the labels of so many shadows—impersonal spirits who did nothing but write and vanish—we can select only those of a few men who seem to breathe the same air that envelops our principal characters.

Such a breathing reality appears in John Augustus Williams, so real in his profound faith in the dignity of teaching, that the chalk-dust seems to swing above his head as a sort of material halo.

To him we find Mrs. Carr writing: "We reached Melbourne in early September, after a long voyage of 104 days! Contrary winds kept us in the Irish Channel a fortnight; but we kept our spirits up, resolved to be content-subjects of the winds. We drifted within sight of the South American shores. We sailed many miles along the mango and palm-wreathed coast of Brazil. We are well and ready for work. Brother Surber was very happy to see us, and the church gave us a most cordial greeting. I will write brother Joe a description of the voyage; you can exchange letters with him. I enclose a little flower and leaf of woodruff. I plucked it at the foot of the south tower of the royal entrance to Canarvon Castle, on Menia Straits, opposite Anglesey. In that castle, the first prince of Wales was born, April 25, 1284."

T. J. Gore writes to the newcomers from Adelaide, South Australia: "I am aware of your arrival in Melbourne. You do not know how I long to see you both—you come from old Kentucky—may Heaven's richest blessings rest upon that dear state! It is hard to realize that here so near, are two live Kentuckians from my far-away home. You will find conditions and customs very different here from America; but it is the Lord's harvest; moreover, Melbourne contains a great many Americans; here in Adelaide, my eyes are hardly ever blessed by the sight of one, but I console myself with the thought that though I am far from my native land I am still in the Kingdom of the Lord. No doubt you and Surber are now talking over days of long ago, at Kentucky University.

"Brother Carr! how I should love to fold you to my heart! Tell Sister Carr she need not fear the hot winds; they are quite harmless. Brother Earl preaches to big audiences Sunday evening at White's Assembly room; he has not found a church yet. Tell Sister Carr she deserves great credit for leaving her home, and coming so far, all for the sake of His Word. My thoughts go to Keith in Louisville, and Albert Myles in Cincinnati. I wish we had an evangelist in New Zealand. Write me something for the *Pioneer*" (which he is editing). "Brother Santo wishes you both much happiness and great success." (Gore has found a sweetheart,—"Brother Santo's" daughter; which gives him a firmer position from which to protest against homesickness.)

At the conclusion of the first sermon preached by O. A. Carr in Australia, two made the good confession. During his ministry in the colonies, he found conversions the rule, while the exception became rarer and rarer, of preaching without visible results. He had not found a house to rent when a letter was received from one who was to take an interesting part in his life—Thomas Magarey, an Englishman, who had settled in Southern Australia:

"Now that you are enjoying a little relaxation from the call of visitors upon your arrival, I may venture an epistle of congratulation upon your safe arrival. May you and Sister Carr be spared to present the old and glorious Gospel. I read your article in the *Review*, and laughed at the alarm of the church at Birmingham, lest any one should 'drop a penny in their collection.' We have very little cause for alarm upon that score, here in South Australia. I have heard that you both are suffering from homesickness. I had that complaint for about twenty years.

"Unfortunately, every one in Australia has suffered from it more or less and, like seasickness, it meets with no sympathy. I never could understand why the most disheartening of complaints should receive no commiseration, but so it is. I cannot think your disease very violent, for the best authorities say, those love home best who have least reason to do so. Thus the Irishman suffers more from leaving his land of potatoes than the Englishman his beef and plum pudding. I need not tell you that the best remedy is constant employment. This is not our home—we are all pilgrims and strangers. My son, just now, was instructing his little brothers and sisters upon Astronomy. I heard him say that from Jupiter, this earth of ours could not be seen. Humiliating thought!"

Fern Brake, Near Melbourne

Fern Tree Gully

Australian Home—Martin Zelius

Prince's Bridge, Melbourne

The man who writes thus abruptly, treading upon the tender susceptibilities of Kentucky pilgrims, calls for more than passing mention. When hundreds flocked to the Australian gold fields, Thomas Magarey established a mill, and sold flour to the prospectors. Gold was found in abundance, and easily parted with; but while others dug it from the earth, Magarey ground his meal and watched the yellow tide as it came his way. "Twenty years of homesickness," on his part, was well rewarded. He owned a palatial home in South Australia, was immensely wealthy, and was a Member of Parliament.

His religious life was diverted into its present channel by reading articles by Alexander Campbell and Walter Scott in the *Christian Baptist*. His brother, some time before the coming of the Carrs to Australia, perished in a fire at sea. Thomas took his brother's family into his own home, where all live as one. His sheep ranch, his cattle, his horses, his milling business, his civic affairs, occupied the greater part of the day, but his evenings were spent with his wife and children.

On Sundays two carriages took them to church in the morning, to Sunday-school in the afternoon, to preaching at night. At the Governor's receptions, the jewels of the Magareys flashed with the costliest; at church, their garments were as simple as the simplest. And if there was no preacher, as indeed was usually the case in this land where preachers were so scarce, Thomas Magarey addressed the congregation, after the Australian manner.

The better to understand this manner, let us return to the Carrs, and take a brief view of their religious life. As we have seen, the preacher delivered a sermon only on Sunday nights. The primary object of the Sunday morning service was the observance of the Lord's Supper. For the Church of Christ, in its desire to do just as the Christians did in Apostolic times, met on the first day of the week to break bread, not "to keep the Sabbath day holy", which they said had been done away, with the old dispensation, but to celebrate the resurrection of Christ.

Besides the communion service on Sunday morning, there would be exhortations to religious life by laymen, who had been appointed a month in advance. These men took pride in preparing brief addresses which they hoped might prove edifying; and so general was the custom, that if the minister failed to be present, his absence was unfelt. Such a custom tended to build up a permanent and fervid religious sentiment in the very heart of the congregation—a speaking Christianity which business men carried during the week into their shops and offices.

The congregation would assemble promptly in the morning, and, a minute or two before eleven o'clock, would sit with bowed heads. Exactly at eleven, all would rise to their feet, and lift up some familiar hymn such as "Safely through another week, God has brought us on our way." Among the five hundred there were not a dozen silent mouths. Following the hymn, a chapter would be read from the Old Testament, another from the New. A third layman would announce a hymn, usually reading it; a fourth would lead in prayer. Still another would preside at the table, to be followed by those appointed for short addresses.

The congregation preferred to take business affairs from their own number, rather than from the minister. As an example—One morning a man rose and said: "Since I have been hearing Brother Carr preach, my Bible has become a new Bible. I never understood it till now. But there is one subject Brother Carr has omitted—the duty and privilege of financially supporting the preacher." Having delivered himself upon this neglected theme, the man concluded: "You know me and my circumstances. I am a shipwright. I will give half a crown a week. My wife will do the same. There are many present who can do as well. Now, will you do it?" And the audience rose and said, "We will do it!"

Before a house had been selected for the missionaries, Mrs. Carr went on a visit to some new-found friends; as a result we have a series of letters between her and Mr. Carr; we trust our extracts from them will be both judicious and interesting.

Mr. Carr to Mrs. Carr: "If my writing proves obscure, remember I'm an obscure person in this country. Brother Magarey left for Ballarat. We all went with him to the depot. Alex. and Vaney" (Magarey's sons) "could hardly keep from crying when they saw their father leave." (Alex. and Vaney are to board with the Carrs in order to finish the course at the University of Melbourne.) "I went to look at that house in Clarendon Terrace, but behold, it was let when I got there! However, the owner said he wouldn't have been willing to have you teach a school in it; and besides, it would have been too far out for the boys (Alex. and Vaney) to walk. There will be plenty of houses to rent when the people go to the seaside for the summer." (By which we mean December).

"We must wait a little longer and be satisfied. I trust in God. We are to do a great work here, if we will be humble and abide the Lord's will. One confession at chapel, today, five at the hall. There are very large audiences. Your class did well. They seemed much disappointed in not seeing you, but they didn't come right out and say they preferred you as their teacher— mighty smart girls! Brother Zelius says I must remember him to you." ("Brother Zelius'" was the first house the Carrs entered on landing at Melbourne; it was he who had sent O. A. Carr the money to come from America. Years before, Zelius had stood penniless, save for one shilling, and entirely unknown, in the streets of Melbourne; but he had done well since he heard and accepted the doctrine as presented by the Christians, and it was natural that he should have a proprietary interest in his missionaries.)[8]

Mrs. Carr to Mr. Carr: "We reached Nutcundria last evening in safety. The day is intensely hot" (November 29). "I do not believe I could ever love the Australian climate. Give me the sunny and starlit skies, the balmy breezes, the snows and winter winds of old Kentucky! There is abundance of ripe fruit here. Couldn't you come for me next week? The trip can be made in a day. I shall never regret placing my heart in your keeping; for every day, I see a new light shining in your character."

Mr. Carr to Mrs. Carr: "Joy came this morning in the shape of a letter apiece; yours from brother Joe, which, I see, came by way of Panama. Mine is from sister Minnie—her news has touched and thrilled my inmost soul: Jimmie has obeyed the Gospel; and dear old father, working hard all day, and going to prayer-meeting at night! Poor mother! I wish it were so that she could attend oftener. Vaney, Alex. and I were at the hall last night. Alex. announced the hymns for me. Vaney says they would take me for a Catholic priest if it were not for my whiskers. Vaney is always cutting at me—we have a good deal of fun as we go along. Say! I would like to see you monstrous well! If you stay up there much longer please send me a lock of your hair! I have a house in view—3 stories, 8 good rooms, just behind Fitzroy Garden, near corner of Clarendon and George streets, price 130 pounds. All rates paid. This house is beautifully situated; from it you can view the Botanical Garden, the Bay, Emerald Hill, etc., but it is a long walk from chapel. I have spent about 3 hours in preparing a lecture for the class, tonight" (we will hear more about that class a little later.)

Mr. Carr again: "Two confessions at chapel, 3 at the hall. The work is going gloriously on. I baptized 10 Friday night. I am very busy. There is great excitement. The Rev. Mr. Ballantyne has issued a tract on baptism. The brethren want me to reply as soon as possible, (presenting arguments for immersion). I ought to get out the tract in 10 days, so I cannot come up for you. If Miss McIntyre will come down in coach with you, I will take pleasure in helping her on the way to heaven; but I cannot come next week. We have no house yet. Brother and Sister Zelius send love."

Mrs. Carr, to Mr. Carr: "I walked out this evening to meet you, and was disappointed. Soon after, I received your letter; of course I approve your conscientious course of conduct. I do not ask your *best* love, Ollie, that belongs to God; I ask only its reflex. Your fealty to our Savior is the foundation-stone upon which my affection is built, sure and firm. How strong is my faith that that foundation-stone will ever stand! Next to my faith in Jesus, it brings me the sweetest consolation. I loved you better than my brother, for I left him to follow you; but I am learning more and more each day, how much better. God knows how my heart yearns toward my dear brothers and sisters; but you are dearer to me, Ollie, than all the world beside. In reply to Mr. Ballantyne, studiously avoid all offense; that which offends will never convince. May God bless your efforts for the promulgation of the Truth."[9]

Government Building, Melbourne

"Take a Look at Diana and the Stag"

Favorite Walk Toward Barclay Terrace

"Last Friday morning we started to the Spur, an offshoot of the Dandenon. The scenery along its sides and summit, is the most beautiful in Victoria. The gorges filled with enormous pines, stately grottos, and gums, and peppermints, are a rich feast to the aesthetic nature—but I saw nothing that so stirred the depths of my soul, as the dreamy hills in autumn along the magnificent Ohio. About 40 miles below the Spur we found good accommodations at Heyfield, which we enjoyed after the long jolting ride.

"We rose at five the next morning to visit the Falls on the Thompson. Their beauty fully paid us for our mile's walk—it seemed three to me. The Falls are magnificent, the lower plunging from 50 to 100 feet, the highest from 200 feet. We made our way with considerable difficulty along the whole face of the Falls. We had to cling to the saplings to keep from rolling headlong into the river. I had a severe headache that morning, and kept my hair hanging, and the bush was so very thick, I wonder I did not share the fate of Absalom. I hope you will get us a house as soon as possible; I am anxious to have a home of our own—if that is possible in a foreign land. I hear that Mr. Surber is going to New Zealand. May God bless you, my dear husband, that you may bring many into the Kingdom."

Shortly after Mrs. Carr's return to her husband, they received another letter from their fellow-countryman, T. J. Gore, who is still afraid they may succumb to homesickness. The manner in which he argues against such a feeling, is very philosophical: "Our home beyond the bright blue sea is lovely; there a father and mother are longing to lay their arms about our necks and say, 'Welcome home!' What a happy meeting that would be!—but not to be compared to the welcome into everlasting arms. Brother Carr, we are going home—we have already embarked—we *are* on the ship, the good old ship, and swiftly we are speeding over the waves of life. We have met a few storms, but the Captain said, 'Peace be still.' The barometer has been low, but He said, 'There's no danger in this ark of safety!' God only lent us our little homes among the hills of Kentucky; it is true they are dear to us; but in a few years He will lend them to others of whom we know nothing."

A sentence farther on explains, perhaps, how the writer can be so calmly philosophical: "You have, of course, heard that I am married. Mrs. Gore begs to be remembered to you; we cannot be as strangers: You and Sister Carr must come over (to Adelaide) to see us soon."

Letters from home may have accented the stress of home-longing, but others came that gave heart for the long separation, such as the following from Mrs. Drusie Ellis of Ghent, Ky.; "Last night, I heard of your safe arrival in Australia. I loaned the paper containing your letters to a friend. She brought it back with the remark that she could scarcely keep from tears while reading it,—and, as I told Doctor, *'Scarcely* keep from crying, indeed!'—when I could not even *mention* the subject in a steady voice! The thought of your wife so nobly giving up home and country for the great work touches my heart deeply. I read of her welcome with streaming tears, and determined to write this word of Christian sympathy, hoping to add one little thrill of joy to hearts so truly consecrated."

Mr. and Mrs. Carr decided to rent the house already mentioned, in Barclay Terrace. It commanded an extensive view of Fitzroy Gardens, through which they walked every day. The way into the heart of the city led among its statues and greeneries. One might sink down to rest on the benches beside the fountains, or loiter on the rustic bridges,—only, alas! there was little time for loitering!—inhale the fragrance of the perennial flowers, and take a look at Diana and the Stag before setting forth for Chapel. From the bandstand ascended, "God save the Queen," to the Southern Cross. Who shall say what element of charm did not steal unconsciously from such beautiful surroundings into the hearts of the missionaries?

We have said there was little time for loitering; the reader shall be the judge. Two nights in the week were devoted to the prayer meetings of the two churches; one night was devoted to those who came to Barclay Terrace to inquire after the truth, or to learn Christian duty; a fourth night every week was the lecture-night at the Collinwood Church—the Church established by Mr. Carr; on Friday night there was a short sermon and then the baptizing of those who had already inquired after the truth and made the good confession, and who had been instructed as to the purpose of baptism, and what would be expected of the subject as to attendance at church, contributing, and the governing of one's household.

As the weeks passed by, the history of the Friday nights presented the appearance of continuous "protracted meeting." Rarely, if ever, did a week pass without the application and acceptance of from one to twenty members. Nor did those who joined the one body, the church, enter upon the crest of an excitement-wave, or with a superficial notion of what it meant to be a Christian. The following note will show that converts were not to be obtained with undue haste:

"The following was passed at the Business Meeting of 23rd March, 1869: 'That this Meeting considers it inexpedient for our Evangelists to invite public confessions, seeing they regard it desirable to have conversation before baptism.'"

"CHURCH SECRETARY."

Besides the work already indicated, there was an "Improvement Class" each week, composed of young members of the church, who read essays, and made short talks, to be criticised by the minister. From this class were selected those who addressed the congregation on Sunday morning. These young men were closely bound by affection to their leader, Mr. Carr. There was something perennially young in his own bosom, that responded to their youth.

His health was delicate, as it had been in Lexington, and the never-relaxing labors of every night in the week, might have made another prematurely old and solemn. But his boarders, Alex. and Vaney Magarey, could have told of many a time when he slipped to the attic with them for a hasty game of marbles. Such innocent, though clandestine sport, heartened him up, no doubt, to deal the more telling blows against ecclesiastical foes. Who in reading his trenchant arguments on the subject of Baptism, would have suspected that at that very moment the marbles might be clinking in his pocket![10]

No wonder the young men felt his spirit akin to their own! After prayer-meeting they would walk with him "part of the way,—" which usually extended quite across the fifty acres of Fitzroy Gardens, and up to his very door. And as they walked they talked, talked with all the earnestness of youth, when youth is in earnest.

Waiting in Melbourne alone. Will go to Hobart

One night when the conversation had become unusually absorbing they stopped and, looking up, found they had halted before the Model School Building,—which corresponds to an American college. The subject of acquiring an education had often engaged them before, but now ideas came to a focus.

"I have a calf, and some carpenter's tools," said one young man, addressing Mr. Carr earnestly; "I will sell them, and buy clothes and books if you will teach me."

Without hesitation the minister cried, "Come on."

"May we come too?" chorused the others.

"Yes!" Little did they realize how much that consent meant; how much of energy, of which there was no surplus; how much of nerve-drain and anxious thought. A number of young men decided to come to Barclay Terrace every day. They came and Mr. Carr gave them the same course he had taken at Kentucky University. This was, indeed, paying back to the world with interest, the good that the world had bestowed! When Eneas Myall carried to Carr's tavern the money that started Oliver Carr on his road to the University, little did he dream of the beneficent influences he was setting in motion on the other side of the globe! It is so with every good deed. One never sows a word of love beneath the northern skies, but he may find it blooming some day, beneath the Southern Cross.

Mr. Carr's boys had studied some—not much—at the public school. They knew something of English grammar; he did not teach it to them; he taught Greek grammar, and it is needless to say that they became good grammarians. They read the New Testament in Greek. They were taught rhetoric and logic from Mr. Carr's notes, taken at the University. Among the class was that T. H. Rix, who is today a successful evangelist. Another—he who sold his calf and tools to buy books,—stands today as the best educated man in the Church of Christ, in Australia, next to T. J. Gore. He is G. B. Moysey. Who will say he would better have kept his calf?

Thus we find O. A. Carr becomes a schoolteacher, though his purposes were all set otherwise. It seemed forced upon him by his consciousness of the good he might do. We are to find the same thing occurring again and again in his life. Duty seemed ever calling him to the desk when his own heart yearned for the pulpit. As yet he was able—both to preach and teach with all his might. Unfortunately that might was not based upon physical resources.

On the other hand, Mrs. Carr must always teach, wherever she was, because teaching was a part of her being. She had opened a class for young ladies in her home. Her accommodations compelled her to limit the number of pupils to about twenty; but, on account of this limitation, she was enabled to select those girls who were most refined, and who promised the best spiritual reward for her labors. This was her second school; and while it was by no means so pretentious as her college at Lancaster, the results were doubtless more far-reaching.

Her system of education,—indeed, her conception of education—differed materially from that found in Melbourne. If her method seemed radical to the most conservative, it filled with delight those open to impressions of new truth. Mrs. Carr's scheme to educate a girl was not to fill her with facts, but to develop her mind and heart. This has not always been understood by those who patronized her various schools. The commonplace test of "how much a pupil knows," did not always apply to her classes. She took pains to teach them how to preserve their health, how to deport themselves, how to preserve their modesty and integrity, how to become forces in the world.

In a word, she did not labor to root in those tender minds a multitude of facts which the passing of time sweeps away; it was her desire to form of each impressionable girl, a noble woman.

It was her conviction that no higher work exists in the world than the development of high ideals of womanhood. If she could have reached young girls in any other way, in daily living, she could have dispensed altogether with the school.

The school was but a means to the end of shaping lives. There were, perhaps, girls in Melbourne at that time, who were learning more facts than Mrs. Carr's girls were learning; who might, it may be, have answered with greater exactitude if questioned as to the dimensions of the planets' orbits, or as to the geological eons.

These things did not seem to her of supreme importance. What to her mind, mattered, was to make world-blessings of her girls. This was so deep a conviction of her soul, that she had little patience with literalism.

It is necessary to understand her purpose, in order to comprehend the relationship between her and her pupils. When Mrs. Carr found in any girl those true and enduring qualities which, however much neglected, promise a harvest of love, and gratitude, and noble deeds, and thoughts, there were no pains too great for her to take, to develop that soul.

But when it was her lot to be thrown with a girl whose life-purposes were all antagonistic to the sphere of the cultured woman—a girl who suspected insincere motives, and watched for faults, and hardened herself against sweet influences, Mrs. Carr felt that she could do more good by giving her time to more susceptible spirits.

Thus it came about that the pupil who reached after the higher standards of life, found Mrs. Carr a woman of motherly tenderness; while she who drew back, found her cold and unsympathetic.

It is difficult to learn the real character of any teacher from her pupils, unless we take into consideration the character and point of view of those interrogated. The pupil in sympathy with the instructress will praise her, one in rebellion will blame her. It seems necessary to say this, because Mrs. Carr has often been misunderstood and misrepresented. An obdurate and intractable pupil usually has a family to espouse her view of the case; and the neighbors share the impression of the family; and visiting guests share the opinions of the neighbors.

It is not always that the pupil wilfully misrepresents; indeed, in most cases, she does not intentionally do so; but she cannot understand, because her heart is not in accord. It would be a strange thing if any teacher should be universally praised by her pupils, and the suspicion would inevitably arise that she had not done her full duty.

On one point all of Mrs. Carr's pupils are agreed; that she was a splendid disciplinarian. Whether you loved her or feared her, or disliked her, she made you keep good order while under her instruction.

As to her success in school work at Melbourne, we shall content ourselves with letting the consul speak a good word for her, then relate a little incident.

Geo. R. Latham to Mrs. Carr: "Knowing the respectable character of the colleges in the United States of which you are a graduate, and feeling a lively appreciation of your thorough education, finished accomplishments, and intellectual and moral worth, and learning that you have opened a select school for young ladies in this city (Melbourne) I most gladly consent to the use of my name as reference."

The terms per quarter for board and tuition were from £18-18-0 to £10-10-0. Mrs. Carr taught the following: "English Literature, Mathematics, Natural Science and all English branches usually taught, Italian, French, German, Pianoforte, Guitar, Drawing and Painting, Leather Work, Wax Flowers." She was the only teacher and, we may conclude, had her hands full!

Port Elliott—Farthest Point South

The anecdote we referred to, related to one of Mrs. Carr's pupils, Ettie Santo. Her father, Philip Santo, lived in South Australia. He was a member of Parliament;[11] and a rich iron monger. He dealt largely in imported agricultural implements. He had the same love of family that Thomas Magarey exhibited; every day at three he would go out to his splendid residence in the suburbs, and play an hour with his children. Then after exercising, he would go to the library. After tea he wrote and read two hours, then assembled the family for Bible-reading and prayer. Ettie boarded with Mrs. Carr. It was the first time she had stayed away from home. She was a very quiet, undemonstrative girl. Her father came to Melbourne to visit her. One day he showed Mrs. Carr a letter he had received from his daughter before his arrival. In the body of the letter was this sentence:

"Father, I love you; I have never told you so; I can write it better than I can speak it."

This is narrated as an illustration of Mrs. Carr's educational ideas. To bring love into being; or, as in the case of this noble-minded girl, where love already existed, to give that love a voice—to teach faithful service and strengthen holy aspirations, these were her imparted lessons. The soul which could not receive them might be hardened against her, but nevertheless she sowed the seed; with her, teaching was a religious exercise.

At this busy time, while Mrs. Carr had her girls, and Mr. Carr his boys, to say nothing of a thousand outside duties to be performed, a character entered their lives like a good fairy. Janie Rainey was born and reared in Scotland. Her sister married a "gentleman" that is to say, a man of means, and for a time Janie lived with them. But it soon became borne in upon her that her brother-in-law looked upon her as a burden to his household. She knew a Presbyterian minister in Melbourne, who, in answer to her letter, encouraged her to come to Australia, where she could find plenty of work. She made the long voyage, and found asylum in his house, until she should find regular employment.

One day she appeared at the house in Barclay Terrace. Beneath her sunbonnet was to be seen a bright face, and shrewd yet kindly eyes. As she sat in the hall in her plain but scrupulously neat dress, Mrs. Carr was charmed by her Scotch accent, and by her manner of dignified dependence. Janie explained that she had heard Mrs. Carr needed a servant; she had come to keep the house for her, to wash, to cook, to do anything. She was received with joy. As Mrs. Carr afterward said, "It was love at first sight."

Before the Carrs came to Melbourne, Janie had gone to hear Mr. Surber preach. "The first time I heard him," she said, "I knew it didn't sound like the kirk! I could understand him; it was so *plain*!" When she had heard him preach about half a dozen times, she said, "I must confess my faith!" She became an intelligent Christian. She knew a great part of the Bible by heart. "I have read the New Testament all my life," she declared, "and never knew what it meant before."

Janie worked for the Carrs all the time they staid in Melbourne. She regularly attended the Sunday services, the prayer meetings, and the other gatherings of the church. From her wages she gave one shilling every Sunday morning. She read the church papers and the daily papers while the Carrs and their boarders were at breakfast. Her room was kept clean and inviting, and a talk with her was refreshing; seldom did a preacher visit the house, who did not ask to see Janie.

Mrs. Carr would sit in the kitchen to hear Janie read "Bobbie Burns," with the proper accent. The servant had seen the places described in the poems; she had known people who had known the poet. She knew anecdotes about him that have never seen the print. She told about a working girl who, on looking into his room, found him stamping upon the floor, and rushing back and forth like mad; how she had rushed down stairs crying, "He's daft!"—how Burns on hearing the cry exclaimed, "*'Daft!* the very word I was trying to think of!"—and how he slapped his knees, and fell to writing.

It was Janie's delight to take care of Mr. and Mrs. Carr,—to stand between them and those innumerable details of daily life, that sap the energies, that waste the time, and ward off the essential objects of life for those who have no Janies.

"She would go to market seeking to tempt our appetites. She would say, 'Oh, you don't eat enough to keep a bird alive!' She petted us. No one regarded her as a servant except herself—but she always held herself to be one. She was, indeed, more of a companion. A beautiful character—one who did her duty because it *was* duty, and who loved us till we felt that she was one of the family. Her disposition was bright and cheerful. We often found her reading while the kettle boiled, or going about her work with an open book propped upon the kitchen table. One day I went into the kitchen and found her laughing outright. 'What is it, Janie?' 'Oh, I was laughing at what Mark Twain says about the Turkish bath!' What ever concerned us seemed as sacred in her eyes as a religious matter, and she would guard it as her own interests. Hers was a life in which we could see no fault."

A high testimonial to one who serves for years in one's kitchen! A testimonial rarely given, rarely merited. Let this be an excuse, if one is needed, for giving so much space to the simple maid from Scotland. Here is one whose soul bursts through the vapors of false pride and unlovely shame that does so much to soil the beauty of the poor. Here is one who recognizes the dignity of service, and who shows by humble acts that mark each hour, she loves her neighbor as herself.

And now that we have one so efficient and willing to admit the visitors, to cook the meals and to do the washing, let us retire to the library and, without fear of interruption, enjoy a sheaf of letters, which lie before us; not, indeed, drinking them to the very lees, but sipping here and there. Our word for it, if the reader be in the mood for mail-opening, he shall not go unrewarded.

Here is a young man writing from the Agricultural College of Kentucky University, whom Carr and Surber have evidently advised to go thither for a Christian education: "I suppose when I told you I would come here to school, you thought I would never come. After hard work I got to England, and I worked hard before I got here; but when there is a craving for an education, no toil or labor will hinder that young man. I come to study the scriptures, to be able to go into the world to preach the Gospel. I work five hours in the A. & M. College on the farm, and the machine shop. I got to this place without one cent of money. What do you think my first work here was? Dropping potatoes—Sir; yes, sir!"

J. B. Myers to Mrs. Carr: "I promised to tell you about the changes in Lancaster," (from which we may glean a little local coloring of Mattie's old home.) "The railroad runs right by the old Methodist church, out by the cemetery; indeed, it took away one corner of the old brick building. The passenger depot is on the Crab Orchard pike." (Then he enumerates all the new houses on the various pikes, tells what girls are going to "set out," and remarks that he pays more attention to ladies since his sister's departure.)

"I am still in the old room over Brother Sweeney's store! I have furnished it up with a $30 bookcase, etc. I have resigned my position in the Male Academy to teach a public school no more forever! I can't live that way—too much time consumed in watching the pupils, and making them keep order,—and the rest of my time, too worried to throw my soul into the work, and give efficient instruction. I begin a private class of about 20 choice boys, right away." Then about some who have died; some who have married; a foolish young girl who has kept her marriage a secret; and a poor gentleman who is growing too fleshy, and the fond hope that—"When you and Ollie come back to old Kentucky, you must keep house, and I will board with you!" "A year of your absence is about gone. May the three pass speedily! Yea, let them all pass rapidly that you and Ollie may be returned to me. How I love you my dearest sister! Tell Ollie I love him; too, and am proud of him!" (Very different does Brother Joe talk, now that he no longer stands hatless upon the pike, stopping our stage coach!)

Here is a letter from our blacksmith, Eneas Myall: "I would not think of writing to you; but I know what it is to be far from home, and the pleasure of receiving a letter when among strangers; and besides, it is my duty to answer your letter. I regret very much that you did not get to see any of my folks when you were in England. I wish you could see more of England. I am satisfied it is the greatest opening for primitive Christianity in the world. Ollie, this will be rather a broken letter as I am talking, selling and writing all at the same time. We are getting along religiously, as well as common. It looks a little odd to see your father and mother attending church; but we are all glad to see it. Your father is always in his place, and so is your mother, when she can get there. And let me tell you, you are not forgotten in our prayers. We hardly ever have a meeting that you are not bidden God's speed. Brother Bartholomew of Philadelphia was here, raising money to sustain a missionary in that city! Not very many were present, so our contribution of $60 was quite liberal, I assure you. Our envelope system is working-well." (Introduced into May's Lick Church by O. A. Carr, who visited personally every member and gave each fifty-two envelopes in which to place the promised weekly offering for a year).

"And now, Ollie, as I am about to close—if we meet never again here, let us meet in Heaven. Let us be faithful to our God. My faith bids me go forward in the unshirking discharge of my duty, and the promise will be mine. All the Myalls send their love to you and your lady. Now, farewell for the present. God bless you both." Thus the blacksmith who beats his money out of iron to spread the Gospel—writing, talking, selling, all at once—the hammer in his hand, God in his heart.

Miss Mary Whittington writes from Daughters' College, and we should find interest in a picture of the scene where Mattie Myers received her education; "I have a faint idea of how you feel, Mattie, off there in Australia, for I took a four weeks' trip to Illinois, and cried to get back to President Williams and the college. You need a correspondent like myself, to give you little suggestive trifles of the college life. We have a baby here, wonderful, blue-eyed and spiritual, not a girl, alas! but a boy—Prince Whittington Williams—the 'Whittington' is for an old maid who, having no children of her own, is thankful when people sometimes name them for her—the writer, in a word. Mattie, I hear the supper bell; I'll run down and eat some battercakes, and drink a cup of coffee—don't you wish you could hear the supper-bell once more?

"Well, I had my supper in the same dining-room where you drank tea, and dieted, of yore, but it was not upon the same old oilcloth, for now we have a table cloth! Moreover the room is neatly carpeted, and the old chairs have been carried into the school rooms to make way for new ones. The girls' rooms have new carpets *all over* them—no naked space under the bed—and have been furnished with neat walnut toilets, and full tin sets for the washstands; and I must not forget the red oil-calico curtains." (The reader must bear in mind that during Mattie's sojourn here, such luxury was unknown.)

"Mrs. Williams is fat and merry. President Williams is also in a flourishing condition—weighs 160. His flesh makes him very handsome; you ought to have seen him several months ago! The secret is that he has quit tobacco. Dr. Williams is still himself. You would have been convinced of it if you had heard him this morning at church-time, when he came storming into the library, crying out, 'Where's Mary? I don't intend waiting any longer on anybody! Is she trying to keep me waiting another half hour?' And there I had been hiding behind the door half an hour, waiting for him! It did me good to rise up, and tell him so."

Here is a letter from our friend Albert Myles, who carried Oliver away from his sick room in Lexington to hold a meeting at Ghent: "When you bade me goodby in Cincinnati about one year ago,"—(how short it seems! and now, how far away!)—"you remember that my health was very bad. Well, it grew from bad to worse, till I lay at death's door. At Crab Orchard Springs I rallied, and grew steadily better until October 20th, 1868, when I—I— what shall I say?—I married! Yes, that was the day that gave me my Ellen for my wife. Two weeks later we took charge at the Mt. Sterling church, where we are still doing what we can in a small and humble way. * * * I could see you two as you braved the dangers of the Irish Channel, and took the long voyage to Australia. I could see you as you star-gazed and moon-gazed; as you promenaded the deck; as you sat and sang with the guitar; as you read and prayed in the raging storm. As you say, none but God can know what you suffered on that voyage; but it is a precious thought that He *does* know.

"Ol., I gather the following impression from your answer regarding my coming out to Australia, 1. Melbourne is the best field in Australia. 2. This field is supplied. 3. Adelaide is supplied by Gore, Earl and others. 4. New Zealand is in danger of a war with the natives, the issue of which is doubtful without help from the government. 5. Whoever accepts the £80 must go to New Zealand. With these facts before me, to be honest, it does not appear to me that Australia is more in need of preachers than many places in the United States.

"In New York, there are only about 400 Disciples; in Philadelphia, only about 300; while in Baltimore, Cincinnati, Chicago, St. Louis and San Francisco, which will average about 25,000 population, there is scarcely an average of 100 Disciples; moreover, in many rural communities, we have not even been heard of! In California are thousands of Chinese who are actually worshiping-idols! It occurs to me, that men who love the ancient order of things, are as much needed here as in Australia. You say also, that the manner of worship there is different from what it is here. This being so, one would have to spend some time preparing himself for the changed condition. If I know my own heart, I never wanted to do anything so much in my whole life, as to go to Australia; but the more I think of the matter, the more firmly I am convinced that if one goes to Australia at all, he ought to make up his mind to stay there. J. C. Keith" (the other member of our "Trio") "has succeeded in getting a comfortable house of worship built in

Louisville. He is doing well." (We have a purpose for presenting Mr. Myles' objections to going to Australia, which will be developed later).

Another letter from brother Joe, written in May, 1868, and of more than transient interest: "The last spike on the Union Pacific Railroad was driven last Monday. Thousands of faces are turning Westward, where large farms can be bought for small prices. New York and San Francisco are at last united by a mammoth railroad that spans the continent. While the last spike was being driven, telegraphic wires were in connection with all the larger cities, and at each stroke of the hammer, the wires rang signal bells from the Atlantic to the Pacific. As I read the accounts of the great demonstrations, of processions and bonfires, my own breast caught the spirit of the age of great enterprises, and I felt like seeking my fortune amid the rich prairies of the West. But then, I thought, man's life does not consist in the things he possesses; so I am resolved to be content in my Old Kentucky Home! I feel inexpressible satisfaction in the thought that while teaching boys, I am exerting a purifying and elevating influence,—an influence that will mould society, and tinge its religious, literary and charitable institutions, long after this heart has ceased to beat. O, what a privilege is ours, Mattie, of setting in motion waves of eternal blessing! How strange that the great mass of mankind neglect such opportunities!

"We are now agitating the question of the removal of the Capitol from Washington. If the Union remains undivided, such a step will be made sooner or later. But wherever they put the Capitol, *my* home shall be three miles from Stanford on the Crab Orchard pike! I like to think how I am going to fill one cellar with choice apples to roast by the winter fires. Wilt come and see us, and help peel and eat, while we talk of Australia? And what rich cider for you and brother Ollie! And there is the garden—oh, what a variety of vegetables! we'll store them away in the other cellar, and keep them for you. And if you should happen to come back home in strawberry time! Cake, cream, berries—oh, you must not think of staying longer than three years! Counting six months for going and coming, and three years for active service in Melbourne, you'll get here in August, 1871. Well, we can visit the Crab Orchard Springs together—they are only distant a short buggy-ride of eleven miles on the smooth pike—and we can take a jug along and bring it back full. You say it will be too warm? But remember, we have a good ice house. Then what a fine lot of chickens and eggs we will have and * * *" But by this time sister Mattie is weary of cleaning off her spectacles, and puts her head upon her arm in that far-away Barclay Terrace, and gives it up, gives it all up for the time—with faithful Janie to ward off visitors. Oh, brother Joe, how could you!"

Do you remember the English Murbys who carried the Carrs away from their splendid hotel in London, and established the missionaries in their own house? Here is a note from Mrs. Murby:

"I often take up my album to look at you both. I think over again the events of the few days we spent together so pleasantly. I always regret your time with us was so short; but we hope to give you a hearty welcome again in old England." (Strange how everything dear to us is "old!" It should be a comforting thought to grandparents.)

"You overrate any little attentions we may have given you. It was a great pleasure for us to make your acquaintance. Our brother" (the Chicago merchant) "returned to the land of his adoption the month after you left. Willie is a bonnie lad now, nearly eighteen months old. Nellie is over four, and quite a little companion for me." (Let us trust she, too, will find primroses in the streets of London).

If you would like a photographic representation of Kentucky University life, do not skip this letter from J. H. Stover. It is nothing to our purpose who the author may be; but he has succeeded in laying before us not a description of that college life, but the life itself. Here is the scene in which Oliver, as a student, so often mingled, and which Mattie, as a visitor, so often looked upon; Lexington in the month of June. Faded, almost gone, are many of the words, but when we rescue them from threatening oblivion, they throb again with the *actual*, which throbs best in trivialities.

"Our exhibition went off last night. Brother J. B. Jones gave his first oration before the public; it was well delivered throughout. The valedictory was by W. A. Oldham, who did the best I ever heard him. Milligan, McGarvey, Meng, Wilkes, etc., sat upon the rostrum. The ladies had helped decorate the house with cedar, etc., very tastefully. Robt. Milligan has just got him a new coat and pair of boots. He has laid aside that old coat which he used to wear, even the first year. He has a new hat, too, but he still keeps on the same old shawl. He comes into chapel with his hand to his head, as of old. He did not have his usual sick spell this spring. The last time we met, he told us that we were to have vacations from our duties, 'but, young brethren,' he said, 'there is no vacation in the school of Jesus Christ, our adorable Redeemer.'

"Brother McGarvey is just the same—same old coat. I went down to the dormitory this morning and, as usual, there were about half a dozen boys standing before Morton's bookstore. They were discussing who had the best speech, and showed the best delivery, at the Exhibition, last night. Brother Jonathan M. came out and said, 'Good morning, young gentlemen!' in that tone bordering on sharpness, as usual." (What a keen observer! We should dread to wear our old coat where he could see us!)

"Brother Myles is here. So is Miss Ella Allen. They were together last night, but I know nothing farther than when you left." (The reader has already seen what *that* came to.) "Professor Neville, W. T. Moore and uncle Dick Bishop have gone to Europe. Professor was excited to death. It was his long-looked for trip. He bought him a new suit of clothes, for the trip. He looked funny in his sack coat. Professor White looks just the same, except his hair is longer. Those same old shoes with holes in the toes, he still wears. His hat, turned down before, and up behind, hangs on the peg on the post yet, during recitation-time. The boys, as of old, went to the board, 'fizzed' and took their seats when he said, 'That is sufficient, I believe!' When I went up to him this morning to inquire my standing, he looked into that *same book*. He told me I had finished the Junior. As I went out the door, I slapped my thigh. Don't a fellow feel good when he studies hard, and does better than he looked for! Alex. Milligan still walks as fast as ever, and the bald place on the back of his head is none the smaller. He is doing well in his book store. Brother McGarvey told me this morning to tell you he would write soon. I heard from Jim Keith a few days ago. He is doing well! Miss Whitie Hocker graduated at the Sayer Institute last week. Our Sunday-school had a festival about two months ago to which the Midway Orphan School was invited. The Bible school was dismissed. McGarvey and Wilkes managed it. I think it was after you left that John Morgan's remains were brought here and interred. There was a very long procession. As I was walking down the street, today, I met J. B. Bowman in his old buggy, behind that same old black, bobtailed mare. He was driving very fast as usual. Next I met Prof. Pickett. Although it was a very hot day, he had that coat buttoned up to his chin. He had that same black cane, and he saluted me in fine military style, then walked on as fast as possible. I met the old darkey who took care of G. L. Surber's room the first year. He wanted to know if I had heard from 'Massa Green Surbah.' I saw old man White with whom you used to board. He still has the grocery on the corner; Kate isn't married yet. He still swings his hands as he walks, and ducks his head forward as usual. Brother Lowber came up and said, 'Well, here is Brother Stover; how *do* you come on, Brother Stover?' I think he has asked me that same question four times this morning, with the same smile. He is a very warm and affectionate friend.

"I saw Bob Neal next. He wore his hat as you remember. Jerry Morton nodded his head at me as he went by. Dick Stohl stopped me to ask where he could find a Horace, and Cottingham called to me from across the street. As I came home, I met Brother Lard returning from Winchester in his buggy; he had 25 additions there. At the table, Brother V. P. told me his prayers were frequently in your behalf. Dear brother Ollie, if I have succeeded in interesting you with these trifles, I am repaid for my long letters. Give Mattie my love, and tell her I claim kin with her." (Which letter, we fear, leaves Oliver about as homesick as J. B. Myers' left Mattie.)

True to his promise, here comes a letter from Prof. J. W. McGarvey: "We published your letter, and a call for packages in the *Apostolic Times*, and have received, in response, enough books, pamphlets and newspapers to fill a medium-sized goods box; we will ship them soon. We now have a circulation of nearly 4,000 for the *Apostolic Times*. I received a copy of your tract, and noticed it in the paper. Innovationists have become rampant among us; they expected to run over our Brother Franklin by affecting superior knowledge, but the *Times* cannot be frowned down in that way. We hope to fill a gap in the ranks of the faithful. You are right in not encouraging the brethren to send to America for preachers while neglecting useful men at home. Teach them to encourage young men of promise. Some changes have occurred in the University. Brother Pickett resigned his presidency of the Agricultural College, and it was offered Brother Errett. The chances are, however, that Errett will take a chair of Bible study, just created at Bethany. He will probably give up the *Standard*, and it will die. It has never more than paid expenses. Brother Graham has resigned to take the presidency of the new female college of which Brother Hocker is proprietor. John Augustus Williams has been elected President of the College of Arts. You both have a large and warm place in the hearts of thousands of the saints. The Lord be with you."

Another note from the Australian student, now at the University: "I am now engaged in the selling of books in the vacation: my object is to make enough money to pay my way through Bible College. My board cost me nothing, for I am stopping at the home of Dr. W. H. Hopson. I suppose by this time you have received the books, magazines, etc., from President Milligan. I preach occasionally at Providence and Bethany. Cannot some of our young brethren in Australia come out here and prepare themselves to preach to poor dying sinners? They may say they cannot pay the passage; but if they love the Lord, they will come, and work their way through."

The following is from Mrs. Carr to her brother: "How my heart blesses you, for almost every mail brings us cheer from your pen! If it be the will of God that we ever again see each other face to face, you will know how grateful I am. You would laugh if you could see us running to the door at the ringing of the postman, or leaping from our seats at the cry of—'*Arrival of the British Mail!* We have many dear friends here, but a word from Kentucky carries our hearts back in a mighty rush, and all is lost in the old and tried affections of home. Forget you, did you say? Ah, we could not if we would. Come back to you, did you say? Assuredly, if it is God's will.

When I come back, brother, I want to sit in your lap, and with my arms about your neck, tell you of my little trials, and of my many, very many abiding joys. Ollie's health and mine, is not good as when we first came here; we fear it may be due to the climate. Ollie is so upright, so gentle and kind to me, that I have strength to bear everything.

"Now a question: Suppose we should establish a College in Australia, exclusively for young men, hoping some day to convert it into a university—and suppose we should cry to America for professors—would you come? Think of the cries of the churches here for education—how they are obliged to send their young men all the way to Kentucky to prepare them for the ministry in the Christian Church. *Would* you come?" And much more to the same purpose, showing that this idea of a Christian University in Australia, has become a fixed idea with Mrs. Carr—an idea which she is not to yield readily.

Now comes O. A. Carr to the charge, showing a little of the heat of battle that has been roused by controversy with the sectarians. It is Thomas Magarey, father of Alex. and Vaney, whom he accosts: "Thanks for candor, but your admonition was unnecessary. I know how it would aggravate a zealous brother to think that my little squirt is throwing water on the fire he is trying to keep aglow. You seem to think that I am desperately bent on doing nothing with a vengeance, especially if it will injure Australia. It may be true I have no more judgment than a pig; I may be showing the pig—or dog, if you like,—in writing this; but like you, if I am wrong, I apologize. And now to the point: What I wrote was solely to argue that we must not depend upon America in the contemplated college affair. My reason for believing that evangelists would not come here from there, was the simple fact of their not coming. I have never written a line home derogatory to anyone's coming to Australia. I wrote a confidential letter to Brother Albert Myles, which he made me promise to do; I gave my first impressions of Australia, and they were more favorable than I ever dreamed I could give, when I was at home. As Brother Myles was to come on Adelaide money, I frankly told him that I could not give him any account of Adelaide. I never believed Brother Myles would come, when we received the call at the same time, for the conviction that he should do so, was not so strong as mine. His mother was a widow, and looked to him for support. Brother Myles is as true a soldier of the Cross as ever drew the sword. Had he seen his way clearly, he would have come, for he wanted to do so. I hold myself free from throwing anything in the way.

"Pardon me for saying it, but I suppose I will always be a '*new chum*' and 'too inexperienced for old English women to sit under,' and 'who ought not to be allowed to write a little Tract till some old, experienced brother had reviewed it to see if it were sound.' I want you to believe that the 'new chum' wrote nothing he could not prove, and that he is anxious for all to come and help in the glorious work, who ought to assume the responsible position of a preacher. So much from the 'bear with the sore head!' There; now! I haven't flared up. I do hope you will send for more evangelists, and that the country will be supplied with a faithfully preached Gospel. Alex. is much better, and is able to eat heartily; Vaney is well. Mattie, I believe, is writing to you."

Back to the charge comes the doughty Englishman, Member of Parliament, and miller from South Australia: "It is a very busy day with me, but I must not leave you under painful feelings caused by hasty words of mine. As I was mistaken, I am heartily thankful, and apologize without reserve. In the first place, you *are* a new chum, and nine out of ten new chums write home under disappointed feelings, as the romance melts from those visions which lend enchantment to the view. But since you did not do so, I am much to blame for hasty accusation. As to the rest, you misunderstood my letter. The fault is with me. I am always getting myself into unpleasant scrapes by my correspondence. Even the newspapers that report my speeches complain that they cannot tell whether I am joking, or in earnest. I have always looked upon you as a great acquisition to the cause of Christ in Australia. I cannot imagine what you mean by talking of 'a bear with a sore head.' I am utterly unconscious of having written anything to give rise to your expression. Will you kindly send me the whole passage. I do not think of you as a bear at all, sore-headed or otherwise. Why, I look upon you as one of the pillars of the Cause. I think,—if we get so much out of Brother Carr at 24, what will we get at 30! Then I think that by the time you are 30, you will have ruined your health, and be fit for nothing. I feel angry that you undertake so much. I know, had it not been for you during Brother Surber's absence in New Zealand, the Cause would have gone to ruin in Melbourne. Then how could I have thought you in the way, as 'a pig,' or as a man? I do not think any of our evangelists are without faults; but if I let them see that I do not consider them faultless, they should not therefore run back to America, as they sometimes threaten to do! I ought to have known better than to take such freedom with our friends from Kentucky. It is said by travelers that a Southerner will allow you to tell him his faults, or his country's faults. But he will not; or can not, understand any playful allusions to them. Now, Brother Carr, I am exceedingly sorry to have written anything that hurt your feelings. I begin to have some dim recollection that I *may* have written something about a bear with a sore head, but I cannot remember what it was. What *was* it? I have Sister Carr's letter; am delighted with it; was afraid she might be cross about that bear. I have no letter from my boys, but hope to receive one soon. But I must close this long rigamarole which I cannot read myself, it is so badly done."[12]

As a last letter in this chapter's mail—what a long chapter it is making!—this is offered from Martin Zelius, he who began Melbourne life with one shilling, and later sent to America the gold that brought over Mr. and Mrs. Carr; it will show that he, too, was interested in that Tract: "I have heard that you intend to investigate, and bring out, the injustice that one of the religious bodies here has done our people. I hope you will do it most effectually, not for the sake of victory, nor of retaliation, but for the love of the truth. Stand up at any time, and under any circumstances, to defend the commands of Jesus. He has said he will never leave us, nor forsake us. When we have our friend Jesus to stand by us, our confidence is raised to the highest pitch. My dear brother, it brings the tears to my eyes when I look back on the past, and see how Jesus has shielded me from many a trial, from many a foe. Stand up for him, Brother Carr! He who is with us is more than all who can be against us!"The way in which the Church of Christ looked at religious matters was so different from the usual view, that the American evangelists felt the pressing need of tracts to disseminate their ideas. One illustration of their effectiveness, may close this branch of the subject.There was a young man whose parents lived in a house passed, every day, by the Carrs, on their way to town. The father belonged to one denomination, the mother to another, while the son, finding the Calvinistic doctrines of both repellant to his bent of mind, refused to accept any scriptural or unscriptural principles. He graduated at the Melbourne University, then took a special course for the degree of M. D. He went into the adjacent country to practice, without having ever met the missionaries. One day he came across one of O. A. Carr's tracts. "I read it with great interest," he said. "I asked myself, is this the truth? I was then unsatisfied with the truths of Christianity."The young man sought his Bible, and began with Moses and the prophets, in a course of systematic and scrupulous examination of the Word. He read himself into the belief of the Christian church. He called upon the neighbors to meet in a hall, that he might tell them what had won him to Christianity. He delivered to them a course of lectures, insisting that everything needful to man's salvation, and life of holiness, was explicitly laid down in the Bible. At the conclusion he cried out, "Is there any one here who believes?"More than a hundred rose and answered yes! He heard them confess their faith in Christ's divinity. He baptized them. Having determined to prepare himself for the ministry, he laid aside his practice, went to Kentucky University, and, thanks to his splendid education, was able to finish the course in a year. Thus Dr. A. M. Fisher became Fisher the Evangelist, thanks to a tract written by one who, not many years before, was gathering up the shavings in Myall's wagon shop.

CHAPTER XI.

BUSY YEARS IN AUSTRALIA.

In the shifting crowds of men and women along our life-pilgrimage, few are those who feel an abiding interest in the concerns of others. We meet and part, each thinking of what he may have gained in the way of social inspiration, rather than of what he may have imparted. It is not indifference, however, which most severely galls the sensitive spirit; it is the active opposition that ever seems the lot of him or her who would help humanity. I do not know if any feet have reached the upper rounds of high ideals, without shaking off detaining hands. In the case of Mrs. Carr, influences adverse not only to her work, but to her peace of mind, were destined to attend her through life.

It is impossible to estimate the good that might be accomplished, if mankind would rally around those souls fired with lofty purposes, and strengthen and make more effective those purposes, by sympathetic encouragement; if it were human nature to add to lofty ambitions, by lending substance from one's own slighter forces. But it appears to be the rule that wherever one is found who desires to do a great good for others, a dozen are found to weaken his influence and to seek to undermine his work. Those physical mannerisms which are presently to perish with the flesh, are seized upon for the purpose of striking dead, influences which might otherwise have been eternal.

On Road to Salmon Ponds, Tasmania

Hobart Town, Tasmania

When Mrs. Carr, experienced for the first time the cruelty of this truth, she was unprepared for it. In later years, having learned her lesson, having been convinced that opposition to truth is inherent to human nature, she was able to hold her courage with a fixed and steel-willed conviction, that cut its way through all walks of opposition. But at first she was not prepared for this unlovely trait of lesser minds. Accordingly, we sometimes find her sinking, wavering, fluttering like a bird in a snare, before the breath of treachery, and the opposition of jealous natures.

To understand the story of this life in its entirety, one must know the details of these struggles and these disappointments. Yet we would rather leave the story incomplete, than perpetuate misunderstandings and misrepresentations. Those who opposed Mrs. Carr in all of her educational plans, share the fate of one who chooses as his part in life, that of opposition. It is not he who opposes, but he who performs, to whom the world owes its gratitude. Those who are antagonistic to good works, court the oblivion that awaits them. Those who, in spite of discouragements and hostility, hold tenaciously to lofty purposes, leave to the world such monuments of their devotion, as the sun-kissed college on the flower-embossed hill overlooking Sherman, Texas.

We shall content ourselves, therefore, with passing by, in silence, the words and deeds of the ill-natured, the unfriendly and the indifferent. One should not go back into the past to gather its thorns. So much is said at this place, that those conversant with the controversies and contentions of school and church life during the last quarter of the nineteenth century, need not expect to find them reanimated in this volume.

The following selection from Mrs. Carr's diary deals with her first trip to North Tasmania whither, two years later, she and her husband were to go for a year's sojourn:

"Jan. 3. Left for Hobart Town, Tasmania, on the ship *Southern Cross*. Sisters at the wharf. Kissed Ollie goodby. Dashed away the tears—may we meet again, dear husband!

"4th. Passed through Port Philip's Bay. Over the Rip, that terrible Rip! what seasickness it brings! Terrible storm! I was crowded out of my birth, but was glad to get the fresh air. The captain and stewardess were kind. The Lord bless them.

"5th. Reached Hobart Town, 7 a. m. Met by the Walworths, to whom Ollie had telegraphed. Saw more vice in two hours than I saw in New York in two weeks. What wicked people!

"6th. Sailed in the *Monarch* to New Norfolk, 22 miles. Scenery along the Derwent is grand, but not to be compared to that of the beautiful Ohio. Hop gardens far up the hills, shrouded in mists. How lovely!

"7th. Visited Salmon Ponds, 7 miles from New Norfolk. Salmons raised here, as they are not native to Australia; 30,000 sent to the ocean yearly through the streams that supply the ponds from the Derwent. Returned to North Tasmania by coach; fine view of the country—how I wished for Ollie!

"8th. Stormy day. Spent it indoors, sewing and gazing at frowning Mt. Wellington, the pride of Tasmania. Attended services on a man-of-war.

"10th. Visited Town Hall and Museum. Saw handwriting of the King of Madagascar.

"11th. Went by coach to Launceston, distance of 120 miles. The grand mountainous scenery compensated for the long ride. Passed the Western ridge on top of which smile beautiful lakes, 1,000 feet above the sea. More like Kentucky than any scenery I've witnessed.

"12th. Visited Cataract Gorge on South Esk. To Prince's Square where stands the finest fountain in the Colonies; it was imported from Paris.

"13th. At Mechanics' Institute saw life-size oil paintings of Victoria and Prince Albert, and the Prince and Princess of Wales. What a sweet, gentle face Princess Alexandria has! Dear woman, she deserves a better husband. These people are so kind to me—Ollie will love them for that.

"14. Visited Mr. Gunn, Curator of Museum, who promised to send specimens to Kentucky University. My husband's Alma Mater is dear to me, because dear to him. Launceston by Tamar. Sick all the way to Port Philip. Scenery along Tamar not so bold as along the Derwent.

"15th. Reached Melbourne, and waited at Brother Zelius' to see Ollie. How glad I am to be with my dear husband once more. May the dear Lord spare him till I die. Only God knows how dear he is to me; God will not take him from me."

At this time, the youth whom we have known as "Vaney" Magarey, leaves the Carrs' household, no longer to play marbles in the third story at stolen intervals, but to take his place in the world as Dr. S. J. Magarey; the "Vaney" quite lost among these dignified initials. Also his brother "Alex." departs, meaning to sail to America. From Adelaide, Vaney writes back; sending Mrs. Carr ten pounds, evidently on her birthday, for he tells Mr. Carr, "I promised Mrs. Carr ten pounds. Please lay them on with your fist with as much severity as you think fitting." Then he tells of £8,000 worth of Adelaide gold just discovered, and sends his regards to all inquiring friends, "except tailors and bailiffs."

Somewhat later, he writes that he will not return; another may have his room. He is interested in Mr. Carr's work as a teacher of prospective ministers,—"For goodness' sake, do not turn them out half-educated. Sometimes students are allowed to leave the Academy before they know enough, and then they cause anxiety to many, and prejudice people against colonial-made preachers." As for Vaney, himself, "We are at the seaside, and have a swim every morning, and drive every day."

An interesting character, this gay young physician, son of the rich M. P. As we have seen, he and his brother were accustomed to address the congregations on Sunday mornings, while they attended the University of Melbourne. When he had graduated, Vaney or "S. J." as we must call him now, went to South Australia and lived with his father, where Gore was editing the *Pioneer*. The young physician married one of Mrs. Carr's favorite pupils. He became successful in his profession, while his brother developed into a splendid preacher. "Alex. preaches and I practice," said the doctor. When it was necessary for Mr. Gore to be absent from the pulpit, he would call on "Dr. S. J." to preach the sermon in his stead.

In the meantime the father, Thomas Magarey, has seen his son "Alex." off to America, in the company of Evangelist Earl. He writes to Mr. Carr, but not now about bears with sore heads: "I have your letter dated 'Washington's birthday.' I have heard something of Washington, but never heard that he had a birthday. I suppose Washington is one of those best kind of demons, more worshipped in America than England. When I go to Barnum's Museum, I will inquire for his birthday.

"I am glad to hear your Forrester's Hall was so hot, because I had thought our White's Room the hottest place in Australia. I am still inclined to think we can sweat freer at White's. I am glad Brother H. makes a good deacon; I am always glad when a Scotchman can be found good for something. Dr. Johnson says the animal ought to be caught while young. You say your health is better, but I cannot believe it, for you give yourself no chance to get better. Go away and take a rest. Why was Paul allowed to waste so much time and energy? Was he not a citizen of no mean city (the Kentucky of his day?) Was he not senior wrangler under Prof. Gamaliel? Had he not graduated with honors and degree of A. M. from the University of Jerusalem? He was at least master of the art of tent-making. Yet with all these accomplishments, he went away somewhere into Arabia for three years. Then he goes from city to city afoot, in danger of being robbed—why wasn't he provided with a buggy? Instead of preaching in a jail, why not have occupied the biggest house in Phillippi? It wouldn't have been refused after that earthquake. Instead of working at his trade for bread, wouldn't it have been better for the missionary cause, if the brethren had paid him a salary, and had him give all his time to preaching? What a waste of time! He might have been writing a "Reply—*a Tract*"—to the Rev. Annanias of the Temple. And think of him at Rome, chained to a Roman soldier (no doubt a Yankee barbarian!) Why, if he had been chained to a Barnabas or Titus, they must soon have got to quarreling. Think of him two years in his own hired house, when the church of Rome ought to have put out handbills that Rev. Paul would preach at the Town Council! But perhaps there were Scotch deacons in that church, for we know there were Britains in Rome. They were too cautious.

"But a thought upsets my theory. Perhaps the Lord saw that Paul's own mind needed the discipline through which he was passing. Perhaps it is so with young men of the present day—sometimes their energy seems wasted; but it may be in order to make the most of their good qualities; that they may learn in time to be sorrowful, yet always rejoicing. Well, I must close my letter and go out into the barren wilderness which surrounds me, in which the shepherd is at wits' end to find pasture for the sheep."

Entrance to Domain, Sidney—Hyde Park.

From Mrs. Carr's diary, Mar. 27, 1870: "Two years ago we made those holy vows to each other that only God can sever. Two years ago, we left brothers and sisters, and all the tender associations of sweet home. May we ever be true to each other, and to God. O blessed Savior, give me more of thy gentleness and of thy humility. Make me a better child and a better wife, as the silent years creep on, leading me closer to the grave,—the dark path that leads to the beautiful mansion in our Father's house. * * * Visited Botanical Gardens, overlooking the Bay. Visited Barrabool hills and along Barwon river to Geelong across the Bay, 50 miles from Melbourne, where we got a cup of milk."

On Mrs. Carr's birthday, her pupils thus testify to their affection: "We cannot permit this opportunity to pass without manifesting our appreciation of the excellent course of instruction you have pursued, and the kindness, perseverance and patience you have combined with Christian love and forbearance, with which you have exercised your arduous duties. You have not only enlarged our understanding, but excited in our hearts a deep feeling of love. You are more like a dear, fond friend than a teacher. The most difficult lessons become, under your guidance, pleasant studies. May you live many years to pursue the noble efforts of your life."—Signed by the young ladies of her class.

From J. B. Bowman, now in Washington City: "I have been prosecuting a claim for damages done the University buildings during the war; I will succeed in getting $25,000, which will be expended in the erection of buildings at Ashland. I have written thanking you for your valued favor of shipping the box of specimens for the Museum. We had the pleasure of opening it to-day at the Smithsonian Institution, and oh! how delighted was I, with the rare and beautiful things in it! It shall be placed in a special case in Ashland. Sister Mattie, how exact they are in the classification and arrangement, showing so much care and skill and science on your part! General Latham arrived after a trip of six months. He called on me to-day at the department. He says Sister Carr is the most highly educated and accomplished lady in Australia. We have about 800 enrolled at the University. The Bible College is a grand success. I propose nominating Jas. C. Keith as Adjunct Professor. Oh, if I had a million dollars, there would be 500 in the Bible College! To this end of enlarging the University, I am working and praying every day of my life."

Mr. Carr to Mrs. Carr—relative to this brief visit to Sidney: "September 27, '71: We will reach Sidney at dark to-night. It is hard to write on the ship. All of us have been very sick, but it is fine now. The wind is fair and we are gliding along most beautifully as we promenade the deck. There is a man on board who has been in Louisville, and *May's Lick*! His name is Smith; a brother of John's I presume!

"28th: After a fine dinner yesterday at five, we had music on deck. Dark came on, and with it the lights of Sidney Harbor. It was the grandest view I ever had of any harbor. The lights were everywhere, and their reflection in the water was like posts surmounted by candles, and we were sailing right into the midst of these posts. We came right up to the wharf and there stood a number of Sidney friends to put us in cabs. After I went to bed, the old steamer was still roaring in my ears, and the floor was moving up and down, as I went off to dreamland. I am now sitting in a little parlor with a headache, waiting for breakfast and fearfully hungry.

"30th: I saw Parliament houses, and fine they are. I walked through Hyde Park, where is a monument to Captain Cook with this inscription; 'Captain Cook, born in Yorkshire 1726, founded this territory 1770.' Just over the monument I saw, away in the distance, part of Sidney harbor, the sun shining on the hills, and glistening in the water. Visited a former servant of the Magareys, who is now independent and owns a mill of his own. His daughter is a fascinating little creature—don't be jealous!—a perfect prodigy on the piano. They insist that I must preach here two Sundays.

"Sidney is the funniest laid-out place I ever saw. Part of the city is compact, the streets running every direction, at all angles, like London, while a short distance toward New Town there is a cowpen or paddock. The houses are strongly and handsomely built of massive stone, and some have stone steps running to the top of the three stories. Some houses look as if they had stood for centuries. It seems to me that the poorest thing the people have is religion. The one thing needful is the only thing neglected. I am not over my seasickness, and even now the table seems to be going up and down as I write. Give my love to Surber and Zelius, etc. If my tooth quits aching, I shall bring it back to Melbourne in my mouth.

"Oct. 3rd: Preached yesterday to small but interesting audiences. At night, three confessions—the first ever had in Sidney immediately after the preaching. The brethren were delighted.

"Oct. 4th: Went to hear an elocutionary effort in a little chapel; I was charmed by the speaker's manner and style, but pained because he did not preach the Gospel. From there we hurried on a boat for a trip up the Parramatta river, and saw Sidney Harbor to best advantage. I never saw such a sight, not even in old Kentucky! It is beautiful beyond description. The river was clear and smooth, sparkling in the sun. As far as the eye could reach were the weeping willows and pines, and trees whose foliage had the appearance of a continuous mountain range, relieved by beautiful flowers and lawns surrounding the prettiest houses, in front of which were the winding walks. The red soil and bright pebbles glistened down to the shore-bridge, where the boat would stop for passengers. We saw many islands where were beautiful houses and gardens, and could see the people walking about in their island homes. The most famous was Cockatoo Island whither the convicts were once sent, from which there was no possible escape. There stood the houses in which they had once lived. As the steamer glided on, we saw the ripe oranges hanging from the trees, and when we landed to go to a hotel at Parramatta, the perfume of the flowers followed us through the streets.

"Oct. 9th: Your two letters came, and I had a rare treat reading them. I was so glad to hear of the success you are having in the matter of raising funds to build the chapel! Hurrah for those sisters at Collingwood! We'll have a chapel, won't we? Certainly, if my wife takes the enterprise in hand!"

Mrs. Carr to Mr. Carr, while he was on his visit to Sidney: "It is very stormy today on land,—what will it be on the sea? I dreamt last night of a sinking ship. In reaching forward to save you, I awoke. May God bring you back safe to me, my dear, dear husband! Jane Nash" (of whom the reader is presently to hear) "is going to Tasmania in about a fortnight to be married to Brother Smith; she wants you to perform the ceremony. Can you not come home by way of Tasmania? Jane will go over any time you can be there. Let us know."

Among the young men who were bound to the Carrs by tender affection, and a common religious interest, was George Smith, a hatter by trade. Some time before the Sidney experience, Mr. Carr met Smith on the street, and the young man grasped the minister's hand, while the tears shone in his eyes. He had been out of a job for some time. "And now," he said, "I have found a position. I answered an advertisement a few days ago, and a telegram has come for me to take a place at once."

"Then what is the trouble?" asked Mr. Carr.

The trouble was that the position offered Smith was at Hobart Town, in Tasmania. There was no Church of Christ at Hobart Town; there was no one known to the young hatter, and, moreover, there was Jane! "How can I leave the brethren?" exclaimed Smith; "and how can I leave Jane?"

Jane Nash had been reared a Roman Catholic. Through the influence of her suitor, she was induced to attend the preaching. She was so disturbed by what she heard, that she resolved to take her Bible, visit the different preachers, and have them point out the places that might tell her what to do to be saved. She visited several; but they could only tell her to read her Bible, to pray, to wait for a divine influence. At last, she accosted Mr. Surber with her oft repeated question: "Will you tell me what I must do to be saved?"

"I cannot tell you," said Mr. Surber; "but I will direct you to those who can; men who ought to know, for the Savior himself inspired them to speak his will."

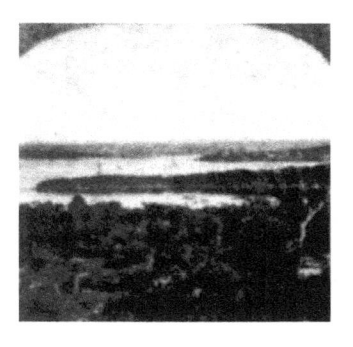

Sydney Harbor

Port Jackson, Sydney

Sydney Harbor

Jane was greatly excited. Mr. Surber took her back to the day of Pentecost, and had her sit under the preaching of Peter. Her question was the very one Peter had been asked. The answer on that day was the answer now. Jane confessed her faith, and was baptized.

It was best for George Smith to leave Melbourne, that he might make a home for himself and his betrothed. Dear as both were to the Carrs, they urged the young man to accept the position, and Jane, to wait till he could send for her. After they were married, they faded for a time from the lives of Mr. and Mrs. Carr; but, as we shall presently see, they were again to enter their history in a way more pronounced.

In the meantime J. C. Keith writes from Louisville, and gives us a melancholy bit of news as regards that Australian student whom we had seen dropping potatoes, to hurry along his education; Keith writes to Mrs. Carr: "I have read with interest all your articles to our different papers. You are doing a noble work for the Master. Few women in this fashion and money-loving age would endure so much for the Savior. Oh, that woman would rise to the dignity of her position! * * * My letter has been interrupted. The life of a city preacher is a checkered, yet a glorious one. One day he exhorts the brethren to be faithful, the next he faces a bridal pair, the next he stands beside the dead; then he visits the poor and bereaved and goes reading, and singing, and praying, on his way. I met Brother Earl and Magarey" (our Alex.) "Earl is working hard to raise the $20,000 for your Bible College in Australia. I saw Mr. Cowley yesterday. He is in this city, working for some Boston book house." (This is our enthusiastic Australian pupil. Note his sequel.) "Don't think the Cause lost much." (Ah, yes, let us solace ourselves as best we may.)

J. W. McGarvey writes encouraging words, not about young Cowley, who, alas! is no longer ours, but regarding another Australian student who is destined to remain in the fold: "Our Bible College is moving on with steady growth. We have 107 matriculates and expect 20 more. The *Apostolic Times* is growing in favor, but not so rapidly as we would like. The tendency among us is strongly in favor of latitudinarianism; our opposition to this rouses counter opposition. *The Standard*, under its free and easy policy, has almost caught up with the *Review*. *The Christian* has at last possession of the *Pioneer*, and has a clear field in Missouri. We have recently had a runaway match of a rather unusual character. A young son of Brother G. W. Longan of Missouri, who was a student at the Bible College, got a dismissal to go home, and slipped off with Emma Lard, Brother Lard's third daughter. Bad for the children of two preachers! All the special friends of the parties are very much mortified. The young couple are poor and inexperienced; they have a poor prospect before them. "Brother Capp" (our young man from Australia) "is making a good student. He is industrious, popular, and recites very well for a new pupil. Much love to Sister Carr, and many thanks for her good letters in the *Times*."

John Augustus Williams is very doubtful about that Australian University scheme; he writes to Mrs. Carr: "I know the Lord, by his tender providence, is guiding you to do a good and noble work. I hardly know what to say in reference to your proposed trip to the United States with a view to raise funds for a College in Australia. No doubt you could succeed better than Brother Earl" (whose efforts for $20,000 came to nothing).

"But you would assume a great undertaking. While I would give you all the help I could, you would have to depend mainly on your own personal appeals. It is impossible to excite any general interest in an enterprise that lies so far away. Though Charity may extend a liberal hand, she does not reach far."

Mrs. Carr, in a letter, gives a sidelight on her busy life: "If you could follow me one day through No. 4 Barclay Terrace, and then through the streets of Melbourne, you would lay your finger upon my lips, should I seek to apologize for not writing oftener. I am discharging some duty every waking hour, and I rarely retire till after twelve. Yet with all my humble efforts, a host of duties unfulfilled is daily pressing upon my conscience. Often in the storm, it is a perplexity to know what should be done first. But I rejoice that I had the strength to cut the cord binding me to the vanities of life. No, I do not complain, for I never *lived* until I came to Australia. When I read, two years ago, Mrs. Browning's line, 'Where we live, we suffer and toil,' I thought it a golden bar of poetry; now I know it to be a diamond of truth. Then, it moved my girl's spirit with the murmur of the outer world; now, it pushes my woman's nature toward the inner significance of all things. Yes, to suffer and toil, is to live!

"So I enjoy this life; but I should enjoy it intensely, if I had but three hours every day to devote to self-improvement. It may be a selfish desire; not having a single hour to cultivate my mind, is a sore trial. I try to smother this longing, fearing it may be wrong; but my every effort seems to give it a brighter glow. It is a part of my life, a part of the life that hungers after the beautiful, the wise, the infinite. If I were with you, I would bore you from morning to night with poetry; for during my summer vacations in girlhood, my store of poetry grew painfully immense. Have you read 'Gold Foil,' and 'Bitter Sweet,' or 'Dream Life,' and 'Reveries of a Bachelor'? If not, a rich feast awaits you. There is a deep, strong poetry in all that dropped from 'Ike Marvel's pen, though he wrote nothing but prose. I thought of comparing that brilliant writer to Washington Irving, but remembered the grave of buried love, and Friendship weeping there, and my hand refused to commit the sacrilege."

In October, 1871, we find that one of our "Trio"—the graduating class of '67—has been attacked by a foe from whom there is to be no escape. The letter is from Albert Myles: "Yes, the notice in the *Times* by Brother Brooks was correct. I am disabled from preaching—my last sermon was delivered April 26th, six months ago. I may never be well enough to preach again, though I try to keep a brave heart and hope on. It was at first a cold, of which I thought little, but instead of getting better, I finally had a cough—the doctors said it was bronchitis. By their advice, I resigned my position and went to St. Louis, as the doctors said a rest would restore me. But shortly after I came to the city, the 8th and Mound Street congregation earnestly solicited my services. They are poor, and only about 200. I consented to preach twice on Lord's day, if they would not ask me to visit; but it was a mistake; the work did not seem heavy, but I grew worse, and worse. I still thought my lungs were sound, and being called to the church at Columbia, Mo., I thought I would go there for the country air. I had been but a week or two, when I was compelled to quit and return to St. Louis. I had the doctors examine me again, and, to my utter astonishment, they said with great unanimity that I had old fashioned tubercular consumption, and that my life depended upon quitting preaching immediately, and that, for a good while. I have not dared even to exhort in prayer meeting, since then. As to my coming to Australia, the dangers of the voyage have never been considered by me. But if I come—for I cannot even yet decide *not* to do so—could the trip improve me sufficiently to labor there? And suppose I came, and could do no more than I do here!

"My headquarters are still in St. Louis; but I am not living anywhere in particular. I am at Mt. Sterling, Ky., now, where I see your brothers nearly every day. They do not look strong, but you can't tell anything about the Carr tribe by their looks, they are such a bony set! I must go to church now—will finish this letter after church if strong enough." The next day he takes up the pen again. "You have doubtless seen an account of the death of my brother James. No man in the ministry did so much work as he, in the same length of time. He was literally the victim of overwork! We have also lost our darling little Allene; she was 20 months old. Not only we, but every one thought her remarkably beautiful. Dear Ol., you have never been blessed with one of these little heavenly messengers; but neither have your hopes, once kindled, been turned to ashes. May the Heavenly Father give us the strength to endure."

So cries out our young Christian soldier, almost fallen in the last trench of the hard battle; a cry for help, but a cry, too, of fealty, to his great Captain. One by one his arms have been stripped from his feeble grasp—he cannot even exhort in prayer meeting!—and how fondly he remembers the date of his last sermon!—and no little Allene ("I shall never love another child so well," he says)—no fighting brother James to carry on the standard. But he still hopes he may get to Australia for missionary service. We, who cannot share his hopes, can at least rejoice that he began duty so young; for consider this; in the few years of his ministry, he has done more for Christ, than many a man of sixty.

His beloved schoolmate, Oliver Carr, stands much in the danger of James Myles. His energies are all gone—we do not say wasted, but spent; a vacation is imperative, and the missionary turns toward South Australia, whence have come the letters from Magarey and Gore, and Gore's father-in-law, Philip Santo. Mr. Carr goes thither on a visit to these three—the rich miller, the evangelist and editor, and the rich iron monger. This holiday furnishes us with the concluding series of the present chapter. The time is the Australian spring (or American Fall) of 1871.

Mr. Carr to Mrs. Carr: "I am in Brother Gore's study at Clapham, safe and sick. I was met by Santo," (M. P.) "Earl" (who failed in his attempt to bring over American gold for our Australian College) "Moysey" (who sold his calf some time ago to buy school books, not in vain) "Gore" (who has a new baby, T. J., Jr., by name, and affords the Australianized Kentuckian a fresh vantage point from which to argue against homesickness) "and many others. I never was so thoroughly seasick. I was on the bed or couch from one harbor to the other. I'm sick yet. Brother Gore and I came near talking all last night through. I've been asked many questions about Miss Ettie" (Gore's sister-in-law, who wrote to her father, "I love you," and who is still attending Mrs. Carr's boarding-school.)

He writes the next day: "I've gotten off my sea-legs, but my health is no better. We drove out to Magarey's and the family were glad to see us" (no talk of sore-headed bears, we may conclude). "Alex. is well," (who preaches while his brother "practices.") "For the first time, I pulled ripe oranges from the tree. We talked incessantly. I ate six before dinner." (The talk, then, not quite incessant!) "This country about Adelaide is a level plain for 200 miles around the seashore, girt by hills like those at Maysville on the Kentucky side. In the early morning, as I look at those hills and the lovely plains silvered with light, all is so much like home that my heart rises in my mouth, and I could almost say poetry! Adelaide seems to have been laid out for about 200,000 people, but only about 30,000 have come; so the spaces between the houses have been made into lawns and fragrant gardens. It is truly a rural place. The houses are principally one-story, with gardens, trees, etc. I only wish you were here to enjoy it. We talked about Kentucky University and the 'boys,' etc., all day long. These are just my kind of folk!"

Mr. Carr a few days later: "I am resting, oh, so good! I'm as easy as an old shoe—I wrote that while looking at Brother Santo, who had just come in to sauce me. He is a good man; I have a deal of fun with him. I get on the scales nearly every day to see if I've fattened. I wish you could breathe this clear, fresh air, and the perfume of the roses! I can hardly stop in the house long enough to write a letter. I baptized one last night. I told you how scattered the houses of Adelaide are—no danger of anybody's getting killed by being run over. This air is so clear that you can distinctly see the bodies of the trees and the cows grazing on the hills, six miles away. Tell Miss Ettie I don't blame her for being homesick for a place like this; all the family are just like Miss Ettie, so you would like them all."

Mrs. Carr to Mr. Carr: "I am distressed over Dr. Campbell's diagnosis. If your right lung is weak, a few more weeks' preaching in the hall would bring on disease. Now, my dear husband, the best thing that you could do, is to act the part of a rational being by taking the doctor's advice. If you will spend the summer in Tasmania" (whither our friend Geo. Smith has gone to make tall silk hats,) "I will gladly stay here in Melbourne for your sake. If you ought to return to America before the building of the Chapel—in other words, before the Cause is firmly established in Collingwood,—I am willing to do that or anything to re-establish your health. These are only suggestions; your own judgment must decide. No consideration could induce me to oppose you in any course the doctor might pronounce. Ollie, take good care of yourself. I am glad you and Brother Gore are going to the mountains. Climb Mt. Lofty, if it is accessible. You won't be able to tease Ettie about her country, when you return, you are so enthusiastic about its beauties. My birthday party passed off happily. My girls surprised me with a beautiful toast rack, butter knife and candlestick. It was a real surprise. We had delightful music. Two complimentary tickets just came for you from the Town Hall. Ettie and I will have the tickets, and you can have the honor. May the Lord bless you, my darling, and give you the strength to accomplish your proposed work in this land. I will be as economical as I can, that your health may not suffer for want of travel. Your large donation to the Chapel Fund will make things a little hard, but the Lord will supply us in a way that we know not."

Mr. Carr to Mrs. Carr: "I have been with Alex. to see such sights from the top of Mt. Lofty, as I cannot describe. The Magareys have done their best to make me happy, and oh, I do enjoy it! We went to church; Brother —— gave us the fall of Jericho. We got home at 9, enjoyed our cocoa, then to rest. Brother Gore is going to give his class a two weeks' holiday; then we will go fishing, and sit on the fence! We have great audiences here, our Cause is very strong in this country; and yet there are only about 350 real members (year 1870) in Adelaide; the faithful are few!"

Mrs. Carr to Mr. Carr: "I miss your wise counsel and kind encouragement in the discharge of duties. I would not wish to live without you; I feel that I could not. I hope you will write to Brother Albert Myles without delay. In his present health, he must be greatly crushed by the death of his brother. If you do not take the rest you require, you will go as perhaps Brother Albert is going. The Lord bless Brothers Santo and Gore for their goodness to you! Ollie, I wish you would write more of what you feel, and less of what you see. I want to know if you are any better, and I want to know Dr. Campbell's opinion *in full*. Ettie and I enjoyed the annual meeting of the deaf and dumb at the Town Hall. We had a representation of a cricket match; and the battle of Hastings. How did you happen to write 'Six shillings are too much for the book?' In my opinion you should have said 'Six shillings are too *many*,' or, '*is* too much.' I called on the American consul's wife; both are pleasant people. I am still determined to keep you in Tasmania two or three months during the summer, even if I have to keep lodgers."Mr. Carr to Mrs. Carr: "I find no fault in what you have written for the *Times*, why you should not have it published. I return you the MS. with my approval. Brother Gore and I went by coach to a fine old English tavern at Port Elliott where we staid till Saturday. I got you some shells. We wandered over the beautiful fields, gathering the wild flowers daily, and hourly left our little (?) footprints on the beach to be washed away. I wish you could have seen that view! Mattie, do you think I would let you stop at home and slave away, for *me* to have all the fun, just because of what Dr. Campbell says about one lung? I am glad your birthday party passed off so well. Many thanks for the flowers from your bouquet."Mrs. Carr to Mr. Carr: "I am sending you an article for the *Times*, for you to criticise. Return it to me and I will send it to Brother McGarvey, as I want to write to him. If there is anything in the article you disapprove, underline it, and perhaps I will omit. That which you cannot *tolerate*, doubly underline, and I will certainly strike it out. Does the little boy really cry for *you*, when you start for town, or isn't it for Brother Gore? Thanks for the nice flowers. I appreciate such a remembrance from my 'prosy husband.' If Ettie returns next year, I will keep you in Tasmania for your health three months. She is such a good girl, I love her more every day. I miss you more than I can tell, darling; but I have made up my mind to do what is best for you. Brother Dick remembered you at morning service, yesterday. It is after eleven now, and I must read some French before I sleep."

Mr. Carr to Mrs. Carr: "I am sorry I wrote you anything about Dr. Campbell's notion—I believe you called it a 'diagnosis.' There is nothing serious. My breathing is all right,—but my *unbreathing* isn't perfect. But I think I'm coming round finely. I shall certainly write to Albert Myles. Brother Santo is teasing me—I can't write. He is such a jolly good soul. He has been put up for the Upper House, and is pretty sure to go in. Much excitement about it. Brother Gore and I tease him all the time."

Mrs. Carr to Mr. Carr: "I still insist upon that Tasmania trip. Sister Smith is confident you can do much good there during your two months' rest." (Sister Smith is the Jane Nash, once a Catholic, whom Geo. Smith left when he accepted his position in Tasmania. Ever since the hatter went thither, he has urged the Carrs to come and establish a Church of Christ; now that he has married Jane, he has a faithful ally in sending the call for help to Melbourne.) "Expenses are running up, and I have no way to meet the bills; but the Lord has helped us in the past, and he will in the future. Your trip to Adelaide has put us in debt; but never mind, we will get out;

just now, we must restore my darling's health. Your letter was read to the church last Lord's day, and all were rejoiced at the improvement of your health. They say it is a shame you have never had a long rest after three constant years of labor! They desire very much your recovery, for they know how much depends upon you at Collingwood. I am writing on your table in Ettie's room. She occupies your study and will till you return. Aren't we saucy girls! But you will be so glad to see us, you won't scold. My eyes are closing—so good night, my love."

In Botanical Garden, Melbourne

In Botanical Garden, Melbourne

**Town Hall, Melbourne
Seats 4,000 on First Floor**

In Botanical Garden

Mr. Carr to Mrs. Carr: "Had a long talk with Sister ——— . She is too despondent to be a happy woman. There's no use in such a thing as that. Be cheerful and happy! I wish you were with me here at Two Wells. I was at the Port yesterday, 7 miles away, and got to fishing and got several bites, and came near catching a fish. I had him near the top of the boat, but he—" (Ah, yes!) "I am now at North Adelaide, at Magarey's. Everybody in the room is talking away, telling me what to write—write this and that—'Tell Mrs. Carr that joke on you,' etc. Such a pleasant visit!—talk, music, etc., and I played drafts and beat them badly every time, and then threatened to beat my antagonist with the board. Brother Thomas Magarey and I had a long walk and talk. He is a fine man and is sorry for ever having misunderstood me, and been led to think strange of us. He shows a great interest in your work."In the next chapter, we enter upon that Tasmanian visit which was destined to be of far greater proportions than Mrs. Carr at first planned. As a final word on the life at Melbourne, we quote from Mrs. Carr's diary, when all were together in the work:"My evening class as usual. Ollie is with his Adelphian that he loves so well. How it has grown in favor under his good and gentle guidance! How delightful to see him yield a Christian influence over the hearts of those destined to become the pillars of the church!"Took two young ladies to Chapel. They had never seen a baptism before, and were favorably impressed."Had a talk with my dear husband on the Baptism of Jesus and John. How hard I try to be worthy of Ollie!

"Ollie went to officers' meeting after preaching, and came home after twelve, much exhausted. Blessed Savior give him health and strength, and keep me humble.

"Wrote to President Williams about my plan for an Australian College. Blessed Savior, give my husband strength to labor for Thee."

CHAPTER XII.

EXPERIENCES IN TASMANIA.

The following extracts from letters of 1872 furnish an interesting account of the removal from Melbourne to Hobart Town, Tasmania. Mr. Carr writes to Mrs. Carr: "Arrived at Lancaster, safe but sick, January 6th. We set out for the Temperance Hotel, but it had become intemperate and gorged with guests before we got there. We went on, and have struck a bargain with an old woman who charges us one-six for each meal, and one-six every time we sleep. I came near stealing a march on my landlady by falling asleep this afternoon without the old lady's knowing it. Pretty high fare, but we are high up in the second story. Called on a Church of England acquaintance; he didn't invite me to his residence, but asked me to his pew. The coach doesn't leave for Hobart Town till Tuesday at 5 a. m. This place is just now taken by storm by pleasure parties from Melbourne; I suppose they will go on to Hobart Town. I am better to-day. I do believe if I stayed here, I could establish a church. The people are delighted to hear of your teaching, and of your plan of teaching. Shall I get you any boarding pupils? I believe this climate will be good for me.

"January 10. We arrived at Hobart Town last evening. Brother Smith was at the Coach Office, by chance or providence. There were 48 passengers. It was a very large open coach and we had a fine view of the country from Launceston to Hobart. All the cabmen and mischievous boys in the country flocked around to see why such a big affair had come to town. We were very cordially received by Brother and Sister Smith, and after cocoa, went to bed, and that was delightful, too. It is raining today, and I feel wretchedly dull and bad. I can hardly sit up.

"January 15. I do trust you are not discouraged. I am not. Remember you are a child of God, and all things work together for your good. I believe I have come to Hobart Town just at the right time, and the Lord will bless my coming to the good of this people, and the restoration of my health. I am enjoying the hospitality of Brother and Sister Smith, who show me every attention. She prepares many nice things for me to eat, and he has given me a fine new hat. I have a front room and a parlor all to myself, and the climate suits me exactly. Brother Smith and I went to the Baptist prayer meeting, and afterwards, they insisted that I preach on Lord's day. They asked me many questions, to which I returned Scriptural answers; I told them all about the church to which I belong, and what I preach; and they agreed, and I came home on tiptoe.

"The next night I went to Town Hall where the different preachers had been preaching all week. Sunday morning I preached at the Baptist chapel to a good audience. Then we ate the Lord's supper. I insisted on the ancient order of things—especially on meeting the first day of the week to break bread. They were delighted, and said I must preach in their chapel whenever I wanted to speak. There is a prayer meeting held every day at noon, and preaching held three or four times a week in the people's hall; but oh, they are so benighted! They don't know the Gospel in its beauty and power. I just burn to preach to them. I will, if I get half a chance.

"January 20. I am called on from every quarter to speak. All seem interested in my sermons. Things look bright, now; but I fear they will soon become prejudiced against the truth.

"January 27. I agree with you about the brick Chapel, and leave it all to you. I do hope they will not put up a wooden one. But they had better not have any Chapel, than to quarrel over it. If the majority say a wooden Chapel, a wooden one let it be. I don't believe in the Collingwood Church's going down. The faithful will remain faithful, despite a Chapel. The people here are becoming enthusiastic. Among my large audience Thursday night, I had two preachers. The people say they never heard such preaching in their lives. I am trying to work them around on Apostolic grounds. Now, Mattie, do not think all for me, and nothing for yourself. I could never forgive myself if I came here for my health, and you overworked. Do not let the building of the Chapel take too much of your strength.

"February 6. Last Lord's day I spoke on [13]'My Sheep' and there were about half a dozen of the higher Calvinists—who own the Chapel—who were not pleased. They will hold a church meeting next Thursday to decide whether or not I am to preach in their Chapel any more. Perhaps if they turn me out of their place it will be for the best, because the people who have been thronging there, do not believe in Calvinism; I am sure none would take steps to the Savior in that church, while I am preaching. I could rent a hall for eight, a week, and think after a while I can have a church here. The people meet me on the street and take me by the hand and say, 'I do wish you were going to live here,' etc. Last Lord's day, I spoke on the wharf to what is said to have been the largest audience ever assembled there. I am going to speak tonight at the People's Hall. But you must not think, dear Mattie, I am overdoing my strength; for it is no harder to preach than to go out to tea and talk.

"February 10. Great excitement in church affairs. I preached on John 10:27, and the audience was much interested, even excited, so that they began to talk in the yard about the absurdity of the church's bringing me to task. But I went in to my trial. One of the deacons made the motion that because I preached that it was possible for one who had been converted, to fall away and be lost, and because I said that Christ died for all, the Chapel be no longer tendered to me.[14] The motion was put, and only this deacon and two others voted for it. One man would not vote either way, and four voted in the negative. The chairman announced that I could use the Chapel when I liked, only three being opposed. But I declined to accept the offer, and yesterday tried all day to get a place to preach in; but was told in each place, "No, it would injure the other congregations, by drawing away their members." I am going to preach on the wharf tomorrow, where I will have a larger audience than I could ever have at the Chapel. The cause of the Master will not be hurt by this opposition. The editor of a weekly paper has offered me one page to edit religiously, and thus I will preach to the people. Brother and Sister Smith and I sat up late last night talking over the situation. She cried like a child and he is so excited over the matter that he doesn't know what to do. They will give us a room as long as we can stay. You must come.

"February 11. To-day has been one of great anxiety. As I could not get a hall to preach in, I thought it best to go to the Baptist Chapel as a hearer. The deacon of whom I wrote yesterday, preached in a vexing manner and Brother Smith was highly wrought up over the misrepresentations of my position. I preached on the wharf to a large throng in the afternoon, and at night heard a celebrated Congregationalist. I was so disappointed at passing one Lord's day evening without preaching the Word, that I was unable to give him a fair hearing. The people are in a furor because I cannot get a place to preach in. One lady whom I have never met, offers to give £5 toward erecting some sort of shed, that I may have a place to preach. I am not discouraged. Not even in Old Kentucky did I ever see so much interest manifested. The Lord will surely make some way here that his Truth may be heard."

From Mrs. Carr to Mr. Carr: "My heart is full of you and your mission, and prayers for your success. I believe the Lord will bless your efforts. I am determined that you shall have a hall to preach in, I know you will never sacrifice any of the fullness of the Gospel, hence you cannot continue at the Baptist Chapel. I send you £8 that you may rent a first-class hall. This I have borrowed, and I would borrow for nothing but to further your efforts in the Gospel. People ask me if you have had any 'Results.' Do not write to any one but me, of your labors, until you have had what the people call 'Results,'—until at least 20 have obeyed the Gospel. I will pay your rent until then, and after that you may be sure of the hearty co-operation of the churches. It is the *work performed* that determines the value of any instrumentality. At least, that is the opinion of the churches; and their idea of work performed is embodied in '*Converts*,' or, as some say, '*Results*.' And they are not wholly wrong. Don't write to others about your work until you have success. The £8 will rent a hall for two months at £1 per week, and by that time you will certainly have some 'Results.' But don't forget to take care of my darling's health. I do trust that your success will be such that you can stay three months longer. A gentleman we met in London at Mr. Murby's, called with letters and papers from Mrs. Murby. She says we must make up our minds to a long stay with her in London, on our return to Kentucky."

We resume Mr. Carr's letters to Mrs. Carr: "I have done it. I have rented one of the best places in the city, Odd Fellows' Hall, for 13-9 per week, including cleaning, gas, etc. Am now at the printing office getting out posters. We are to have six hymns printed for next Lord's day. I will ask baptized believers to remain after the sermon, to see how many members of the church there will be. Tell Brother Dick to send 50 hymn books, with bill. And tell him to send my baptizing suit in the same box.

"February 19. Our first day at the hall was a very successful one. The house was crowded and the people stood at the door. Poor Brother Smith is hardly able to contain himself for joy. On Tuesday we meet to organize a church. Don't forget to send that baptizing suit.

"February 20. To-night (Tuesday) we met in a side room of the Odd Fellows' Hall and talked on the basis of union. I answered their questions, and we had a happy time. Then I asked all to hold up their hands who were in favor of taking simply the New Testament as their rule of faith and practice, and nearly every one held up his hand. Fifteen of those who had been baptized, gave me their names, pledging themselves to live by the Word of God. So you see, we have a start even in Hobart Town.

"February 27. Lord's day evening the hall was crowded; some stood, some sat on the floor. There are some candidates for baptism, but a difficulty has arisen. The three who objected to my preaching, do not want to let me have the use of the baptistry. They have called a church meeting to which I am invited to explain what I make of baptism.[15] In the morning we met at the hall to break bread, so I regard the church as begun in Hobart Town. Our collection from the 15 who have taken their stand with us, was 1-6-0 last Lord's day morning. Pretty good for a start, isn't it? I will soon be able to return that money you borrowed. There is no communion service in Hobart Town, and I had to send to Melbourne for one.

"March 5. Our evening audiences are increasing, but only a few meet to break bread in the morning. The people are so ignorant of everything pertaining to Christianity, that I have to teach them as if they were children, sure enough. Many never heard of what I preach; and while they admit the truth of it, they stand aloof. About 500 read each week my religious page of the *Advance*. That is better than tracts. Come to Tasmania! I am sure you could do a good work here, and this climate would restore your health. We will treat you, oh so well! Let me know when to expect you, and I will go out and sit on the wharf and wait for you."

Mrs. Carr to Mr. Carr: "The *Southern Cross* leaves Melbourne the 26th of March, the anniversary of our wedding. I wish we could be together in Hobart Town on that day. I will bring my piano. If you are on the wharf at 6:30 Thursday morning you will see your wife. But I'll not expect you there, for I remember your motto—'He who cannot rest his head upon his pillow and enjoy his forty morning winks, is up to knavery, or else he drinks!' At the tea meeting everybody asked about you, and expressed joy at your success. The brethren are delighted that you have established a church in Tasmania. No, I will not bring Sister Smith a half dozen *reams* of cotton; paper is sold by the ream; but thread by the gross; perhaps you meant reels. It does seem strange that in less than a week, I'll see my husband! I scarcely know how I'll behave myself! An appeal was made to the Lygon street church for assistance to Collingwood, in the erection of a brick chapel. All thoughts of a wooden building have been abandoned, and harmony is prevailing. I am sure I'll get pupils on the piano and guitar when we are established at Hobart Town. President Williams' last words to me were, '*Only believe*, Mattie, and the light of his face will always shine upon you.' I believe the Lord will open a way for our support, if not through my labors, in some other way. I am going to have your faith, Ollie, and I know I'll be happy. Take good care of yourself. I'm sure you work too hard. Remember your work and your wife, and *take care of your health*!"

The reader who has followed the preceding pages does not need to be told why the Carrs finally left Australia. The admonition which each constantly gave the other—"Take care of your health,"—could not be observed. Even on holidays, as we have seen, hard work came pressing at the door; and the climate was never favorable to the constitution of the missionaries. They left, at last; but the Collingwood Church established through their efforts, remains to perpetuate their influence. At Hobart Town, success came in spite of active opposition. When Mr. Carr was challenged with the inquiry, 'What do you think is the design of baptism?'—his reply was as follows:

"'He that believes and is baptized shall be saved.' That is what the Savior says. That is what I think."

This reply was so unsatisfactory that he was refused the use of the baptistry. The town, less scrupulous in its views, proffered the use of public baths. The public would assemble upon the porch of the bathroom, and, in the salt water, the converts would be immersed. It was not in vain that Mr. Carr preached on "My sheep hear my voice." The entire Baptist Church with the exception of six came to the congregation at the rented hall. At the end of three months, Mrs. Carr joined her husband. During the year in Tasmania, they lived with the Smiths. Mrs. Carr taught music, and she and Mrs. Smith made sailors' caps and sold them to help on with the missionary work. Whaling ships came in there, and the demand for sailors' caps was unceasing.

But while Mrs. Carr thus lived in partial seclusion, sewing and teaching music lessons, her thoughts reached far beyond the straitened opportunities of the colonies. Five years from the native land had resulted so far as visible results went, in the establishment of two churches, one in Melbourne, one in Hobart Town. Such accomplishments were well worth the sacrifices they had demanded, but they were achievements aside from those definite ideals which she had formed at the beginning of her school life. Her boarding school in Melbourne had done much good, but it was not a permanent institution; with her departure, it passed away; and she was resolved that out of her life should come a monumental school, which, though she departed, should remain. Her plans conflicted with her husband's intense zeal for souls, hence she quietly worked away at sailors' caps, and agreed, if he thought best, to go next to New Zealand for the Cause. But at last, when it became manifest that his health demanded a rest from work too great for even a strong man, and a decided change of climate, she declared for a return to America. To go back meant not only the probable regaining of his health, but the carrying out of her educational ambitions; and in order the better to perfect herself in her chosen work, and to secure the needed rest for both, she resolved that they should spend the next year in travel, studying the countries of the Orient, and dwelling among the hills round about Jerusalem.

Mr. Carr to Mrs. Carr, from Hobart Town, January 17, 1873: "Last night we had our Tea Meeting and oh! such a Tea it was! Everybody seemed pleased with everything but one abominably long address. The speech of the evening had much about you; 'a lady of such rare abilities,' 'your condescension in coming amongst them,' 'they would never find your equal,' etc. The good you have done, your kindness to all, your talents, were dwelt upon by nearly every speaker. Poor Brother Jones could hardly restrain his feelings. He said he had never seen your like. The singing was splendid. The room was most tastefully decorated. 'Farewell to Brother and Sister Carr for a season,' and 'Welcome to Brother G. B. Moysey,' were the letters hanging about." (Mr. Carr's successor at Hobart Town was that Moysey who had sold his calf for learning.) "After Brother Moysey's first sermon on Lord's day, there was one confession. It was a grand sermon,— he is just the man for the place and I am sure will do a splendid work here. Everybody sends love to you. I am so excited,

I'm ill. I do hate to go from here. I never knew before how much I thought of this people. I have spent three days taking Brother Moysey around to see the people in their homes. I am so sorry to hear of your illness. Take good care of your health. Love to Brothers Gore, Santo, and everybody—dear me! I can write no more."

CHAPTER XIII.

TRAVELS IN THE ORIENT.

An account of one's travels in lands far from the scene of one's life-work, has no proper place in biography, unless such travels reveal or develop characteristics of the traveler. No matter how wide-spread may be the interest in the countries traversed, the biographer has no right to convey his reader from land to land, simply because the feet of his subject have gone on before. We would, therefore, pass over the oriental experiences of Mr. and Mrs. Carr with but a word, if we did not have before us extensive notes on the journey, in Mrs. Carr's own hand.

The fact that she wrote of her experiences, makes them at once of biographical value, for we are enabled to observe the reaction of peoples and countries upon her own mind. While it is true that these notes were made that she might tell others what she had seen, it must be remembered that they were not intended for publication.

"On a beautiful May morning, the pet steamer of the Peninsular and Oriental Line, with all canvas spread, was skimming the smooth waters of the Indian Ocean. No albatross of ill-omen hovered round our ship. The passengers, light-hearted and joyous, were chatting under the awning,—when the man at the wheel shouted, 'Fire! fire!'

"At that awful word, every man of the crew was at his post, while pale passengers stared at each other, fainting women fell into trembling arms, and the children caught the contagion of fear. Suddenly our Captain turned his wide-mouthed trumpet upon us and shouted:

"'Ladies and gentlemen, I beg your pardon; the crew is on a fire drill!' Those who had fainted, never forgave him for his failure to notify them of what was to happen.

"A night of excitement succeeded. About ten o'clock, while we were on deck, enjoying the balmy air of the tropics, the sharp report of a pistol was heard, its flash gleamed for an instant on the waters,—and a suicide had cast a gloom over all. A night of watching by the dead passed, and at the rising of the sun we witnessed a burial at sea. The body, enclosed in a canvas sack and weighted with iron, was laid upon a latticed bier close to the opened gangway. It was held in place by two guards lest, even in that calm sea, a sudden tilt of the ship send it into its grave before the time. The service of the Church of England was read; then the body fell heavily into the waters, there to remain until the coming of that sound which is to penetrate even the depths of old ocean.

"A few days sail brought us to the luxuriant shores of Ceylon. We spent several days driving over the beautiful island, through cocoanut and banana groves and cinnamon gardens, inhaling the spicy breezes, and sorrowing over the degradation of the people.

"From this beautiful but sin-cursed isle, our ship soon brought us through the straits of Bab-el-Mandeb, and anchored at Aden, on the barren shores of Arabia. Near Aden are situated the immense tanks holding millions of gallons of water, without which the land would be uninhabitable. Continuing our voyage up the Red Sea, we passed Mocha, renowned for its coffee, and in due time arrived at the gate-entrance of the great Sinaitic Peninsula,—Suez.

"Suez, washed upon one side by the sea, is encircled upon the others by the barren wastes of the desert. No tree, shrub, or blade of grass, relieves the gloomy sterility of the landscape. We hasten on by rail. Soon a long, low line of water appears, just beside the railroad track. Behold, it is the Nile—that river cradled in the depths of mysterious caverns, forcing its way through granite ledges and mountain barriers, rushing over cataracts, foaming through narrows, then flowing gently onward, singing amid perpetual sunshine, until it empties by its seven mouths into the great blue sea. A river which has a place in history by the side of the Euphrates and the Jordan; a river which the Egyptians worshiped, and the miracle of whose waters made a Pharaoh tremble; a river on whose banks perished Thebes with her hundred gates, and Memphis with her monuments; a river that has seen the coming of Ethiopian and Persian, Macedonian and Roman, Saracen and Turk, in fulfillment of the curse God spoke through Ezekiel.

"After stopping at numerous stations where we were greeted by sights, sounds, and odors peculiar to the coarse civilization of the Orient, the minarets of Cairo and the pyramids of Gizeh looked down upon us. After a minute examination of the pyramids" (I omit a thoughtful and logical disquisition on the various problems presented by these monuments) "we drove back to Cairo under the grateful shade of the lebbekh trees, over a fine macadamized road, built in 1868 in honor of the Prince and Princess of Wales. After a pleasant and profitable talk with the American consul, who kindly came to bring us our passports, and to invite us to dine with him, we reviewed, as usual, the scenes of the day, and rested as only weary sight-seers can rest.

"Early the next morning, we drove through the Esbekeeyah, the Corso of Cairo, on our way to Heliopolis. It is easily identified from a distance by the oldest obelisk in Egypt, bearing the name of the founder of the XXII. dynasty. In Scripture, Heliopolis is called On. Moses is said to have studied here, and Joseph's father-in-law was a priest of its renowned temple. Here Plato lived for thirteen years. It seems to have been literally a city of obelisks, for it furnished all that have been transported to Europe. Its destruction was prophesied by Ezekiel.

"The way to the magnificent palace of Shoobra lies along a beautiful avenue of sycamore, fig, and acacia. The Shoobra road is the 'Rotten Row' of Cairo. It is perhaps the most republican promenade in the world. No vehicle or animal is excluded. The Khedive and his outriders are jostled in most unseemly fashion by bare-boned donkeys whipped along by ragged urchins. Ministers, consuls, bankers, money-changers, speculators, singers, actors, ballet-dancers, adventurers, and not least conspicuous, English-speaking tourists, form a curious medley. After a drive to the tombs of the Caliphs through sand that buried our carriage wheels almost to the hub, we spent a pleasant evening with the American consul and his accomplished wife in their beautiful oriental home, then slept the dreamless sleep of the weary traveler.

"In the early morning we mounted our donkeys which were ornamented gorgeously in oriental style. These donkeys, in honor of our nativity, had been christened Uncle Sam and Yankee Doodle. We expressed our appreciation of such patriotic names, when, lo! almost every donkey in Cairo, in the neighborhood of our hotel was suddenly transformed into an Uncle Sam or a Yankee Doodle. But Mr. Carr and I would not desert the first of the name.

"I wish you could have seen us flying along the Nile at the rate of the Western Lightning Express, Eli, without either bridle or mane to cling to, our English tongues crying, 'Stop! stop!'—which the Arab ears of our muleteers interpreted into, 'Faster! faster!' Our muleteers were very accommodating fellows, and their interpretation encouraged them to renewed efforts to increase the speed of our donkeys, by applying, every thirty seconds, a sharp-pointed steel instrument. Our English-speaking dragoman was too far ahead to hear our cries of distress as we rocked in the cradle of (on) the donkey.

A New Year's Reception

"After an hour's most exciting ride, we dismounted at the Museum of Egyptian Antiquities. Here is a mummy coffin, whose hieroglyphics demonstrate that the ancient Egyptians had a conception of hell and heaven, and a belief in the immortality of the soul. There is an inscription proving that the Sphinx existed before the time of Cheops; and that even then, the people were rich and civilized. Here are ancient knives, scissors, needles, etc., but nothing is made of iron, which they thought a bone of their evil genius. Here on exhibition are the magnificent jewels found on the mummy of Queen Aoh-Hotep, the mother of the first king of the XVIII. dynasty.

"Here can be found the confirmation of many narratives of the Old Testament. The first great event in the Kingdom of Judah, after its separation, was the invasion of Shishak, king of Egypt. According to the sacred record, Shishak came against Jerusalem with 1,200 chariots and 60,000 horsemen, took the fenced cities, and was about to invest the capital, when Rehoboam made his submission.

"On the outside of the great temple at Karnak, hieroglyphics commemorate the success of Shishak against Judah, and records a long list of captured towns—the fenced cities of Scripture. The picture Moses gives of a Pharaoh ruling over an absolute monarchy, finds confirmation in the ancient Egyptian tombs. From vast numbers of papyri, we learn in detail of that old civilization—records which even Herodotus was not able to read.

"In these we find a counterpart of the picture of that country presented by Moses. After a slumber of 3,000 years, these records present the people prostrating themselves, the laborers storing away grain, the baker with his three baskets upon his head, the brickyards with Jewish laborers supervised by Egyptian taskmasters, etc.

"In the Museum of Antiquities are statues of kings and queens who lived in the era between Moses and Abraham. In front of them is an immense glass case in which is deposited their crown jewels, artistically executed. Among them is a massive gold chain, more exquisitely beautiful than anything I saw in the Tower, among Victoria's crown jewels, unless I except the Kohinoor. It was more beautiful than the jeweled swordhilt, breast plate or crown of the Shah of Persia, worn at his reception at Milan, though they represented nearly half the wealth of his kingdom.

"Thus it is proved that in the era in which Joseph received the chain of gold from Pharaoh, such chains, of rare workmanship, were already in vogue. Less than a century ago, critics were hurling their shafts of contempt against the so-called blunders of Moses; but monumental history substantiates his credibility. Truly, Egypt is one of God's historic books. His handwriting is on temple and tablet and tomb. Here dead men speak, and stones rise up to testify. Bricks of unburnt clay, torn up from the ruins of centuries, tell of Israel's bondage and labor.

"Of course we went to the bazaars and parks, cathedrals and mosques, the missionary schools, and the College of Cairo—the principal University of the East. And then to Alexandria—to which the ancient city has, indeed, bequeathed nothing but its name. Though earth and sea have remained unchanged, imagination can scarcely find a place for the ancient walls. Little vestige remains of the magnificent days of the Ptolomies and the Cæsars.

"One-fourth of the population is foreign; the city seethes with the scum of all the cities of the Mediterranean. Here luxury and literature, the Epicurean and the Christian, dwelt together; but now, in the Oriental part, one finds only dirty, narrow, tortuous streets, mud-colored buildings with terraced roofs, varied by fat mosques with lean minarets.

"Here once stood the renowned library of antiquity. Here the Hebrew Scriptures expanded into Greek under the hands of the Septuagint. Here Cleopatra, '*Vainquer des vainquer du monde*' reveled with the Roman conqueror; here Mark preached the truth upon which Origen attempted to refine; here Athenasius held warlike controversy; here Amer conquered, and here Abercrombie fell.

"In company with our intelligent dragoman, we sailed from Alexandria on a Russian steamship, and, after a voyage of a day and a half, beheld the queer stone city of Joppa, with its fort-like houses rising tier above tier on the hillside.

"I cannot describe the enthusiasm we felt at the thought that we were at last to walk upon the soil hallowed by the feet of patriarchs, prophets and apostles and to visit the scenes where they lived, labored, and communed with God. We walked through the winding, slanting streets of Joppa, and called at the house of Simon the tanner.

"So well preserved were the vats of his tannery that one would hardly have been surprised to find the distinguished guest of Simon walking on the housetop in the twilight. But we must confess that we could not identify this house by the description given in the tenth chapter of Acts.

"Leaving Joppa early in the afternoon, in a German spring-wagon, and passing through the only gate on the land side, we set our faces toward the Holy City. Gardens and orchards, groves of orange, fig, and pomegranate, made the country delightful. Our road lay directly across the plain of Sharon.

"Isaiah prophesied that Sharon should be a wilderness, and the black huts of the Bedouin tell the fulfillment of that prediction. We look in vain for the beautiful flower to which Solomon likened his beloved. But although man is no longer regaled by its fragrance, the true Rose of Sharon still unfolds its charms to every believer, whether he be a child of the plain, or the mountain.

"We passed by Ludd, and refreshed ourselves at the Arimathea of Joseph. We approached the hillside village of Kirjath-jearim, with its terraces of olives and fig trees. Leaving the valley of Ajalon, the rough macadamized road led us up the rocky sides of Judea's hills. We traveled nearly all night; and, just as we reached the highest point in the road, between the sea and the river, the rising sun unveiled to us the minarets and domes and massive walls of Jerusalem. I cannot tell you how inspiring, how deep, were the emotions that came crowding upon brain and heart.

"When we were about five miles from the city, a young man, mounted upon a beautiful Arab steed, brought us to a halt, with a courteous wave of his hand, and, in broken English, presented us with the card of the Mediterranean Hotel. We learned that the proprietor was a convert of Dr. Barclay, and decided to make his house our home during our stay. In a little while we entered the Joppa gate amid cries of squalid beggars, and, a few yards from that entrance, dismounted before our hotel. It stands on Mt. Zion, in the shadow of the Tower of David, and here we received that cordial welcome accorded to those willing to pay $3 a day.

"Standing on the heights of Mt. Zion with your face to the east, you have before you the Tyropeon Valley, now so full of debris as scarcely to appear as a valley. Looking a little to the north you behold Mt. Moriah where now stand the Dome of the Rock and the Mosque of El Akra. Beyond these to the east, is the deep Valley of Jehosaphat with the brook Kedron and the supposed Garden of Gethsemane, and beyond rises the beautiful summit of the Mount of Olives. Northward is Akra, and east of it Bezetha, two of the hills on which the city originally stood, and a part of which it still covers.

"We have lingered at Bethesda, whence the angel has departed; at Siloam's fountain; at the Wailing Place where the Jews, every Friday afternoon, lament in the language of their poets, the misfortunes of their people; at the Dome of the Rock with its marvelous Moslem wonders; at the Church of the Holy Sepulchre, that centre of enslaving superstition, whose annual triumphs cast a ray of hope adown the narrow halls of the Vatican. Through a hole in the wall of the Chapel of Angelo, a torch is annually passed out, supposedly lighted by fire from heaven. The pilgrims wait in the darkness with wax tapers, to be lighted from celestial fire. The devotees bathe their hands in the flame, to secure a special blessing; and the extinguished tapers are carried to 20,000 distant homes, to be as devoutly reverenced as the pilgrims who carry them.

"There is nothing in the Church of the Holy Sepulchre that is not saddening to the heart of the enlightened. Through our visit to this building we had the honor of making the acquaintance of the Bishop of Jerusalem, and receiving from him diplomas testifying to our Oriental travel. I fear I should forfeit mine could he know my unorthodox opinions of the 'sacred spots' of the Church.

Woman of Bethlehem

"I loved to walk along the Via Dolorosa, to visit the home of Mary and Martha. I wept under the shade of Gethsemane's gnarled olive trees; I climbed to the summit of Olivet, and listened to the French prattle of the Countess de Bouillon; I took a donkey ride over the hills of Judea; I lunched in the shadow of the rock where the man who went down from Jerusalem to Jericho, fell among thieves; I tented in the valley of the Jordan with the Stars and Stripes and the Crescent and the Star waving above; I stood on the whitened shores of the Salt Sea, and gathered dead sea apples along the shady banks of the Sacred River; I had a cooling draught from Elisha's Fountain at the foot of the Mount of Temptation; and in the shadow of Mount Tabor, I thought I heard the angel of death calling me to another Canaan. The flowered slopes of cedared Lebanon, the snowy top of Hermon, the clear waters of Abana, the ivy of old Damascus, Tyre and Sidon, Mt. Carmel and Nazareth—in short, from Dan to Beersheba, we saw all.

"And for all the Holy Land, the most accurate guide-book the traveler can have, even to this day, is the Old Testament. So perfect is the agreement of the land and the Book, that frequently when standing upon some elevated spot in Palestine one could read the story of Joshua, Judges and Samuel, and follow accurately with the eye the movements from place to place, as readily as on a modern map.

Mrs. Carr in Jerusalem

O. A. Carr, Arab Gentleman's Garb

"Since the first siege of Jerusalem by Joshua thirty-three centuries ago, it has undergone twenty-six sieges, and in almost one-third of these, the city was utterly devastated. The great explorer, Captain Warren, has sunk shafts through the immense mass of debris accumulated at the wall penetrating stratum after stratum of debris of successive devastations.

"Descending eighty feet, he found the road that used to lead from the gate, in the time of Herod. Sixty feet farther down, was discovered the road of the time of Solomon. In the foundation-stones were found the marks of the quarries of Tyre. They came upon the arches of the viaduct, that, in the days of Solomon, connected the palace with the temple.

"There is no discord between the voice of the ruins, and the voice of inspiration. These wonderful voices of the dead, coming not alone from Egypt and Palestine, but from the exhumed capitals of Assyria and Babylonia, awakened after a score and a quarter centuries of silence, bear testimony in unmistakable tones that 'Jehovah is God, Jehovah is God alone.'"

CHAPTER XIV.

WORK IN KENTUCKY AND MISSOURI.

The five years following the return to America were years of transition, of experiment. Mrs. Carr was, as always, bent upon devoting her energies to educational work, and Mr. Carr was content to preach in whatever surroundings might be best adapted to her talents.

Fortunate is he who discovers anywhere in the world, a situation which calls for the exercise of all his highest faculties; usually such a setting must be made, fashioned from a part of that energy which, might, if not thus deflected from creative work, have wrought the more.

It was so with Mrs. Carr. Endowed with gifts of high order, gifts that the world always needs, she had not, as yet, found the vantage ground for their full exercise; nor was she ever to find that highest development, until she had fashioned from her own heart and brain, the battle-ground of service.

As yet, she did not know this, but sought in various fields for a ready-prepared equipment, a sword sharpened, and a breast plate polished by other hands, with which she might fight for the truth. Returning from Australia she naturally looked about in Kentucky for the background of her ideals. It was not to be found there, and she came presently to Missouri; first to Fulton, then to Columbia.

She entered into various school relationships, but we find her restless in association with presidents whose ideas of school-government were different from her own. We trust the following extracts from letters will prove of interest in themselves, and at the same time tell the story of these years in the words of those who were chief actors.

May 27, 1874, about eight months after the return from Australia, A. B. Jones writes to Mr. Carr from Madison Female Institute, Richmond, Kentucky: "If I should conclude to resign here, would it be worth while to nominate you and Mrs. Carr for the position?"—which shows that Mrs. Carr is making no delay in seeking her sharpened sword and polished armor.

She is in fact, impatient in the search, as witness this to her from Mr. Carr, May 27th: "I am having big audiences at Sycamore, Kentucky. At the conclusion of the sermon, last night, eleven came forward. You must try to be reconciled with your lot until next fall. This constant moving about from place to place, is best for the present. As to Hocker College, they want you and I will hold myself liable to an engagement at Cincinnati, for my wife's sake. Do not worry over the matter. Teaching must be attended to, just as the institutions of baptism and the Lord's supper. I am sure you will be one of the happiest women in the world, if you are settled at work; and this shall be, if we are spared to see next fall."

He writes again, June 25th: "Your letter came yesterday. A man named Carr, opened it by mistake, and when he saw that ribbon and those flowers, he must have thought it from somebody's sweetheart,—and so it was! Brother Crenshaw has a flourishing Ladies' College at Hopkinsville. These institutions have sprung up rapidly in Kentucky. Here at Princeton is another. Warrendale College at Georgetown is to be sold for debt. From all I can see, these Colleges do not promise much. I am sure a certainty at Hocker is preferable to an uncertainty elsewhere."

Extract from the *Kentucky Gazette*, Lexington, Ky., August 18, 1874: "On the second Monday of September, Hocker College" (of which Robt. Graham was President) "will begin its sixth annual session. The immense outlay of more than $100,000 has made the building perfectly adapted to its purposes. To the faculty of the fall term has been added Mrs. O. A. Carr, a Christian woman of untiring energy, and zeal in the education of women. She is a graduate of St. Catherine de Sienna and Daughters' College and holds a Traveling Diploma from the Bishop of Jerusalem. She purposes delivering a series of lectures, extending through the collegiate year, upon the wonders of many lands. She is eminently qualified as an educator and disciplinarian for the position of Principal in Hocker College."

M. W. Green, writing from Australia, throws a confirmatory light on why the Carrs were obliged to return to America: "You say you are so busy you find it difficult to get time to write. It is to be hoped that in doing so much you will not again overtax yourself, and bring on another time of weakness. I am beginning to feel somewhat as you did, before you left Melbourne. Nature is beginning to wear out, and calls for a rest. I cannot get that rest on land, for if I see an opportunity to preach, I feel myself unfaithful if I do not avail myself of it. Sometimes I think I will never get a rest unless I take a long sea-voyage. It must be hard for you to have your study in Lexington, and your books in Hobart Town. Brother Earl writes me of his sorrow at hearing that protracted meetings are being introduced into Australia. 'They,' he says, 'often bring unconverted people into the church; and they are discouraging to the regular preacher, for the people get into the way of not uniting with the church, except at the exciting time of a protracted meeting.' We are pleased that Sister Carr has obtained so good a place for usefulness as the one at Hocker. We had Brother Magarey over in Melbourne to preach for us. I was much pleased with him, both as to piety and ability. His style much resembles your own, and I cannot tell his handwriting from yours." (This was the miller's son, Alex., whose brother practiced medicine and religion, as we have seen.)

While Mrs. Carr is teaching at Hocker, Mr. Carr writes to her from Vanceburg: "I cannot tell when I will be home; this is the time for work. I would be miserable hanging about Hocker College, doing nothing, and you hard at work. I will hold two or three meetings before I return. Miller is blazing away at Greenup; he is giving me a drumming, I hear; but he can't hurt me. I understand that Brother Sweeny has agreed to debate with Miller. I can assist your young ladies on the Argonautic Expedition as well from here, as if I were with them. I advise them to write sensible essays, and have their papers strictly original. This advice is all I could offer them, no matter where I am. This is an odd place. The farmers bring their produce to town every other day, which consists of a few bundles of hoop-poles for barrels, and these they trade for something to eat. They leave the city with a long slice of fat bacon under the arm, and a little bag of flour, enough to sustain their families for the next day. Then they come, and go again. I am amused at the merchants, who give their goods for poles, tar and tanbark, and then run cooper-shops in connection with their dry goods and bacon. One of our sisters here is a milliner. She says she doesn't take tanbark in trade for bonnets, but she has ladies' hats for ten cents a piece, and carries on a lively trade. Don't you want me to bring you up here, to do some shopping?"

Standing: Matt (Mrs. W. B. Smith), R. A. Carr, Mrs. O. A. Carr, O. A. Carr, Mrs. H.P. Carr, Owen Carr. Sitting: Mary (Mrs. Goddard), Wm. Carr, Mrs. Wm. Carr, Capt. H. P. Carr, Minnie, (Mrs. Jno. W. Fox, Sr.) HOME AGAIN—ALL HERE

We learn from the following that Mrs. Carr found one year at Hocker College (now called Hamilton College) enough to convince her that it did not afford the opportunities she sought; the letter is to the Trustees of the Midway Orphan School, and is written by Robert Graham, May 10, 1875: "Having heard that there will be a vacancy in the principalship of your institution, it gives me pleasure to say that Sister Carr has been associated with me in Hocker College during the session now coming to a close, and that she is a lady peculiarly fitted to have charge of girls in the classroom and in daily life. She is a lady of refinement, intellectual culture, and energy. I think her conscientiousness, experience, and religious devotion, point her out as one raised of God to do a great work in the intellectual world, and spiritual education of women."

September 9, 1875, Mrs. Carr, now at her old home town, Stanford, receives a letter from John Augustus Williams: "If you had consulted me as a daughter should consult a father, you would have saved yourself some trouble. I received several letters from the Missouri Orphan School recently; they wrote for my advice regarding teachers,—but I thought you engaged at Hocker College. School must be in session now, so it is too late. But you and Ollie, having no children, ought to be in charge of that school. It is 150 pupils strong. What to do this session? Well, address yourself to study, and prepare yourself to take charge of your sister-women in any branch. Daughters College is full. Over 100 boarders have applied, and we cannot take them. You and Ollie come to see me. Yes, come *home*, and let's have a talk!"

Mrs. Carr was never associated with the Missouri Orphan School, but she was convinced that Missouri offered her better opportunities than Kentucky. Accordingly, when in the fall of this same year, Mr. Carr was called to preach for the 17th and Olive Street Church, at St. Louis, it meant a final departure from the state of their birth, so far as permanent work was concerned.

At the St. Louis Church, Mr. Carr was the successor of Dr. W. H. Hopson, and the predecessor of T. P. Haley. It was an interesting and a critical time in the history of the St. Louis Churches. J. H. Garrison of the Central Church was laboring night and day to keep the infant *Christian* upon its feet. The faithful members of both congregations stood loyally by the little weekly, and took their turns in ministering to the mission churches, such as that at 13th and Webster.

Of the Church for which Mr. Carr preached, there were three elders, who were interested in this missionary work: John G. Allen, the father-in-law of Albert Myles; Dr. Hiram Christopher, former teacher of Chemistry at Bethany and author of "The Remedial System" as we have seen; and Dr. J. W. Ellis, who practiced law during the day, taught in Jones's Business College at night, preached on Sunday afternoons, wrote "Jarvis Jeems" articles for the *Christian* between times, and edited the St. Louis Ladies Magazine.

The matter of finding board for Mr. and Mrs. Carr was a difficult one. Albert Myles and his family lived with J. G. Allen, hence Mrs. Allen did not feel that she could receive an additional family, however congenial. In the end the Carrs went to her hospitable home, but for some time they lived with Dr. and Mrs. J. W. Ellis.

To this association of a month, the present writer owes his personal knowledge of Mrs. Carr. He had never seen her until the fall of 1875, he never saw her after the spring of 1876. Inasmuch as his sixth birthday fell within those extremes of time, he cannot be expected to speak of Mrs. Carr's mental and spiritual characteristics, from his own observation. He remembers her, however, not as a mere name, or as a vague shadow of the past, but with clear-cut distinctness. Of all the women who flitted through his boyhood days never to reappear, Mrs. Carr's personality stands forth best defined.

Perhaps it was because she had no children of her own, that she was able to impress children, from the interest she had in the children of other people,—her absorbing thoughtfulness for youth itself. This was with her no transient pastime, but belonged to that deeper part of her nature which started the stinging tear at little bits of childhood-verses. Her manner with children was not gay and buoyant, but gentle and untiring.

The child felt that her interest did not spring from impulse, to pass with the hour, but that whenever he should be ready, he would find her. In that inherent dignity and seriousness of her natural character, kindliness for the young shone with a steady light which, if it did not flash out in sudden radiant mirth, remained unclouded from any other interest.

Those who have proved restive under Mrs. Carr's unrelaxing discipline, those who may have opposed her in school management, those whom she has faced from the public rostrum in state addresses with logical argumentation, may have found in her a fearlessness that seemed at times the indication of an imperious and unyielding disposition. Doubtless those who opposed her were unable to understand the wounded heart behind the stern, accusing eye. But however brave and determined, there was one thing she feared,—to wound the heart of a child.

During Mr. Carr's ministry in St. Louis, Mrs. Carr devoted herself to study and travel. A large composition book, filled to the last page, shows her indefatigable labors with the German language, under the guidance of Dr. J. W. Ellis. In 1876, she went to the Centennial Exposition at Philadelphia, where we find her studying the exhibits with the same thoroughness she had shown in London and Cairo. While she is on the wing, Mr. Carr writes to her from Sedalia in June:

"I'm all right here, a little sick. Friday night I lectured at Mexico. Brother Hardin and I took the freight to Moberly; and then here, in time for the meeting. Dr. Hopson is in the chair and there are twenty-nine preachers present. I met Brother Longan last night, and he laughed as we shook hands. He and I will have a private dig. What do Brothers Wilkes and Rogers think of his 'One Word More' in the last *Christian*? Do they think Longan is right on the ghost question? This is a charming city. The country around looks like the best part of Fayette County" (of course he is speaking of Kentucky.)

"The little I have seen, is bewitching. I am on for a speech tomorrow, and have been too sick to prepare it, and here I sit with my finger in my mouth! I hope I'll do as well as —— did last night, and I think I will! Brother Monser is my roommate, and we did talk last night! I think he likes my wife better than he does me. Well, I let him. He is a good man. He spoke of the time Brother Mountjoy conducted you to the platform at Mexico."

The following, from Fulton, Missouri, signed by three citizens, shows that while at the Exposition, Mrs. Carr was making plans for future work: "In compliance with your request, we report as follows,—We have interviewed the members of the church in town, and find them quite favorable towards patronizing a school of our own; we think 30 or 40 may certainly be counted upon at the opening. We cannot do anything until we first ascertain that we are going to have a school taught. Desks, seats, etc., can be easily secured when we find there is to be a necessity for them. If preparations be commenced at once, we think a very good school can be founded here."

September 7th, Mrs. Carr wrote to Mr. Carr from Washington, D.C.: "I am writing in the celebrated Washington Post Office. I have learned a great deal during my short stay in Washington. I have made a pilgrimage to the American's Mecca,—but I boiled my peas,—and have visited all the places of interest in the city. I will reach St. Louis to-morrow afternoon. Tell Sister Childers I would rather have the room over the parlor, for you know how wakeful I am. The room over her room we can have for a study. May the Lord abundantly bless my dear husband, and grant me the happiness of seeing him once more face to face."

On the same day, Mr. Carr wrote to Mrs. Carr: "Brother Franklin preaches at Fulton to-day, so I have run down here to Louisiana, Missouri, to try to get a pupil for you" (for the prospective school, perhaps to be established at Fulton.) "You say you will be in St. Louis soon—then in Fulton, I suppose, about the 12th. Is it possible that I shall see my dear wife so soon? I do long to see you and have your encouragement, and enjoy your counsel, your comfort and your love. You say, 'I have just called on H. W. Longfellow. What a grand old man he is! His poetic soul flows through every word he utters. I wonder if he *ever* did anything that was wrong?' I wish I could have accomplished more in our St. Louis work. I believe our new field at Fulton is promising."

Mrs. Carr's fourth experiment in the educational world was at Fulton, where she established Floral Hill College for girls. Her note book shows that her rules of discipline were as wise and as rigid, as if her attendance had been much larger. The attendance was not indeed large, but it was sufficient to place the institution upon a paying basis.

At this time the Orphan School was at Camden Point, and Floral Hill College had no rival in Fulton. However, at Columbia, not far away, Christian College proved a formidable check to any thought of future greatness. Christian College had long been established; it was handsomely equipped, and could make the appeal throughout the State, that Floral Hill College could not offer. Mrs. Carr found herself at the head of a college whose management depended solely upon her own wisdom; but as an offset to this advantage, she knew that her institution could never become a mighty force in Missouri.

"I Want to Educate you"—"Absorbing Thoughtfulness."

The spring of 1877 saw the close of her first year's work, and the following, written by Mr. Carr, in August, shows that she intended to open school in the fall; he writes from Maysville, for he is on a visit among the scenes of his youth:

"Mother and I went by Mill Creek, where Brothers Jno. I. Rogers and I. B. Grubbs are holding a meeting, on to Mt. Carmel. Thursday I dined with Brothers Grubbs, Rogers, Loos and Myall at Sister Mayhue's—she was one of my schoolmates at May's Lick. The meeting at Mill Creek closed last night with several additions. Everybody asks why I didn't bring you. Kate would 'give anything to go to Floral Hill College'. Grandfather is nearly 86 years of age, and has been very ill of late. I talked long with him, as he lay there, and read 2 Cor. 5, and prayed with him. He wept for joy and simply said 'I am waiting for the Lord's will to be done.' I am so glad to find father and mother able to go about. They are still working for their children. You must be encouraged about your school. Brothers Grubbs and Rogers praise you for your work. But nobody praises you more (I mean *prizes*) than I!"[16]

Mrs. Carr had not been teaching long on her second year, when she received a request from Mrs. P. F. Johnson, President of the Christian Women's Board of Missions, to make an address at the St. Louis convention, to be held October 19, 1877. The subject given was, 'Children in Mission Work.' The request was seconded by Mrs. Sarah Wallace, who made this interesting comment:

"From the very beginning of our work as a Society, we have had to battle with the habit of 'giving nothing' among our churches. The people are not stingy, but they do not realize the necessity of systematic giving. When we wanted to add to the amount for Brother Darly's school (the mission school in Jamaica), it was asked, What can the children do? Our board advanced the amount, then issued an appeal to the Sunday-schools. We wanted the children to have a work of their own. Brother Darly's school proved more than a success, passed the examination in six months, and is now under the patronage of the Government. As a result of the appeals, the Sunday-schools gave, first quarter, $12; second quarter, $23; third quarter, $36; fourth quarter,—not yet reported. It is now decided that a school be established at Kingston. It will call for about $250. The Board desires to continue this as children's work. Mrs. Jameson feels confident of meeting you in St. Louis, when she will tell you the whole story. Her illness is not violent, but lingering, as malignant fever usually is."

In the meantime, O. A. Carr had been preaching for the Fulton Church. The following from Geo. W. Longan of Plattsburg, Mo., shows the activity of both, and that "private digs" about ghosts had no place in public work for the Cause:

"March 6, 1878: Of course, I can't consent to take the burden on my shoulder! It falls of right on yours, and you can carry it as easily as any one. The objects of the convention are to discuss themes of living interest, and general utility as a sort of preachers' drill. We aim to assign subjects according to the known tastes of the individuals chosen. I suggest that no one be selected who was on the program last year. Of course, the country around Fulton will furnish most of the speakers. The subject, 'Phases of Current Unbelief' would be both interesting and profitable in the hands of the right man. I think J. Z. Taylor would write a good paper on that, or A. F. Smith, or President Geo. S. Bryant, of Columbia. Procter had nothing last year; you might get him to preach at night. Experience proves that two papers with discussions following, and a sermon at night, is the best division of time. I will try to compel my mind to think of other objects. Write to Edgar for suggestions as to men."

(We may state parenthetically, that the reason the present writer never again met Mrs. Carr, though she often returned on visits to St. Louis, is because Dr. Ellis moved from the city, first to take charge of Woodland College at Independence, later to assume the presidency of Plattsburg College at Plattsburg, Mo., where Geo. W. Longan was still preaching.)

Mrs. Carr had not finished her second year at Floral Hill College when a series of letters were exchanged between her and the President of Christian College at Columbia, Geo. S. Bryant. These letters show a consciousness on her part that Floral Hill College, if continued, was destined to remain overshadowed by larger institutions; and a conviction on his part that Christian College must inevitably suffer from the nearness of Floral Hill. President Bryant seeks to absorb Mrs. Carr's institution, and to employ Mrs. Carr as Associate Principal,—the same relationship she had held toward Robt. Graham at Hocker. This correspondence is interesting, and throws light upon Mrs. Carr's ability as a woman of business. Not only does she gain the various points for which she contends, such as the number of hours she is to teach, the amount of salary she is to receive, etc., but she is jealous of her official position, and will have none of its privileges abridged. President Bryant is a man who loves his joke, and is inclined to illuminate contested ground with the glow of good-fellowship; but Mrs. Carr will have none of his humor until all her propositions are definitely accepted. At last, May 23, 1878, President Bryant writes:

"The propositions of yours of the 21st—eight in number—are the propositions of our agreement, as I understand them. So Christian College and Floral Hill College are one! I congratulate Christian College upon the accomplishment of so desirable an end. Please allow me to say that your spirit of self-sacrifice has not gone unnoticed. Instead of assigning reasons to the 'Fulton Public,' would it not be better,—'To the Public?'—For Floral Hill College was not an institution of Fulton simply. I will gladly publish in the catalogue a statement over your own name, of the reasons."

This agreement was reached after months of negotiations.

Floral Hill College was absorbed by Christian College, accordingly; but Mrs. Carr's personality was one that refused to be absorbed by any association, or institution. So definite were her ideas of the management of a school, particularly in regard to its discipline, that her position as associate principal could never have been satisfactory in any school. Mrs. Carr was a woman of intense conviction, and when attempts were made to persuade her from her principles, she felt that she was being persuaded to error. Those who are by nature fitted to lead, find their inborn talent curbed, when this leadership is clogged. In any school, there can be but one real head. Mrs. Carr would not look upon her position as associate principal as an honorary title; nor could she feel that she was doing all she could for the education of girls, when her ideas of education, which emphasized conduct, clashed with those of others who insisted rather upon grades in recitation. As at Hocker in Lexington, so now at Christian College in Columbia, she grew restive before the year had expired.

In the spring of 1879, Mr. Carr again went to Kentucky to hold meetings, and we find him lingering among the scenes of his boyhood, and naturally thinking much of the past.

"March 17. As I walked about the streets at Mt. Carmel, many familiar objects met my gaze. There was the road along which you used to take your morning walks, and the woods in which the birds sang for you their best early songs. They put me to sleep in the parlor where you said to me, '*I will go with you!*—that room in which I first became acquainted with you, and asked you to go on an excursion with me to Æsculapia. I thought of the past and tried to sketch the future, and prayed that you may be happily situated. I expect to have a happy meeting at Carmel, for those old familiar faces inspire me. If you were here, I could preach much better.

"March 20, Stony Point. This is my sister's home, midway between Paris and Winchester" (the sister Minnie, now Mrs. John Fox, Sr., whom we heard of in the May's Lick days). "I am sitting at the old desk where, seventeen years ago, I conned my Greek grammar under the instruction of my brother-in-law Jno. W. Fox, who is the head of this house, and the head of a school here, of eighteen years' standing. He has a family of ten children all of whom, except the infant, have been taught by him. One son, Johnnie, passed the Harvard examination last spring, and is now at Lexington. Professor Neville brags on him, and says he knocks '95' every time in his Greek class. His half-brother Jimmie, is one of the public school principals of Lexington, and is much respected there. He has taken Johnnie with him, pays his board and tuition, and assists him in his studies." (The reader will doubtless recognize in "Johnnie", the author of "Little Shepherd of Kingdom Come," and "Trail of the Lonesome Pine.") "President Graham was out here, and stayed one night. He enjoyed it! He says, in talking of us, 'Ollie and Mattie.' The children all fell in love with him, and gave him cakes. My father is able to walk, and my mother's general health is good. At Lexington, I saw many of your old friends: Grubbs, Cox, etc. Doctor Hopson and Brother Graham say that you ought to take a good rest. *Now do you hear?* That is from headquarters! My visit at Lexington was too short. I fell in with some Australian students who came near monopolizing my time. One young man, Charlie Thurgood, used to work in a baker's shop all week, and come to my house in Melbourne, Saturday nights, to learn grammar. Now he is in Lexington, preparing to preach the Word.[17] The Bible College has 45 students, College of Arts 65, Agricultural and Mechanical 105. Professor Neville says it is the most pleasant session he ever had. Hamilton College" (formerly Hocker College) "has moderate success. I gave them a Bible reading at Broadway Church, Wednesday evening. The audience was very good. It was like old times."

When her first year's work ended at Christian College, Mrs. Carr, though dissatisfied with the restraints upon her, had not decided to relinquish her position as associate principal. However, she and President Bryant were unable to agree upon terms, and in July she definitely terminated her engagement. "I would not insult President Bryant," she wrote him, "by supposing for a moment that he expected Mrs. Carr to accept the propositions in his last letter."

She observes that she would have considered a re-engagement because of Mr. Carr's earnest desire to assist L. B. Wilkes, then in poor health at Columbia, and also because Mrs. Carr's work in the College had been greatly appreciated by patrons. But the curtailment of her privileges and authority, is intolerable; the matter of salary is of no moment, in view of this obstacle; nor will she hesitate to make the matter clear to all who seek enlightenment. As she remarks, "I do not know exactly what you mean by burying the past. In the course of the sad work, you may cast a few clods over the remains of Mrs. Carr's once prosperous school. If by burying the past, you mean, stop all discussion of our differences, I have only to say, it is impossible to bury that which is not dead. Be assured, I would not bury it alive if I could. When I am asked why I do not remain at Christian College, I am constrained to tell the whole truth, though I would rather be silent." Let us hope that President Bryant's sense of humor enabled him to enjoy this keen sarcasm.

About this time, Dr. S. S. Laws, President of the University of the State of Missouri, situated at Columbia, became desirous of associating Mrs. Carr with the University. He had been deeply impressed not only by her scholarship and wide experience, but by her reputation as a disciplinarian. As she was now free from Christian College, he expressed to her his hope that she would consider an offer. Such an association could not but be looked upon by her as a high promotion in her beloved calling.

September 1, 1879, Dr. Laws wrote to Mrs. Carr as follows: "I mentioned the case to our Local Board, and their favorable action I now send you. Your answer will, of course, be addressed to the Board, but I'd be obliged for a note by bearer, informing me of your acceptance—I should say, of your *answer*, as I will then be able to leave on the evening train for St. Louis."

With this note, the present chapter properly terminates; it has been a chapter of changes, of rapid transitions. We have now reached a period of stability, of advancement, of growth,—the ten years of Mrs. Carr's connection with the University of Missouri.

CHAPTER XV.

LADY PRINCIPAL OF THE UNIVERSITY OF MISSOURI.

During the ten years of Mrs. Carr's connection with the University of Missouri, we find her busy mind occupied by three entirely distinct sets of interests.

In the first place, of course, there was the University work, into which she threw herself with tireless energy and splendid success. The position she occupied was Professor of English, and Dean of the Young Ladies' Department,—a two-fold work, which threw her into contact with both sexes in the classroom, and called for the exercise of rapid judgment in the government of the young ladies.

As Lady Principal, she not only preserved order in the study, looked after the health of its occupants, shaped the literary exercises of the various organizations, and gave as much energy to procuring new students as if she were conducting a private school; but she strove to win the confidence of her girls, that she might lead them to higher spiritual planes of life; and we find her making the same religious impress upon the minds of the young men.

We need but refer to two letters written to Mrs. Carr in later years, leaving the reader to judge of the positive results of such a character as that of Mrs. Carr; results too significant and lasting, to excuse a lack of appreciation, or to palliate the breach of unkind criticism. One is written by a distinguished citizen who states that he was on the eve of committing suicide, when he came under Mrs. Carr's influence; and that she, unconscious of his darkened mind, saved him by the clear radiance of her daily life. The other tells of a young man who entered the University with no ambitions and no purposes in life.

"All that I am now," he writes, "I owe to the time spent with you in the classroom." He occupies a high government position.

In 1882, Mrs. Carr, writing to Hon. J. S. Rollins, states what she regards as her most important duties at the University: "The subject of my salary was thoroughly discussed last year by your Executive Committee, and it was reported to me by Eld. J. K. Rogers, that my salary of $1,500 should remain unchanged. The avenue to my highest success in my supervisory work (which is indeed, my chief work), is my social intercourse with the young ladies under my charge; and this can be best secured by having a home in which I am free to invite them at any time. My classroom work, as Adjunct in the English Department, and as teacher of calisthenics, entitles me to $1,200, and the classwork is the least important, and the least embarrassing, of all. My supervisory work demands the most constant and harassing thought and involves great responsibility."

The following from Mrs. Carr, to the Board of Curators, will show how thoroughly she threw herself into the interests of her young friends: "I hereby testify that the appropriation asked by the Philalethian Society, is needed to complete the furnishing of their Hall. I need not tell you that the work for girls in our University is yet in its infancy, and needs especially, therefore, your guardianship and helping hand. I have encouraged the young ladies to appeal to you, through President Laws. If you hesitate to grant the petition on the grounds of financial pressure, will you please allow $138.60 of my salary to be deferred, until after the next appropriation by our Legislature?"

Mrs. Carr began to lay great stress upon the physical developments of her pupils,—a neglected branch of education in her own case. Her entire work at the University was destined to strengthen those powers of government, already highly developed, for the future scene of her greatest usefulness; and, in after years, we find her views on physical culture, carried out in concrete form. In addressing the young ladies of the University, she said:

"If you will stand for one day at the corner of Washington Avenue and 4th Street, St. Louis, or Broadway and Fulton, New York, and watch the passing multitude, you will see scarcely one in ten who is erect, or well-built. The large majority of Americans are born of imperfectly developed parents. After six years' association with the robust women of England and the Continent, the physical degeneracy of American women appeared more marked to me than ever before. In London, the broad feet of robust women make the flags resound in the early morning; in New York, the tiny feet of pale-faced ladies trip along Broadway at stated fashionable hours. An Englishwoman thinks nothing of walking from six to ten miles a day. After climbing and descending the Cheops of Egypt, I was unable for three days to ascend an easy flight of stairs. An Englishwoman who went up the Cheops as I did, rowed up the Nile, the following day, to the Boolak Museum, enjoyed a donkey ride back to Cairo, returned to the hotel, and spent the evening in nursing my aches and pains. Physical tendencies, whether toward beauty or deformity, like gentle dispositions and moral obliquities, are inherited; remember that you are the coming mothers of the nation."

It is not our intention to dwell upon Mrs. Carr's daily life in Columbia. Any young lady desiring to attend the University, is asked to correspond with her. She delivers lectures in the University Chapel; she contributes to the Missouri University Magazine; she corresponds with Miss A. M. Longfellow, daughter of the poet, concerning their work—for Miss Longfellow holds at this time, practically the same position at Harvard, that Mrs. Carr does at Columbia; she advises with Representatives concerning the passage of bills at Jefferson City; she is in frequent consultation with Dr. Laws regarding the perplexing problems that are always arising in University life.

In presenting the portrait of Dr. Laws to the young ladies of the Philalethian Society, in 1886, she compares the ladies department with its status ten years before—the year before Dr. Laws became president. It was natural for her to attribute the secret of the great development to the doctor's labors. Whatever may have caused the wonderful growth, there can be no doubt that much of it was due to Mrs. Carr. She says: "In the catalogue of 1876, all announcements concerning the young ladies are restricted to 33 lines. It records 39 lady students, only four of whom lived outside of Boone County. The catalogue of 1885 records a special service for young ladies; generous provisions for their physical education; a Girls Academic Course, equivalent in honor to any other academic course of the University; a neatly furnished and convenient study, on the first floor, and another in our elegant library room; a handsomely furnished society hall, lighted by electricity; and many other conveniences, and luxuries. We have 73 young ladies now attending the University. They represent 28 counties of Missouri, and four states. In 1875, no girl took a degree. In 1885, four received academic degrees, four, professional degrees, and one read the McAnally English Prize Essay. On Commencement, 1886, one read the Astronomical Prize Thesis, and another delivered the valedictory of the Normal graduates."

A large and interesting volume could be filled with the lectures of Mrs. Carr. For biographical purposes, they need be simply referred to, as an indication of one form of her activity. The preparation of such discourses, replete with classical and historical illustrations, must have consumed many of these late hours snatched from the rightful claims of repose and relaxation. One might suppose that this woman, always frail, always wakeful, liable at any time to fall the victim to headache, would have found the University work with its many-sided life, much too great for her strength. For her physical strength, it was, no doubt; but that untiring mind found leisure, after its thousand details, to turn in another direction. As we have said, she had three separate sets of interests, during the ten years at the

University. We are now to consider the second—her connection with the women's missionary work of her church.

We have a threefold purpose in dealing with Mrs. Carr's work for the Christian Woman's Board of Missions. In the first place, it formed a large part in her life; in the second, the work in itself is interesting; and in the third, it proves how erroneous were the circulated reports that Mrs. Carr was opposed to organized missionary work. Concerning these reports we shall speak at another time. At present our difficulty is to select from among the many appeals to Mrs. Carr to speak at conventions; from reports of her addresses; from accounts of money sent in by her for the missionary magazine—the *Tidings*; and from the various conferences held by her with the members of the board,—lest our narrative be overburdened with a mass of similar instances. It seems almost incredible that one so absorbed as she in the University work, could have given not only her vacations, but special days during the school year, to the labor of organization, and platform addresses, appeals for money to the missionary cause, and for subscribers to the *Tidings*.

That strangers to the Christian Woman's Board of Missions may understand just what it was, and that its friends may know how much it had accomplished at this time, we present a condensed account of the organization, delivered by Mrs. Carr at the Annual Convention, at Carthage, Mo., in 1885; by this means we are not only enabled to introduce the subject, but to give an adequate conception of Mrs. Carr as a public speaker:

"I want to talk to you directly about our mission work, giving a historical sketch of the Christian Woman's Board of Missions from its incipiency to the present time.

"In July, 1874, Mrs. Cornelia Neville Pearre suggested the desirability of effecting a missionary organization among the ladies of the Christian Church. The sisters were exhorted to consecrate monthly little sums of money from their allowances, or salaries, as individual means to the spread of the Gospel. The idea at once became popular. A little Aid Society in Indianapolis seized upon the thought, and discussed it. At their meeting a stirring letter was read from Mrs. Pearre setting forth the purposes and basis of the proposed society. At the same meeting, a brief article of incorporation was drawn up, to which eight names were signed. A president, secretary and treasurer were elected, and a meeting appointed.

"The women composing the new society were inexperienced in the work. Not one of them had ever lifted her voice in a convention; all of them were wholly unskilled in parliamentary address. They were simply housekeepers, wives and mothers; but their hearts burned to do more for the Master, and they had the rare sense to know that organized effort is the surest and shortest road to success. Not long after, Brother Isaac Errett espoused their cause, and sounded forth the entreaty, 'Help these women!'

"This led to a mass meeting of Christian women, held in Cincinnati at the same time as the General Convention of the Christian church. About seventy-five composed the meeting, over which Mrs. Pearre presided; in a most earnest and prayerful manner, she presented the purposes and plans; and then and there, the Christian Woman's Board of Missions assumed an organized form, and entered quietly upon its humble yet glorious career.

"Indianapolis was made headquarters for the general officers. Five States were represented, and a vice president, a secretary and managers, were elected for each. After a full and free discussion it was resolved that Jamaica should be the first object of their care. The unanimous vote for the revival of the Jamaica Mission, which Brother Beardsley had been forced, in sorrow, to abandon, and whose resumption had long been postponed, brought delight to many hearts; though some present had hoped that a field nearer home would be chosen.

"The following December the Executive Committee held its first meeting at Indianapolis, and determined to make an effort to establish Auxiliary Societies in every State and Territory of the Union. The following January $1,500 was in the treasury, and Brother W. H. Williams of Platte City, Missouri, sailed with his wife and child, for Jamaica.

"The day after his arrival in Kingston, though debilitated from the rough voyage, he preached to about thirty, in a dilapidated Chapel. His audiences increased. He established prayer meetings, Sunday-schools, teachers' meetings, and carried the Gospel from house to house. Through his instruction, several native young men were soon prepared to render valuable assistance. When, in 1879, Brother Williams was forced to resign on account of his wife's ill-health, he was succeeded by Brother Isaac Tomlinson, under whom the work steadily advanced.

"In 1882, Brother W. K. Azbill was appointed. Through his association with the Baptist ministers, he soon ascertained that the differences between their doctrine and his was merely nominal. His proposal that the name 'Christian' be substituted for 'Baptist' was joyfully accepted by several of the oldest and most intelligent ministers, who, with their entire congregations, planted themselves upon the Bible, and the Bible alone. A building-fund was established looking toward the permanent establishment of the work in Jamaica.

"We are especially anxious to put our schools upon permanent basis, for the educational work is, after all, the best and most lasting missionary work.

It is our earnest prayer that we may see, after a few more patient years, the desire of our heart fulfilled,—the cause of Jamaica, the oldest born of our love, self-supporting, under the exclusive management of native talent.

"Brother and Sister DeLauney have, for several years, been supported by the Foreign Christian Missionary Society, at Paris, France. In the summer of 1879, the Christian Woman's Board of Missions, with hearts stirred by their success in Jamaica, determined to contribute to the French mission. At the Bloomington convention they pledged $500 to the salary of Sister DeLauney's assistant. Immediately after this, our beloved Brother Timothy Coop of England, without any knowledge of our purpose, presented us with £100. God put it into our hearts to promise $500, and He put it into Brother Coop's heart to pay it, so that the following year we were able to give $500 more to the French mission.

"In 1881 we enlarged our mission by establishing a mission among the freedmen of the South. At Jacksonville, Mississippi, Elder R. Faurot is carrying forward the evangelical and educational work, among a large colored population.

"In 1882 the Christian Woman's Board of Missions became a happy stockholder in the India Mission. The Foreign Christian Missionary Society sent Brother Albert Norton and Brother G. L. Wharton and their wives; we sent Miss Mary Greybiel, Miss Ada Boyd, Miss Laura Kinsey and Miss Mary Kingsbury. These offered themselves for that remote corner of the Lord's vineyard, without any stipulated salary. There is a work there which only women can do. In Oriental countries, the home must first be captured for Christ; and in these homes, men cannot give instruction to the hedged-in women.

"Missouri had the honor to suggest the next field to be occupied—the far West. In June, 1883, Brother J. Z. Taylor assumed control of this department, and in a short time Brother M. L. Streator was established at Helena, and Brother Galen Hood at Deer Lodge. These two congregations were at that time the only ones in Montana. The Western field is immense, and the sooner it is occupied, the less the difficulty of occupation.

"As I spent six years of my life 10,000 miles from home, helping my husband in his labors for the Master, I will not be thought sectional or narrow, though I say that I regard the Western mission as our most important one. Indifferentism, skepticism, Mormonism, and almost the whole catalogue of *isms* are growing rank in the busy, rushing, money-loving Western heart; if the children of God do not eradicate these poisonous weeds, American civilization must inevitably deteriorate, for the character of a country's civilization depends upon the character of its people.

"In the midst of infidelity at home and heathenism abroad, the Christian Woman's Board of Missions is pushing forward, in a quiet, womanly way, without the sound of trumpets, or the gleam of arms, its blessed work for the Master. We are doing something; but a completer organization will help us to a completer work. The best results can be accomplished only by a systematic plan, a comprehensive grasp and a disposition of forces: We must organize ever new auxiliaries; we must strengthen the weaklings, revive the dying, and, by the power of the living Christ, bring the dead from their graves of idleness. Let us have more and better societies. The gifted Mrs. Browning says:

'The world wails For help, beloved. Let us love so well, Our work shall be the better for our love. And still our love be sweeter for our work.'

"Daily, we pass into the likeness of that which we believe. Very soon, Faith hangs out a label, and the whole woman becomes a confession of its truth. If you have faith in God to save souls, you will certainly be transformed into the perfect likeness of the missionary woman. You may have much to discourage you; it may be better for you, if you do. Those from whom you have the best right to expect sympathy, may be those who will misinterpret the truest purposes of your heart. He who engages in any work worth the doing, must antagonize somebody. But what of that? Is not woman the best burden-bearer? Can you not weep tears of bitterness,—yet press on, in the midst of all discouragements, to the beautiful likeness of the Great Missionary, who left the solemn injunction, 'Go ye into all the world, and preach the Gospel to every creature?'

"We scatter the seed. But when we are old and feeble, who will gather in the golden sheaves? Where are the future reapers and sowers? They are in the Children's Bands. In them you will find the sure prophecy of the future of the Christian Woman's Board of Missions. Whether that prophesy be radiant with promise, depends upon how we are educating the girls of to-day, to be the women of tomorrow. Some time, our brains will grow dull, our hands helpless. Shall not the daughters receive the torch of truth from the hands of the mothers?

"In conclusion, let it be felt as inevitable that we should often feel tired by the way; that we should hunger for human sympathy; that our best efforts at times prove barren of results, through the indifference of God's children; that the purest purposes of our hearts be impugned by those we love best; for a public work, however unobtrusively performed, and painful criticism, cannot be divorced. It is said that there is a grape which, transplanted from its native soil, loses its taste; but possesses the flavor of the soil, when grown upon the banks of the Rhine. It is only when our lives are planted in the aromatic soil of the love of humanity, that our lives shall be identified by the richness of Christianity; and no human hand, however unkindly strong, shall be able to transplant our affections into an alien soil, or take from our lives their flavor of piety and devotion."

Having now placed before the reader the object and accomplishments of the Christian Woman's Board of Missions, in Mrs. Carr's own words, thus showing her attitude toward it, we come to speak of the third great purpose that influenced her life during the ten years' work at the University.

It was none other than the same central idea of her life which we found developed in the Daughters College days of her girlhood. She realized that in her present position at Columbia, she had reached the highest step in her educational career; the highest, because she was thrown into touch with the greatest number of young lives which it became her privilege to shape toward lofty aims.

Indeed, her entire history shows advance steps. The tentative experiment of her first school at Lancaster was fortunately relinquished for her work among the girls of Australia, with its broadening experiences. Having acquired that broader view of life that comes with the extended horizon of foreign lands, it would have been unfortunate, had she not returned to America to communicate the fruits of her observations. Hocker College was, accordingly, an advance upon the Melbourne work, just as Floral Hill, where she was sole authority, hence better able to carry out her original ideas,—was an advance upon Hocker. Her keen foresight, and unalterable determination to sacrifice personal feelings for the development of wider aims, led her to merge Floral Hill into Christian College, thus losing her identity in swelling the general good. As we have seen, the promotion from the Christian College to the State University was one of far-reaching importance.

And yet, Mrs. Carr was not content. She had not reached that ideal toward which she had directed her gaze when a mere girl; and, in the elements of her nature, there were traits that refused to be satisfied by anything but the great object in view. Success did not for an hour swerve her aside from her fundamental purpose; to establish a college for girls in which she might develop her original ideas of government and tuition.

Hence, all during the Columbia days, we find her seeking a promising opening. Her eyes were turned toward many fields. Her caution and prudence prevented her from relinquishing a great responsibility for an uncertain experiment; but her indefatigable mind, while rejecting one expedient after another, never wearied in the quest. Hence it is that during those years, we find her absorbed not only in University work, not only in missionary interests, but always, as well, in the great object of her life.

It was particularly in the latter that her husband proved of invaluable assistance. Called to preach in many diverse scenes, it was his pleasure, and his care, to look about for a suitable opening where a college for girls might be established; a college whose foundation stone should be the Word of God, and whose every day's instruction should be permeated with the love and power of its truth.

CHAPTER XVI.

PURSUING ONE'S IDEAL.

The letters presented in the present chapter are not only interesting in themselves, but are valuable as illustrating the threefold bent of Mrs. Carr's mind, as outlined in the preceding pages. They cover her University experiences. Here is a manuscript revealing Mrs. Carr's struggles with the Greek language. She has evidently just taken up this study; her exercises show the same thoroughness she exhibited in her German commonplace-book.

Here is a receipt from the Christian Woman's Board of Missions for $50 which Mrs. Carr has sent on subscriptions to the *Tidings*. And Mrs. S. F. D. Eastin writes from St. Joseph, 1880, requesting Mrs. Carr to read her essay before the Moberly convention. "I know it will be worthy the attention of that erudite body," says Mrs. Eastin. Worthy *any* erudite body it should have been; the subject is "John Stuart Mill and C. W. B. M."

Mr. Carr to Mrs. Carr, October 23, 1880, from the Louisville convention: "Your letter was handed me in church just before Brother McGarvey's excellent address. Your words rang through my soul all the time he was preaching. The devotion to the Cause expressed in your letter is an echo of my heart, and I second your motion to go to Paris next summer, but I fear you will exhaust yourself in such abundant labors. Your spirit is too strong, and too active, for your body. I gave Sister Eastin your message and she says it is the very thing. This has been a glorious convention, most orderly and deeply pious. I delivered to the convention the messages of Brother and Sister Rogers and Brother and Sister Wilkes. To-day the convention closed in tears and in high hopes, for the future. Brother Magarey" (our "Alex." of Melbourne association) "went to Bethany yesterday. He looks a little older, but is the same blessed man. I love him. We had long talks. Brother Gore will visit home before long. All well at Brother Santo's. I got this sheet of paper from Jimmie Fox's desk. He is doing well—Adjunct Professor in the Male High School. I am writing at the office of the *Old Path Guide*. Brothers Hardin, Allen, Cline, et al., are talking all around me. Hardin goes to St. Louis tonight; I send this by him, that you may get it soon. Collis and Thurgood asked of you especially. I told Brother McGarvey of your work, of Brother Wilkes' estimation of you, of your position in the University, of the high praise President Laws gives you, etc., and Brother McGarvey says he wishes you could have a work directly in the interests of Christianity; but all he can advise is, to stay in the University until such a position opens up."

W. W. Dowling to Mr. and Mrs. Carr: "I am publishing in the *Sunday School Teacher*, biographical sketches of some of our prominent Sunday-school workers. I want a sketch of both of you—a synopsis of your lives and labors."

J. W. McGarvey to Mr. Carr, June 30, 1883: "I am glad you have the heart and ability to care for your aged parents as you do. In regard to educational affairs, I doubt the possibility of legally removing the Canton Institution. If you need an institution for the education of preachers, you cannot do better than to build a house, and endow two chairs in connection with the University. But I do not see that you need it for many years to come. Our College at Lexington can receive all your young men, and do a better part by them, at less expense. An attempt to have a Bible College in every State where we have a strong membership, will result in a large number of weaklings. The Baptists in all the South aim at but one; the Presbyterians, the same. We are now aiming at six or seven, and ours, the largest, has only 94. Since Geo. Bryant has gone home, I hear they are expecting 250 guests at Independence. I am surprised so many are expected. I have not heard whether Brother Oldham made a good reputation at first, or not. I am sure, however, that he will establish a reputation and secure success. I hope the preachers will help him." (Oldham was Bryant's successor at Christian College, Columbia. The institution referred to, at Independence, was Woodland College.)

November 4, 1883, O. A. Carr issued a circular addressed to the Alumnæ of Christian College, urging them to send matter for the forthcoming book, "Biography of President J. K. Rogers, and History of Christian College." This was a book Mr. Carr had undertaken at the request of President Rogers's widow. The work was attended with much difficulty and many delays, on account of the alumnæ pursuing the usual course of alumnæ, by refusing, as a whole, to answer request or entreaty.

Mrs. S. E. Shortridge, from Indianapolis, to Mrs. Carr, February 20: "I have been working all day steadily on the *Tidings*, and tonight, being too nervous to sleep, I take advantage of this halt to write to you, though the midnight hour is not far away." (Mrs. Shortridge was the Cor. Sec. of the C. W. B. M.) "Accept my thanks for the kindness and patience with which you have gone over the whole ground. I quite agree with you in the main; the only difference between us is, I believe, in the exceptions to the rule. I must assure you that we are of one mind here at Indianapolis. Perfect harmony and confidence prevail. This is particularly true of Sister Jameson and myself." (Mrs. Jameson was the president of the C. W. B. M.)

"From her I have no secret. We are very near neighbors; I see her almost daily; yet I am continually finding new beauties of character to love and admire. I find the *Tidings* cannot be enlarged this year: I wish it could." (At this time the *Tidings* was a small four-page sheet, four columns to the page.) "We are not able to rent a room, or office, and we work at great disadvantage. I never look at the paper that my conscience does not stir uneasily, it reminds me so much of a motherless child. And yet—I am doing the best I can. I have no journalistic genius, Mrs. Goodwin always insisted that I had, but she was blinded by love. If I have talent, it is still dormant. I do believe in you, and trust you fully, my dear Sister Carr. I think of you as a lovely Christian woman, incapable of consciously doing an unjust thing."

L. B. Wilkes, from Stockton, Cal., to Mrs. Carr: "I am better—nearly well. Still, if you were here to rub my head, I believe it would hurt me pretty often yet. You are in earnest—you would like to come to California—and will, if I can find a place for you and the doctor" (meaning Mr. Carr, of course.) "The school business is overdone among our folks. We have three colleges, all mixed schools, and pretty badly mixed. Just come to our house and stay till you find a place, let that be long or short. I don't know how to write a letter, so leave the gossipy part to my wife, she is good at it. I will start the doctor a paper in which I have a small piece on the organ." (For in those days one could write about the organ, when all other subjects failed.)

To which letter, Mrs. Wilkes adds a postscript—"He says I am good at gossip; I deny the charge. He would have you both come on here; but selfish as I am, I cannot insist on your coming, for fear you might not like the place."

In 1884 O. A. Carr was appointed State Evangelist for Missouri, and the following notes are taken from his letters to Mrs. Carr. The names of places are generally omitted:

"March 3. We are poorly represented here. The people don't seem to believe the Bible. A woman, though, has been taking the rag off the bush. It is said she can out preach a man—goodness! my wife could beat nine-tenths of the preachers, but I'm glad she's a woman who wouldn't preach publicly before a promiscuous audience. There is a gloomy prospect here. Ignorance—you never saw the like. At Trenton I tried to raise money to seat the meeting house at ———, but they said, 'That is in the midst of a good agricultural district—why don't they build their own church?' They don't know that infidelity stalks abroad in daylight there, and that infidelity does not build meeting houses or anything else that is good. I have been talking to an old brother with his wife—mine host—on missionary work, trying to show that I am in as legitimate a business as the editor of the

Review when he publishes a paper. The woman yielded at last—said at least there is no harm in it. Good! My desire is to meet some more of such people, and convert them. I believe I can do it! I will have a heft at it here, I think. Some good old men have tried to preach and farm, and have not done either very well, I presume. It will be difficult to persuade these people to give $200 for once-a-month preaching, when they have been giving about five dollars. I have not done a thing on the Biography of President Rogers, nor do I see how I can at this rate. I have a bad cold. The door is warped and won't close, and last night the wind whipped around into the bed, and everywhere. I've got the stove between me and that crack in the door now, and some of the atmosphere will have to get warmed, before it reaches me. Brother A. B. Jones says I'd better stay at —— and work it up; but there's nothing to work up, and the only chance I see is to get that place joined on to the congregation here.

"March 6. I've tried to introduce the envelope system of contribution in the church here (Gallatin) and have run myself down today; from house to house. I am in a cold room, writing after speaking tonight at the Christian convention. I enclose $25 for you to forward to father, Wm. Carr, Maysville, Ky. Brother S. P. Richardson says, 'Give my love to Mrs. Carr.' He says he was in your class at the University, and thinks a great deal of you. He says he had a good time in your class. He was a law student. Will Sister Rogers be satisfied with delay of the Biography till fall? How I do wish I had the material for a complete biography. I don't like to blame anybody, but I have tried faithfully to collect it. I do not like to think of anything incomplete in connection with that grand, good man.

"March 9. Thank you for that nice letter; there was great encouragement in it. A vision of you comes before me—it is a charming picture. You say you are anxious that I should succeed. But in my case, what is success? If adding members to the churches is a success, I have failed already. I have been setting churches in order, and teaching the brethren. Here at Gallatin, we meet in a hall. There is no house, and the members are poor. From Trenton I go to Breckenridge, or Grant City. Brother Floyd of the *Christian Herald*, of Oregon asks me for a Missouri sub-editor. I have recommended you to him. I have written my notes for the *Christian Standard* and *Christian-Evangelist*. I will watch for your article and see if it sounds like I wrote it. That was a big joke! Did *I* know what you could say about John Stuart Mill and the C. W. B. M.? I don't suppose Mill ever heard of such a thing as the C. W. B. M., and I don't know how you thought of both names at once. I wish you would write a dozen articles for our church papers—divide them around. Write on Women's Work, for the *Quarterly*.

"April 15. I rode twelve miles horseback for your letter, which heightened the joy of receiving it. I am utterly discouraged about that Biography of

Brother Rogers. I cannot find time and quiet to write. For instance, I walked nearly two miles to church, then two more to reach a place to stay all night—where I had to sit up, and be sociable till I was worn out. The people are generous here, and I think, religious. The church is ajar, and I am expected to set it in order. It is rather discouraging for me to have to do the hard work, then leave to set another church in order, while some one else follows me up, and holds the meetings and gets the additions. I am here, trying to get the members to act decently toward one another. It will take a week to warm them up, and then I will have to leave.

"April 19. It rained so much last night, I could not get to meeting, and I am compelled to stay in doors. Mine host is a good man. He and wife and six children are all crowded together in two rooms, and we have confusion worse confounded. I have to cross a swampy valley to and from church (distance two miles) and a muddy, snaky river that is to be despised. Our toilette arrangements consists of a washpan outside the house. It will take a week to get the Christians to be friends with each other. I heat up in church and cool off walking home, and cough at night. Between coughs, I think of you, wondering if you are wearing yourself out with toil and anxiety. Learn to take life more leisurely! My idea is for you to become author—write a book or two, if you please, and contribute to the journals. Our papers need your talent. Please forward the enclosed $25 to mother."

From J. W. McGarvey, Lexington, Kentucky, to Mrs. Carr, April 29, '84: "Brother Patterson is to continue at Hamilton College at least one more year. He is making money out of the school at a very handsome rate; but the fact that he is building a fine dwelling on the place he bought from Brother Lard's estate, indicates that he will not remain much longer than a year. When the time comes, you may rest assured that I will present your claims and merits before the Board, in all their attractiveness. I have no doubt you could make a success of it. I am sorry I cannot accept Brother J. A. Lord's invitation to lecture on 'Bible Colleges' at Columbia."

The following of July 15th, shows Mrs. Carr working in a fresh field—the Women's Christian Temperance Union: "As Corresponding Secretary of the Columbia Union, I send you the following resolutions, which were unanimously adopted at the last session of the Union: * * * Be it resolved that we as an individual Union protest against the resolution passed at the Sedalia Convention, namely, 'That the White Ribbon hosts of Missouri work for woman suffrage.' The woman suffrage attachment will necessarily complicate the nature of our plea. An organization already exists entitled, 'The Woman Suffrage Association', whose exclusive purpose is woman's suffrage. Many of our friends, and many in our own ranks, oppose the plea of woman's suffrage, as a part of our plea for temperance."

Mrs. Carr writes to Mr. Carr concerning a church quarrel which he is striving to quell—judging from her letter his efforts at warming up the members has taken an unfortunate direction. The letter is interesting as showing Mrs. Carr's wisdom in such delicate affairs: "I cannot tell you how deeply I deplore this church difficulty. Deal with the matter very gently. Don't write sharply to any one, for if you do, you will be misrepresenting yourself, and injure the work. Let the matter readjust itself. I advise you to so arrange your work as not to be present at the county meeting. Your presence at this juncture might do harm to you and to the Cause. Stay away, and write them a good, fatherly letter, to be read before the convention. I'm sure, intuitively, that this will be best. Your success is the burden of my prayers. After a few more years I hope we shall be more together; we shall see each other every day."

Robt. Graham to Mrs. Carr, from Lexington, July 9: "Your letter was duly received, and I immediately set to work to see what could be done to get you into the Midway Orphan School. I handed your letter to Brother McGarvey, and he agreed with me that there is little likelihood of the trustees placing the management under the control of a lady. I consulted members of the executive committee, and find they are resolved upon a man. It is very difficult to find the right one. Keith of California refused at once; Bartholomew of Louisville has a better position, etc. It is suggested that you buy the now vacant school at North Middleton, Bourbon County, and while I could not advise you to such a step, I mention it, that you may know of that opening. I see that Corinth Academy is for sale, but I don't suppose you would want to put your means there. Brother Patterson holds on for another year at Hamilton College. I can easily understand why you seek to be engaged in a school where you could work for the Cause we love; were it in my power, I would soon have you in a position more congenial to your tastes. As it is, you must be content to labor and to wait, till God opens up the way. I write this, knowing you have a position of great honor and emolument, one that many would gladly obtain; but I know your desire, and sympathize with it."

More notes from Mr. Carr, as State Evangelist, to Mrs. Carr—July 18: "Letters forwarded. You don't miss me any more than I do you. I am going to hold some meetings during pleasant weather. I have very few additions to report. I have spent most of my time trying to set up torn-down churches. As to Vice President of the C. W. B. M., I don't object for that honor to be thrust upon my wife. I think it very complimentary; get up the program, and preside at Kansas City. How about that Biography? If *you* could work on that, we would get it out. You ought to write much for the Brotherhood. Women can do that work, and not trespass on I Cor. 14:34-35. Drive out to church and hear Brother Powell, Sunday. Don't forget to fix up the genealogy of the Rogers family. Don't try to drive that horse by yourself. While you are resting, select the essays to be added to the second part of the Biography. Don't work hard, just lounge around, for this is your vacation, you know.

"August 6. While at Savannah I received some letters forwarded by you to '*Sullivan*.' How they came to Savannah, marked thus, I don't know, I suppose there is no such postoffice as Sullivan, and they might as well come here as anywhere. Halt!—I had to go out to preach my ten o'clock sermon. I am preaching day and night. It's a hard row to hoe. The church is in a deplorable condition, and of course nobody will 'join.' But I am expected to stay up here, and keep digging. Brother J. H. Duncan asked me to help make out the C. W. B. M. program for the State meeting. Isn't he impudent? I told him you are president, and will manage it; but I helped him on the *male* part.

"November 27. This is Thanksgiving Day, and I am to eat at a hall—a dinner by the Methodists. I'm a good hand to eat for the benefit of a church. I hear they're going to have ice cream. Well, I can't help it. I must go. You will have to be thankful without me; I'll be as thankful as I can. We are to have a Thanksgiving sermon by a North Methodist preacher, and coming so soon after Cleveland's election, it is anticipated he will give us a gloomy kind of thanks. He will doubtless feel somewhat as Dr. Pinkerton did, when he told his wife he had nothing to be thankful for because there was no butter. Our meeting drags. I had to get this part of the county fixed up and friendly. There is a good prospect now. Received account from Brother D. O. Smart. Sorry I could not be with you and the young ladies and gentlemen at 'Narrow Gauge' today."

From the Missionary *Tidings*, September, 1884: "Mrs. O. A. Carr of Columbia has been appointed vice-president of the C. W. B. M. of Missouri, to succeed Mrs. J. W. Morris, who was compelled to resign on account of ill health." The reader is referred to past files of the *Tidings* for a full account of Mrs. Carr's labors as organizer, platform manager, speaker, and her committee work in the C. W. B. M. She was vice president in 1884, 1885, 1886, after which she became a State manager. During her first vice-presidency, the managers were Mmes. Hedges, A. B. Jones, J. H. Garrison, J. W. Monser, Dr. Petitt, T. E. Baskett, T. D. Strong, E. C. Browning, Kirk Baxter, Wm. Pruitt; during each of her terms, the secretary was Miss M. Lou Payne. In 1887 she was succeeded by Mrs. J. K. Rogers.

On the 20th of March, 1885, the St. Louis publisher, John Burns, writes to O. A. Carr: "Last Friday I went to Columbia and had a pleasant interview with Sister Rogers about publishing her book. We agreed that the matter should be delayed no longer. The MS. should be in my hands with the least possible delay. It should be in type by the first of May, and the books ready by June 1st. As you are so constantly engaged away from home as our State Evangelist, it is thought best for Brother Mountjoy to read the proof. As to compensation for labors, Sister Rogers stated that she is anxious for you to be satisfied. I have agreed to bring out the work in first-class style. There is to be a steel engraving of Brother Rogers, and a wood cut of Christian College. The work will be in two bindings, one to be full Turkey Morocco, gilt. The John Burns Publishing Company will have entire control of the work, and have agreed to push the sale to the best of their ability. I expected to meet Mrs. Carr, to discuss the matter with her, but could not delay my stay in Columbia."

At the foot of the foregoing, Mr. Carr writes a hurried note to his wife, on enclosing her the letter: "I wrote Brother Burns that I would rather trust you to read the proof than anybody. I am afraid I cannot get the work done, even next month. I have to settle a church here."

While churches are thus wrangling among themselves, and sinners are standing aloof, taking notes on the War of the Christians, and the Biography is apparently fated never to get itself into type, Mrs. Maria Jameson, national president of the C. W. B. M., writes to Mrs. Carr: "I read your letter to the Board, and there was a unanimous expression of gratification at its contents. You are one of the women among us who can make public addresses. Now, if you are willing, we will utilize this talent. Public lectures, properly advertised, designed to attract attention to missionary work, particularly to the work of our women, might do great good. Of course, you will have to use judgment in selecting the places for the addresses. No provision has been made for an outlay of money in this matter, as we can ill afford to divert a dollar from regular work. I believe, as a public speaker, you will spread the name, and strengthen the influence, of the Christian Woman's Board of Missions."

W. B. Johnson of the Christian Publishing Company, St. Louis, to Mrs. Carr: "Your C. W. B. M. notes will appear in next week's paper; and I will also speak of the University, and of your work there."

M. B. Mason, Principal Meadville Public Schools, to Mrs. Carr: "We intend to celebrate Whittier's birthday with suitable entertainment. Will you please send some suggestions regarding arrangements, program, etc?"

Mrs. Maria Jameson to Mrs. Carr, November 1: "Ever since our parting, I have purposed writing to express the pleasure given me by an increased acquaintance with you. During our recent convention, I learned to feel constantly that I had an able ally, quick to see what was needed in an emergency, and able to act intelligently and promptly. I wish you would write occasionally to me during the year; so many new sides of things are evolved by talking them over. My daughter and son-in-law are back from their trip abroad, and, of course, I have not had time for much, besides talking to them; but in a short time my thoughts will be turned to our work. With the help and blessing of God, I will do everything in my power this year for its development. Let 'For Christ's sake' be our motto, and in his blessed name we shall do many wonderful things. Pray always with me, and for me, my dear sister, that we may prove faithful until the end."

Enough has been said about Mr. Carr's work as State Evangelist—his work of several years,—to suggest the arduous nature of that labor. Passing by any further details, we turn for a moment to the Biography, which did, after all, find its way into cloth and Morocco, in 1885, under the title, "Memorial of J. K. Rogers and History of Christian College."

The book is divided into three parts: the first, of about 200 pages, is devoted to the Life, Letters and Addresses of J. K. Rogers; the second, of some 30 pages, is called "History of Christian College"; while the third of about 100 pages, bears the title—"Some Essays and Poems of Pupils of Christian College, Edited by Mrs. O. A. Carr, Principal of the Ladies Department of the University of the State of Missouri."

This Part Third of the Memorial, is the only work left by Mrs. Carr, in book form. As we have seen, she undertook the editorship of the collection of essays and poems of the Alumnae, at the request of her husband, in order to hasten the publication of the book.

Joseph Kirtley Rogers was born in Fayette County, Kentucky, in 1828. When he was two years of age, his parents left Lexington on a thirty days' journey to the wild and Indian-infested West, pitching their tent finally about twelve miles west of Palmyra, Missouri. Here they lived in their log cabin. "Game was abundant," says the Memorial; "panthers screamed, wolves howled; bears roamed the thick woods; deer were a common sight, and wild turkeys hovered in the tree tops." It was near the birthplace and boyhood scenes of Mark Twain, and the author of "Tom Sawyer" had no need to go outside of Marion County to find the original of his "Colonel Mulberry Sellers."

When William Muldrow with others, borrowed $20,000 to establish "a great college"—Marion College—on the western prairie, purchasing therewith 4,969 acres, and confidently expecting a future hay crop to reimburse the teachers, he fathered a scheme that the "colonel" might have joyfully laid out with his toothpick upon his tablecloth. To this college Rogers went,—until it died; then he attended the University at Columbia.

Christian College was the first institution for the collegiate education of Protestant women to receive a charter from the Legislature of Missouri.

The enterprise was largely due to the work of D. P. Henderson, minister of the Christian Church at Columbia, and Dr. Samuel Hatch and Prof. Henry H. White of Bacon College, Harrodsburg, Ky. When Jas. Shannon of Bacon College, was elected to the presidency of Missouri University, he recommended a former pupil for the presidency of the contemplated college. This pupil, John Augustus Williams, held the position from the opening of Christian College until 1856, when he resigned to establish Daughters College at Harrodsburg. It is an odd coincidence that Williams should have gone from Columbia to Harrodsburg in time to shape the educational life and ideals of Mrs. Carr, and that Mrs. Carr should, in the course of years, have come from Harrodsburg to Columbia, to act as associate principal in the college inaugurated by her favorite teacher.

John Augustus Williams was succeeded at Christian College by L. B. Wilkes. During the latter's administration, J. K. Rogers from Marion County, Mo., acted as instructor; at the close of President Wilkes' second year, Rogers became the third president of the institution; a position which he occupied for nearly twenty years, and which only a fatal disease compelled him to relinquish. During his administration there were 174 graduates, and it was the difficulty of hearing from so many, that delayed the Memorial.

George S. Bryant was the fourth president,—from 1877 to 1884. His successor, W. A. Oldham, had scarcely finished his first year, when the Memorial was published. The book is true to its title; it is rather a Memorial than a biography, the work of a friend, who prefers to quote such men as G. W. Longan, J. W. McGarvey, etc., rather than to substitute words of his own.

And if the life of a minister who, for twenty years, occupies the same chair in a school of learning, lacks the variety which gives to biography an interest to the general reader, still less can the history of that school be offered as a work of entertainment. Something more may be said for the part edited by Mrs. Carr. Whatever lack of merit her collection of essays and poems reveals, may be charged to the paucity and immaturity of the material in her hands. It is fair to conclude that she gave us the best that the alumnae gave her; and the impression that most of it might just as well not have been preserved, is dissipated when we are told that President Rogers was anxious to have the writings of his girls published as his memorial, even if no word be said about himself. Viewed, then, not as literature, but as the fruits of his instruction, these writings, breathing the deepest piety, and revealing both learning and grace, hold their fitting place in the memorial to the Christian teacher.

But it is because this Part Third reveals the mind of her who edits it, that it is of moment to our biography. In the first chapter she gives us an indication of what she regards as of the utmost value in a woman's life:

"In looking over the scores of letters I have received from the Alumnae of Christian College, I find that I have written on the envelopes of about nine out of ten, the word, *Christian*; on two out of ten, the word, *teacher*; and on each without exception, the golden word, *home-worker*. In this statistical catalogue of three words, is found the grandest record of Christian College. That the life-work of its Alumnae has been chiefly confined to the church, and the school-room, and the home, is its honor and renown."

Mrs. Carr thus sues for toleration of "a wrong spirit" manifested in an essay on the "South." "Though the author evinces a little bitterness, we should forgive her. She wrote at the close of our sad civil war. When she writes vigorously and touchingly of 'A Washington, a Jefferson, a Calhoun, a Clay, a Breckenridge, a Benton,' when she proudly says, 'Behold on Virginia's consecrated ground, noble Bethany College, and Virginia's magnificent University,' when she turns lovingly to 'Kentucky University, one of the proudest in the Union,' and when, in the full bound of her loyalty she clasps to her heart her 'own Missouri University,'—then indeed we forgive, and our heart rejoices with hers in a common love."

Mrs. Carr thus introduces her third chapter: "If no George Eliot was found in the previous chapter, so no Elizabeth Barrett Browning will be found in this. If the reader be generous, he will find some very sweet poetic thought expressed in verse; but he will feel no deep stirrings of an angelic genius, that looks through Casa Guida window up to the very gates of heaven. He will find only the rhythmical outpourings of ambitious girlish hearts; and if he laugh at their imperfections, he will only prove that his heart is old—" Reader, let us not delve into these ambitious poems, lest we laugh and prove ourselves no longer young. Let us come away, after noting this comment on a poem entitled 'Longfellow.'

"Having once met him in his poet-home," says Mrs. Carr, "having felt the warm pressure of his hand, heard the low music of his voice, looked into the clear depth of his poetic eye—having felt, in short, the benediction of his presence, I find in the following simple dirge, a peculiar charm. That the modest author so tenderly loved her nation's poet, whose song like his own flower-de-luce, shall 'make forever the world more fair and sweet,' evinces both a refined taste, and a cultured heart."

Gone, now, that good white poet, to mingle in the poesy of the past; and vanished is she who felt the warm pressure of his hand, and looked into the clear depth of his poetic eye. But the world is here as when they trod it beneath its daily sun; and here are you and I. Happy are we, if we find the world more fair and sweet because of those who have breathed their influence upon it.

So we lay aside this Memorial, the joint work of Mr. and Mrs. Carr, the only book they ever produced, and go on with the story of their lives—a story full of incessant work, its routine broken by some such adventures as is suggested by the following from Anthony Haynes to Mrs. Carr: "You are invited to read a paper before the State Teachers' Association which meets at Sweet Springs, March 22-24, 1886. Your cabinet is just the thing we wish to see at the Display—bring it."

From Mr. Carr to Mrs. Carr, June 6th—showing that Mrs. Carr has her eyes unalterably set upon the future: "There is no advertisement of phonography in the *Cincinnati Enquirer* or the *Courier-Journal*. So you have learned the shorthand alphabet! Well, I am sure it will require a great deal of practice to report verbatim. I do want you to take a rest this summer, whether you learn phonography or not. The truth is, you ought to be resting now."

But the report of the Fourth Annual Convention of the Women's Christian Temperance Union shows that Mrs. Carr was doing anything but resting. The "Irrepressible Conflict" of this year, shows her laboring sturdily for temperance. Further letters show her struggling at spare moments with shorthand. What will she do with *that*? This from Mrs. S. E. Shortridge of the C. W. B. M., suggests a new activity:

"Sister Jameson was very much pleased with the card of flowers you sent her. She is very greatly improved—able to see and enjoy her friends. We had a most delightful conference with her last Sunday afternoon. Brother Azbill, Dr. and Mrs. Pearre, A. M. Atkinson and wife were there, besides the member of the board, and others. Mrs. Jameson is still confined to her bed. She sends her love and says she will write very soon. Perhaps you can get your leaflet printed at Kansas City. The C. W. B. M. will highly appreciate your kindness in the preparation of a leaflet, in the midst of your various duties and obligations. There is a growing demand for such information. I am anxiously awaiting its appearance."

In the same year, O. A. Carr attended a meeting of the Alumni of Kentucky University, and in a public address, thus referred to his own graduating class: "The class of 1867 has never appeared on this rostrum since commencement day nineteen years ago. We were three then; we are two now. We were called the Trio. For nigh six years of student life we were boon companions. We shared our mutual joys, our mutual burdens bore, in a most intimate friendship. We planned our future so that our paths might often cross each other, but duty called us to labor in fields as far apart as Colorado, California, Australia. When James C. Keith, President of Pierce

Christian College, California, and I were corresponding, concerning this meeting of today, our hearts cried out for the absent one—the noble, generous, gifted, brilliant valedictorian of our class. In the hearts of those who knew him, there arises, as a sweet fragrance, the memory of Albert Myles."

Not long after the delivery of this tribute, Mrs. O. A. Burgess wrote to Mrs. Carr: "I was in Indianapolis a few weeks ago, and found our dear Sister Jameson better than I hoped. I had a delightful visit with her. She realizes that she is soon to leave us, but is as bright and cheerful as she ever was in her life, and her interest in the C. W. B. M. is unabated. Allow me to congratulate you on the rapid growth of the C. W. B. M. in Missouri. You certainly must have efficient workers. Your article on 'How to Organize an Auxiliary' will meet a long felt need."

November 27, 1886, Mrs. Shortridge wrote: "Am sending you our amended Constitution and the December *Tidings*. In the list of Missouri officers you will notice your name as a manager. I hope you will approve. The relation between yourself as Vice President, and the Executive Committee, has been so pleasant and congenial, that we are unwilling to sever it altogether. We need your help, and will be grateful at any time for suggestions. Your leaflet, you so kindly prepared, has been most useful to me in answering the question, How to Organize; and it has been a means of encouragement to a great many timid sisters. Indeed, my dear sister, when I think how promptly you have responded to my requests for help, how your loving words of appreciation have lifted me up when almost discouraged and ready to give up the struggle,—the tears come to my eyes, and I ask God to bless you abundantly."

The leaflet referred to, is by Mrs. Carr, as President of the Missouri State Board, and is addressed to "The 39,000 Missouri Sisters who wear the badge of the C. W. B. M." It is an eloquent and logical presentation of the value of organization.

From Mrs. Maria Jameson, came the following, October 4, 1886: "Your loving message with the pretty card was received with heartfelt thanks to God, who has given me the love of so many warm hearts. Surely in this regard, never was woman more blessed. With humble heart I accept it as one of the ways the kind Father 'is making his grace sufficient for me.' Of course, I am thinking much of the Kansas City convention. You and I have begun an acquaintance so pleasant—you enter so readily and heartily into my views and plans—so ready to render me judicious and active assistance, that I looked forward with increased pleasure to the labor of coming years. But 'man proposes and God disposes.' I almost dare think that He wished to give me a special lesson of the absolute dependence of all my plans upon

His sovereign will. When I knew beyond a doubt that I could not be present, the question rose, Who will occupy the vacant chair? One day it flashed across my mind that now we had the opportunity of making a graceful public testimonial of our respect to the woman whom the C. W. B. M. delights to honor—Mrs. Pearre, who is this year, for almost the first time, free from school duties. You, as Vice President, will open the convention's sessions with the usual exercises. Mrs. Pearre's name will be received by acclamation, and you will conduct her to the chair, and give her all the help and encouragement you would have given me, staying beside her, informing her and supporting her according to requirement. What shall I say of myself? I have through all my life received wondrous good from God; shall I not patiently receive evil, also? Pray earnestly for me, that I may cheerfully yes, joyfully, submit to His will."

In 1887, O. A. Carr went to Arkansas to look about for a promising field, where he might labor in the ministry, and his wife, in her own chosen profession. He writes from Fort Smith: "I lectured last night to a moderate audience. We have a neat little frame church here. The preacher has been re-elected; 22 for, 12 against. I am sorry for him; but he is going to stick to them. He is a pleasant man, and very kind. They are remarkably hospitable here. I send you a little bouquet from the front yard. Think of violets and roses, a month ahead of the Missouri bloom! You will recognize the two large leaves; they are maple! It is now about as warm as a June day at home. I don't believe you could have any success here during the summer, in teaching elocution and phonography; for I am told that the people take holiday during the summer months, and take it very extensively—even the laboring men, because they are afraid to work much. People are dropping in here quietly, buying, and slipping out. There will probably be a rise in property after the bridge is built into the Indian Territory. Work is begun on a U. S. court room and new post office. There is tied up in this nosegay a great deal of love for my wife. I go to Alma tomorrow." (So *now* we begin to understand what that short hand meant! There are to be no more vacations, it seems.)

April 13th, Mr. Carr wrote from Fayetteville, Arkansas: "Brother Ragland tries to convince me that we ought to come here, and establish a Young Ladies' College, in connection with the University—but young ladies attend the University. He says our church has no school in Arkansas, and Fayetteville is the educational center, etc. Brother Robt. Graham started a college here in 1858 and continued it successfully until the war broke it up in 1862. His college building was burned. He had five acres, most beautiful site. His residence is standing yet. I attended the opening exercises at the University. Some of the professors remembered you; they heard your lecture at Sweet Springs. The University is upon a hill and is imposing. I could not make an arrangement for a meeting at Fort Smith, because it is cotton-planting time, and the people are very busy. After preaching at Alma two days (and receiving $6) I came here. I will stop at Springfield, Mo., tonight, and may remain over Sunday, as I am told they have no preacher. I have seen several young ladies and talked up Christian College, distributed catalogues, etc., but they object that Columbia is too far away."

Mr. Carr, from Springfield, Mo., May 13th, showing that Springfield is beginning to enter largely into his life; "I preached last night on 'Quench not the Spirit,' and ended the Ash Grove meeting. The sale of the college is postponed sixty days. Sister Bander said my sermon was much needed. There now! she is a judge. They want you to send some of your tracts on 'How to Organize an Auxiliary' here, to Springfield."

Mr. Carr from Paris, Ky., June 9th: "I received your good letter, and was reading it in Morrison Chapel, as I sat beside Alex. Milligan. He saw the flowers enclosed, and said, 'I thought you were over that!' I told him that was an old bachelor's idea of the matter—just as though true love would ever get over it! I told Brother McGarvey what was in your letter. It is all right; but Brother Graham asked at first, if it was wise for you to give up your work at the University. When I see you, I'll tell you about Hamilton College. I am here over night with Minnie Fox. John is home from New York on a visit. We talked so late last night that I could scarcely get up this morning! Saw Brother Grubbs at Lexington. Monday I take the boat for Cincinnati, and expect to be in St. Louis at the Union Depot, Tuesday morning next. I had a fine sleep on the *St. Lawrence*, and didn't wake up till the boat whistled for Maysville. I hurried up and found mother busy skimming milk. She can not walk far; her ankle seems to be ossifying. She is all the while anxious about the children for whom she has worn out her strength. If I had not engaged at Springfield, I might have gone to Mt. Sterling or Louisville. I don't know but what Springfield is as good a place for regular employment as the other places. The idea is to be content, and do the work well. I want you to have a year's good rest. Now is your time to rest. Get the good out of old Jeff. Make him flutter around. I think he had better be sold to some one in Columbia where he is known. Minnie Fox is a fine girl. She says she would love to be with you in Springfield. John is home now for vacation, but is going to the coal mines in Southern Kentucky" (where his fancy is one day to follow the trail of the Lonesome Pine, and discover a little shepherd herding the sheep in "Kingdom Come.") "He says he would like to be one of the Assistants at the University. I told him you are going to rest, and he wants to know whether there would be a chance for him to get in. He could bring testimonials—his Harvard diploma would be something. If you think well of it, you could present his name. He took the honors at Harvard, and has been tutoring in

New York ever since. He is a teacher by education and by nature. Do as you think best about it."

From the foregoing it is clear that Mrs. Carr has definitely decided to relinquish her post of service at the University of Missouri. That she needed rest, there can be no doubt. That she needed undivided time in which to mature plans for her future college, against the day of opportunity, is equally certain. At Springfield, Missouri, Mr. Carr entered upon a three year's service. As soon as Mrs. Carr could sever her connections with the University, she joined him.

Her work for the C. W. B. M. still continued. We find her delivering addresses, arranging programs, and lecturing. Mrs. Jameson, Mrs. Pearre, Mrs. Shortridge, etc., continue to write her for wise counsel, in grave times of anxious consideration—for instance, when the Constitution was altered, when plans were on foot to make the *Tidings* a stronger magazine, etc. When Mrs. Carr ceased to hold an official position under the C. W. B. M. the appeals to her for advice and help came just as frequently as when she was President of the State Board.

Her work in the W. C. T. U. was also unabated, and during 1888, she took an active part in the prohibition candidacy of John A. Brooks for the governorship. A letter from E. C. Browning requests Mrs. Carr to do the C. W. B. M. work of Mrs. Browning, whom ill-health prevents from performing her duties as manager in Southern Missouri. She is also engaged in lecturing on her tour of the world, taking opportunity as she goes from city to city, to investigate the prospects for a new college.

In the *Nevada Daily Democrat* of October 11th, we find this estimate of Mrs. Carr as a public lecturer: "The lady reads her lecture from manuscript, and has a very plain, clear voice which can be distinctly heard all over the room. Her diction is fine. She is, indeed, a pleasant reader, almost perfect in her pronunciation and emphasis."

CHAPTER XVII.

ACHIEVING ONE'S IDEAL.

The six years following Mrs. Carr's connection with the University of the State of Missouri, might be characterized as the time of preparation, struggle and victory; preparation in the definite formulation of plans for her last educational experience; struggle to find the suitable place and the requisite means for the establishment of her college, and the victory of final achievement. This period extends from 1888 to 1894.

As we have seen, it was Mr. Carr's earnest desire for his wife to take a long rest, on his acceptance of the church at Springfield; and no attentive reader of Mrs. Carr's life can doubt the need of rest at this time—a rest which, in her case, meant keeping house—the every-day work of many women.

While she rests, this biography may also rest, in the respect of dealing with events, since the occurrences in the simple life are most enjoyed in proportion as they make dull reading, and the days at Springfield were happy days.

To illustrate Mrs. Carr's force of character it may be related that one day when her finger was cut off, she found the dismembered part in the folding door, quickly fastened the end back in place, and held it there till help could be summoned.

A brief note from the Ladies Aid Society of Sheldon, Missouri, asking if Mrs. Carr can come to deliver a lecture in their interests, must be taken as an example of countless others of a similar nature. The following statement from the President of the Missouri University, fitly serves as a transition from former experiences, to the new phase of Mrs. Carr's career. It is addressed to her:

"During my administration of the Missouri University for thirteen years, you occupied faithfully and efficiently and acceptably the position of Lady Principal, for eight or ten years. This position you resigned of your own choice. It was not done at the advice, or the instance, of either the Board or the President of the institution. You had always done considerable teaching, as well as serving as Principal, and it was always my understanding that it was not your pleasure to hold the position apart from teaching; and as the care had so grown as to make that overburdensome, when you withdrew, a successor was appointed who has never done any teaching. As a matter of fact, when you resigned, I did not fully understand your reason for doing so. Allow me to express my appreciation for your great worth as an educator, and to assure you of my earnest hope that your enterprise at Sherman will more than realize your purposes and expectations."

This letter from Dr. S. S. Laws was written in 1891, which brings us rather prematurely to the subject of "Sherman." The reader will find that in the course of events, all interests will presently center in that Texas city; but, as we have said, Mrs. Carr is now resting (1888-9) and the biography, as a chronicle of events, rests with her.

But while household cares engage her time, her mind is ever active with that great idea of her life which has attended her since childhood days, and which we are, in the course of time, to find bringing her to the highest fulfillment of her powers. We have seen how that tireless nature has fought its way from battlefield to battlefield, ever progressing in its educational career. It is not clearly defined to her judgment how, or where, she is to take the final stand in her work of improving the greatest number of girls in the most effective way, yet, by following the clews given in the following letters, we may trace out her course to its final destination.

But if Mrs. Carr has temporarily entered into what we may call—as distinguished from other years—her period of rest, the following clipping from a newspaper dated, May, 1889, will indicate that Mr. Carr has been far otherwise engaged:

"Sunday night, O. A. Carr stated to his congregation that he had a secret of several months' standing which he was agonizing to disclose. The long cherished hope of his congregation, and indeed of the North Town disciples was about to be realized—the erection of a church building in North Springfield. He said the money is already raised and the building will begin as soon as specifications are determined upon. He stated that the disciples of Christ with whom he had been meeting in the Good Templars' Hall, for nearly two years, would begin, next Sunday, regular church work preparatory to entering their new church home in the near future. With the dawning light of the permanent prosperity of the church of North Springfield filling their hearts, the congregation was dismissed, and the scene of rejoicing that followed cannot be described."

Mrs. Carr in commenting upon this news, adds, "North Springfield has a population of about 10,000, and a struggling little band of Christians have been praying and working for the above happy consummation, for years."

This brief news-item reveals, to those who have built churches, years of labor, anxiety, and suffering. In the meantime, the quest for a suitable college opening is never relinquished. Now that the church is built, one is freer to look about. Mr. Carr, having served three years at Springfield, Mo., is invited to come to Arkansas and examine the field.

"The brethren will help support and establish a college here," writes G. W. Hudspeth. "I would like to have it at Little Rock, but do not know that she would offer as much encouragement as a smaller town with no college. I have about 400 lots in a railroad town of which I will give sufficient grounds for a college building; and allow the other lots sold, and donate one-third of the proceeds to the support of the college."

In December of the same year—1890—Mr. Carr writes from Bates City to Mrs. Carr: "It seems to me that the Sherman proposition is the best that has been made you, and I want you to see your way clear, and at the same time I want you to act on your own judgment. You say you will accept the terms, if they suit. I hope you will have some word of cheer to send before long. Do not be gloomy and downcast."

A few days after, the following from J. W. McGarvey is written to Mr. Carr, showing that the terms of Sherman were far from persuasive: "Your letter surprises me, for I thought that you and Sister Carr had already moved to Sherman, Texas, and were at work there. The Broadway Church has engaged Brother Bartholomew to preach one year, and superintend the erection of a new house of worship, after which he returns to St. Louis to build a new house there. I hope the school at Sherman has not gone amiss, and that it will not be affected by the college boom at Dallas."

Mrs. Carr, in explaining why Sherman was chosen as the site for her important venture, wrote: "After a long and arduous term of labor as Adjunct Professor and Principal of the Ladies Department in Missouri State University my nervous system broke down, and I am compelled to suspend my work. Mr. Carr accepted a call to preach at Springfield, Mo., believing the altitude would conduce to the restoration of my health. Breathing the ozone of the Ozarks, I was soon a new creature, and I determined to resume my professional labors. The thought, like an inspiration, came to me, 'Build a college for girls, consecrate your life to it, and *leave it as a bequest to the Church.*' I told Mr. Carr of my heart's desire, and after prayerful consideration, we resolved to devote our united lives to the work. I visited a number of towns and cities in Missouri, Tennessee and Kentucky, seeking a suitable location. After I had spent a year thus, Mr. Carr went to Sherman, Texas, to conduct a series of meetings, and some of the prominent citizens, having learned what we purposed, expressed a desire to have the college located at Sherman. A proposition was submitted, which Mr. Carr forwarded me at Springfield, advising me to come and look into the matter. I came, amused at the idea of locating our life-work in Texas; but I was then ignorant of her marvelous developments, and of her still more marvelous undeveloped resources. I visited a number of her splendid towns, and ascertained that in the wide territory of the State, the Church of Christ owned no college exclusively for girls."

It would be a brief story to say that Sherman was finally selected and the college built there; but how, in that case, could the reader gain a knowledge of the almost insuperable difficulties overcome? It is by such a knowledge that we gain the clearest view of Mrs. Carr's character. She was, no doubt, often despondent, but she never relinquished her determination; nor did her zeal cause her to act too hastily. Although Sherman now appeared desirable, no stone must be left unturned to discover if there were towns more promising.

January 18, 1891, we find President J. W. Ellis writing from Plattsburg College, Missouri, to Mr. Carr: "I wrote you a hasty note on receipt of your last. If you had carried the letter a little longer in your pocket, you might have weakened it so it might not have got here! In regard to Sister Carr's quest—Plattsburg College is now prosperous and has been for eleven years. I would be willing to sell it at a nominal price, to get rest from the long-continued service of a teacher and his wife. I see no reason why Sister Carr could not continue the flourishing condition of the school. Campus, four acres, unencumbered, non-taxable."

February 12, 1891, Wm. Frazier wrote Mr. Carr from Calusa, California: "At the suggestion of Brethren J. C. Keith and W. P. Dorsey, I address you this note to say: For some 14 years, Brother Keith has been President of Pierce Christian College; lately he sent in his resignation; we will have to supply his place. I feel at liberty to ask if you will be open for engagement next session, beginning September 1st. I am President of the Board of Trustees, and the Board looks to me to attend to these matters. The church at College City will be without a preacher in June; so the President of the college will most likely be called to preach for the church. I ought to have said that Brother Keith's health has been poor for three years, and his physicians advise a change and rest."

O. A. Carr, in forwarding this letter to his wife, adds, "The above received to-day. I answered by saying, 'Send on your proposition, I will consider it.' Why not get an appointment to lecture at Galveston? You could easily run down there from Sherman, and see the place."

Mr. Carr to Mrs. Carr, March 2nd: "I have just written to Brother Keith in full asking all the questions you suggested, and several besides. I told him we would come, and I could begin preaching for the church right away. I asked him to send you a catalogue at Sherman. It may be that the California plan is better than the Texas one. I have but one objection, which I waive for your sake—I will be so far away from my kin, and the friends of early days. Besides, you know I prefer preaching to teaching; but I suppose I could do both at College City, after a fashion. So Brother Capp is to be at Springfield! Well, I would rather have him succeed me than any one else, for the good of the church. Address me at Omaha."

L. B. Wilkes, at Stockton, California, to O. A. Carr: "I wrote to Brother Frazier. The place at College City is yours, it seems, if you want it. You had better have them as a *Board*, send an official letter, saying just what terms they mean to propose. If there's anything I can do, I am ready."

Wm. Frazier to L. B. Wilkes, March 16th: "I have written to Sister Carr, making Brother Carr an offer to take our college, and am now anxiously awaiting an answer. What a grand service you could be to us, Brother Wilkes, if you could write to Brother Carr and induce him to come and see our college."

Instead of quoting further, the Pierce College incident may be summed up as follows: The Executive Board called Mr. and Mrs. Carr to Pierce Christian College of California. The call was accepted. Mrs. Carr gave up the Sherman idea; all property at their death was to go to Pierce Christian College; an accident policy in favor of the college was arranged. She accordingly wired to College City that she would be there by the 30th; sold the ponies and carriage and the household goods at a sacrifice of about $1,000 (Mr. Carr was then in Nebraska), and was in due time joined by her husband.

The ticket agent secured their tickets. They were on the eve of departure when a message from the President of the Board called off the agreement. Opposition had arisen on the grounds that Mr. Carr did not, in some of his opinions, accord with all of those on the Board.

Mr. Carr, under the blow of this disappointment, wrote to Mr. Frazier as follows: "Your reasons for withdrawing your offer are as great a surprise to me as was the telegram announcing the fact. I stand where Brothers Wilkes, Keith, Graham, McGarvey and Grubbs stand. I emphatically encourage and practice progression heavenward. I will not desert the cause of Christ for the fashion of the giddy world. Having no children, Mrs. Carr has been planning for several years to locate in a college which, at my death, would receive our money. We had decided upon Pierce Christian College. I tell you this that you may know how completely you have upset our plans."

The foregoing is introduced into this biography merely by way of illustrating the difficulties with which the Carrs were forced to contend, before the final victory.

Thus is the California incident closed. The Carrs once more find themselves beset by uncertainties. Mr. Carr writes to their Springfield friend, Mrs. Weaver, showing how one pauses irresolutely before various openings:

"I have been preaching at Council Bluffs, of late. I haven't yet decided where I shall labor. I am waiting to hear from different points, and then we'll go somewhere. President J. W. Ellis of Plattsburg, Mo., offers us his college. I don't know about it. There is no offer so good as Sherman, I think. Tell Miss Kate to write to me in shorthand if she likes. I leave the other side of this sheet for Mattie to say her say."

Mrs. Carr adds: "It is good of you to say my room is waiting for me. I shall never forget your kindness, coming just when it was most needed. I do try to be cheerful and hopeful. We have the comfort that we have tried all along to do our duty, to the best of our ability. I believe the Lord has a bright day in store for us, by and by, if we will only be patient and stand for the right."

June 23rd, F. W. Smith wrote to Mrs. Carr answering her questions regarding the Tennessee Female College at Franklin. He hesitates to advise her to accept it, but believes she could make of it a success, and assures her of his hearty support should she undertake the work there.

About the same time, W. J. Loos writes to Mr. Carr from Louisville: "We have your article from the *Guide*; had just received a note from Mrs. Carr covering the same ground. I will keep an eye on the field, and if I see any favorable opening, will let you know. I think you ought to appear more frequently in the *Guide*."

In 1891, the Carrs are thinking of going to Kentucky with their enterprise. In September, Mr. Carr writes to Mrs. Carr from "Brother McGarvey's study": "Brother Bartholomew says he will prepare you a prospective so that a cut can be made from it, of the college building, if you will give him the idea as to size, etc., and that it can be done in three or four days. For his work, he will charge nothing, but he will have to pay the man who does the drawing for the cut, and the cut will cost about $15." Tentative diagrams at this time, show that Mrs. Carr was making her own designs, arranging the rooms of her college—wherever it was to be—to suit her own ideas. It is no easy matter to make the cut of our college before there is any college. Still it must be done, to bring the scheme tangibly before the public, and one's imagination must become fixed in steel.

September 9th, Mrs. Carr writes Mrs. Weaver from Omaha: "I hope to be with you next week. I shall be in Springfield only a few days, I presume. Then I shall go on to Sherman, to begin the College enterprise. My love to Tillie." (Tillie was Mrs. Weaver's little daughter.) "Tell the dear child to have a dozen kisses ready for me."

Affairs seem to be crystalizing in and about Sherman, Texas. A site is provisionally chosen for the proposed college, "on a beautiful elevation," says Mrs. Carr, "in her eastern suburb, overlooking an immense circuit of country, as charming as the bluegrass region of our native State."

A mass meeting of the citizens of Sherman was called, which Mrs. Carr addresses in the interests of the enterprise. The arguments she produces appear to cover all the ground in sight, and all probable contingencies of the future. She says:

"If another girls college be established in Sherman, it will bring among you many more girls. They, in boarding-school vocabulary, will 'get awful hungry,' and must be fed. Our grocers will have to order a large supply of boarding-school staples, and our meat markets will have to multiply their sirloin roasts and porterhouse steaks. These girls will have boxes of roast turkey and French candies smuggled to them by sympathetic mamas, and nature in her mercy, will send a wave of nausea, and a cry will go up for our Homeopathic M. D. with his pleasant little pills, or for our old school dignified Regular with his calomel and quinine, or for our cautious Eclectic with his 'best' from all schools, and each will add to his list of patients, and our druggists will multiply their prescriptions, and their profits. These girls will delight in pretty dresses and becoming hats—." And so the dry goods stores will have their innings, and the milliners. Hope is next held out to the bookstores, the music supply companies, the opera house, the street car lines, etc.

Perhaps it is not so apparent what advantage the new college may be to those institutions already established in the city. But Mrs. Carr promptly takes up this point, and elucidates it with faultless logic:

"For example, Miss Smith, who is a member of the Christian Church, comes from Galveston, and attends the Christian College of Sherman. She is pleased with the school and delighted with our town. When she returns home, at the close of her session she tells her intimate Baptist friend, Miss Jones, and her intimate Methodist friend, Miss Brown, what a delightful place Sherman is, and how 'jolly' it would be for all to go to school in the same town, etc. What is the result? The following September Sherman Institute opens its doors to Miss Jones, and North Texas Female College welcomes Miss Brown. But that is not all. Miss Jones of Galveston has a brother who must be sent to college, and, with the true impulse of an affectionate sister, she says, 'Oh, brother Jimmie, get papa to send you to Austin College, or Mahan's Commercial College; and you can come to see me every Saturday.' Therefore, all the Baptists and Methodists of Sherman ought to encourage our enterprise to the extent of their financial ability."

Mrs. Carr proceeds to point out how the building of her college will give employment to carpenters, brick masons, carters, etc., how it will help fill the purses of the dealers in hardware and furniture, and carpets, and coal, etc., until most of the industries known to man are shown to be directly concerned.

"What I have said has been chiefly from a financial standpoint," she concludes, "but I know you love Sherman for Sherman's sake, and glory in her educational and religious progress. I believe you have the gallant Southern pride, and the intensely earnest desire for the education of women, to prompt at least one hundred and fifty of you to contribute to this enterprise at least $200 each, especially when you get in return a good-sized lot in one of the most beautiful suburbs of one of Texas' most beautiful cities."

So the success of the enterprise is to depend, it seems, upon the sale of college-lots—an old story, and usually, a sad one! We shall see how it succeeds in this instance.

In the meantime, Mrs. A. M. Laws, wife of the President of Missouri University, writes to Mrs. Carr, January 16, 1892: "I am glad you feel so much encouragement in your new enterprise. If there is such a thing as a fire-proof building, you ought to build fire-proof. I suppose you have heard of the calamity that has befallen our University. It is all in ruins. Last Saturday night a fire destroyed the entire building with its contents. Only the museum specimens, and law library, were saved, and not all of that. But already steps have been taken to rebuild and on a grander scale than before. In the meantime the classes are meeting in various places, all over town. All the portraits and statuary are gone to ashes. Mr. Laws' large oil portrait, and two other crayon portraits of him in the society halls, and one of myself, are destroyed. We will be glad to hear of your success in the new enterprise. Mr. Laws joins me in love and best wishes for a new year."

At last, O. A. Carr comes back from holding meetings in Kentucky, and joins his wife at Sherman. Mrs. Carr, on February 2nd, writes to her Springfield friend, Mrs. Weaver: "I need not attempt to tell you how happy I am to be with my husband once more. He says it is almost like being married over. Nothing but the good work we are trying to accomplish could have persuaded me to stay away from him so long. I have been hard at work all winter, and have got the College enterprise into good shape, and it bids fair to be a splendid success. If we can only stem the tide of our financial troubles a year longer, I think we shall be safe. We think we can get the college in operation by September, 1893. If Brother Porterfield will keep our house until then, or sell it for us, or if we can get the Omaha property off at half-cost price, we will be safe. I believe the Lord will put it into the hearts of our friends to stand by us. When the college is up, we shall be able to return their kindness tenfold. How happy we shall be, when the college is built, and we have you and our dear little Tillie with us every winter! Pray without ceasing, dear Sister Weaver, that the college may be built, for we are so anxious to do a good work, and we want to *work together*, the remainder of our lives. The Reid case at Omaha will retard the college enterprise, for I will have to go there in April; but we trust in the Lord, since the work we are doing is for His Cause, and we believe He will give us success in His own good time.

"We shall be hard pressed, for we are borrowing money, and indeed will be borrowing until the college is up, but after that, we hope to have plenty to live on and give to the Lord. Mr. Carr and I have keenly felt our financial embarrassment, but remember we have told no one but you just how great is that embarrassment; keep it locked up in your own heart. Keep your health and strength for Tillie. She is the special charge God has given you. Keep your energy for her. Is she taking music lessons—or do you think she is still too young? Bless her heart! how I wish I could kiss her this minute! Tell Brother Capp to bring you each *Homiletic Review*, after he has read it."

About this time, J. W. McGarvey, President of the Bible College of Kentucky University, wrote: "It gives me great pleasure to learn that Brother and Sister Carr have undertaken, in connection with the brethren of Sherman, to establish a female college of high grade in that city. Their removal to Texas will not only promote the educational interests of that State,—for which work, Sister Carr has eminent qualifications and experience,—but it will add very materially to its evangelizing force. Brother Carr has had a great deal of successful experience as an evangelist, and his skill in organizing churches for effective work is not inferior to his presentation of the Gospel. I wish them abundant success in their undertakings, not for their own sakes merely, but for the sake of the cause of truth."

Mrs. Carr's reference to money stringency may be explained by the fact that the payment of college lots did not fall due until the college building was actually begun. As our story advances, the reader must imagine the hundreds of attempts to find buyers for the lots, the hundreds of rebuffs, excuses, refusals, which cannot find place in this work, lest it sink under melancholy monotony.

April 4th, Mrs. Carr wrote from Farmington, Texas, "I don't want to write to you, I want to talk to you, face to face. Tell little Tillie to help you pray for our success in the college enterprise. Sherman takes 150 lots; and if we can sell 100 additional outside of Sherman; the thing is a success. May our Heavenly Father be with us, and speed the work of our hearts. If our

Springfield property could be sold, it would be such a help. Tell Brother Capp if he can sell ten lots for us, we will thoroughly educate one of his daughters, board and all, free of charge. Several preachers here, and one in Kentucky, have undertaken this, and I believe they will succeed. If he will undertake this, let me know at once, and I will send him map of lots, picture of building, and all necessary information."

To this letter Mr. Carr adds a postscript: "We are in Grayson County, in the interests of the college. Mattie has lain down to read, after we had a talk about you, of the time which we hope will come, when, the college built, we shall have a home, and you and Tillie with us in the Sunny South. I had a visit from Brother J. D. McClure and his son-in-law from Iowa—where I had a vacation on leaving Springfield. I wish you could know these people. They are the right kind. He wrote before coming, 'I shall be as proud to see you as if you were my own brother.' You may be sure I was proud to see these true men and to introduce them to Mattie. They are booked for five lots in the college enterprise. Remember our address is Sherman, Texas, and letters will be forwarded us, wherever we may be."

On October 10th, the following from the Sherman Soliciting Committee to Mrs. Carr, suggests some of her difficulties: "After a full discussion of the matter, the Soliciting Committee decides that it would be inopportune to try to sell the remainder of the College Park lots. It is thought best to defer this until after the November election; and, in fact, the opinion prevails among the majority of the Committee that it would be better, if possible, for you to finish selling your 100 lots, return to Sherman, report that you have carried out your part of the agreement, and that if Sherman does not come up to her part of the agreement, that you will proceed to go elsewhere with the college."

Mr. Carr to Mrs. Carr, January 13, 1893: "What a surprise to receive your card announcing that you are in Kansas City and will go to Springfield before returning to Sherman! Still it's all right, if you can sell the lots. I have had a fearful time, I sold only three at Clarksville. We will have to take off the names of —— and ——, who say they cannot take their lots! All in all, I have sold 90 lots. Dear me! I have done my best, and have lost a great deal of time—rain and mud. I think we can close it up in about two weeks when you come. Sell all the lots you can, but do not delay, do not waste time. I don't believe any lots could be sold in Paris or Bonham. I tried faithfully. Joshua Burdette, son of Geo. Burdette of Clarksville, Texas, lives at Eufaula, Indian Territory. He is a member of the church and is making money; you might sell him a lot. Tell those Springfield preachers Jimmie Pinkerton" (son of our old favorite professor and doctor) "and John Hardin and Tom Capp, I say for them to put their names on your list for a lot each."

In short, one thinks of little but lots, these days; one dreams of lots; one writes always, speaks always, of lots. People must learn that these lots are for sale, they must be persuaded that the purchase of them is for individual good, for educational enlargement, for the advancement of spiritual interests. The Carrs believe all this. Will others believe?

Fortunately others are found to enter heartily into the project.[18] But, as one might naturally expect, there is great opposition, which one always finds as the shadow to bright deeds. It would seem that no light can shine in the world without casting the shadow of opposing forces upon the ground. There are some who treat the Carrs with rude incivility; will buy no lots, and will, if possible, persuade others from buying.

On one occasion, Mrs. Carr was obliged to walk to the station from a distant farm-house—do you know those muddy Texas roads in the "Black Lands?"—because the farmer is opposed to buying the college lots; he watches her grimly as she makes her way along the difficult road, with no intention of offering his horses. We have before us letters written to Mrs. Carr by members of the church in good fellowship—men of recognized standing in their communities, and who, without doubt believe themselves to be excellent Christians. But alas! these letters, in refusing to buy the college lots, are not, as it would appear, the letters of gentlemen, so we must pass them by.

These were in truth times of pressing need. Mrs. Carr often found it best to walk that she might save the expense of a cab. The Carrs had just suffered a loss of $12,000 in property at Omaha. Often Mr. Carr was obliged to go hungry in his expeditions of lot-selling, and on his way to hold meetings. There were taxes to be paid on vacant property, interest to be found that borrowed money demanded, while traveling expenses were necessarily large.

"Will you please tell me where I can get a meal for twenty-five cents?" Mr. Carr inquired of a stranger in a town whither he had gone to lecture.

The man indicated a restaurant. Mr. Carr went away, but soon returned to the stranger, saying,

"Will you be so kind as to tell me where I could get the quarter?"

"Yes," was the glum response; "at the bank."

"And," said Mr. Carr, when referring to the incident, with a twinkle in his gray eye, "he wouldn't even promise to come to hear me lecture."

In the meantime Mrs. Carr was also traveling, in the prospects of her future college. "Wherever she went," one writes, "she carried good cheer and a blessing to that home. There she would give instruction, impart advice, there she would help with the sewing, and, with pleasure, would teach and care for the children."

But the thought that she should be thus financially embarrassed and placed in a dependent position, was most distressing to Mr. Carr. Yet there was no help for it, until the lots should have been sold. We do not dwell upon these days of heartache and suffering, to inspire remorse in the breast of anyone who offered obstacles to the great enterprise. We would, instead, pay a tribute to those who gave a welcome; who cheered up the way; who, instead of doubting the outcome, hoped for the best; who, instead of waiting for ultimate success, helped in time of need. It is he who smiles at his open door, who joins his song to that of the singer along life's highroad, and reaches out his hand to help, and waves to the departing traveler his confidence of victory,—he it is, who finds the world growing better. For the world is always growing better for him who makes it better for others. Those who helped the Carrs with friendship, and with a participation in their college-plans, cannot be named in this book; but we should like to think that those still living might read these lines, and each take them to himself.

January 30, 1893, Mr. and Mrs. Carr issued this typewritten manifesto to subscribers for lots:

"When you purchased one of the Christian College lots, we promised you that you would not be called on for the first payment before September, 1892. Because of Mrs. Carr's protracted suspension of the work, on account of sickness, the sale of lots has been, of course, retarded. We shall be ready, however, for the distribution of lots by March 1st, 1893, and write to you at this early date, that you may have ample time to arrange for making at that date the FIRST PAYMENT ($100). Please make your draft of $100 payable to Hon. T. J. Brown and Judge H. O. Head, Trustees, Sherman, Texas, who will make you a deed to your lot. If you desire to pay all cash, and it will be best of course, if you can, send the draft for $200 (the full amount) payable to the said Trustees. We shall begin the college building by the middle of next March, and open the first session in September, 1893."

But if the reader supposes that all now glides smoothly forward, let him read this of May 20th: "The distribution of the Christian College lots has been unavoidably postponed until the first of July next, when it WILL POSITIVELY TAKE PLACE in the court house in Sherman, Texas, at 2 o'clock p. m.

O. A. CARR,
M. F. CARR."

At last the ground is broken for the foundation of the college building, and Mrs. Carr proudly walks behind the plow, and guides it in the making of one long furrow. Can you not see her marching thus, grasping the handles with all her strength, her eyes aglow with the realization that she is digging deeper than a foundation of stone?

O. A. Bartholomew is called upon to undertake the construction of the building, July 27th. He shows hesitation and remarks—while our heads nod mechanically, *Ah, how true!* "I do not know what to say. The churches for which I have made the completest plans, have found the most fault. Especially, if I did not charge them much!" And we who have never built churches, yet feel like crying, Ah, yes, how true!

Let us pass over the months of sleepless nights, of anxious days. There was one matter that brought great hindrance to the scheme. It was currently reported that the college was merely a private enterprise of the Carrs, like any other private school; and the Carrs would reap all its advantages and profits: and that the claim that it was deeded to the church was a specious pretense made in order to induce people to buy lots. These charges were made, not by the enemies of education and Christianity, not by unfriendly denominations, but by the members of the Christian church; in other words, by the very body to whom the college was deeded, to be theirs forever.

This accusation had its staunch adherents, men who for years were ready to argue warmly, if not dispassionately, in its support. The fact that it could have been disproved by simply glancing at the records, seems to have lessened none of its force. It wrought much delay in selling the lots, and, after the college was built, it served to lessen the attendance. Carr-Burdette College was, indeed, a free and loving gift,—given, one might almost say, in spite of the reluctance of the beneficiary, and held in his possession while he disclaimed its ownership.

It is not our wish to lessen the patient helpfulness of many of the members of the church. Had the Carrs worked themselves to death they could not have disposed of the lots, had not people been found to buy them. People there were found, as we have seen, who co-operated with the Carrs to the extent of their ability, and many of these were among the most illustrious of the Texan brotherhood. But for years, one might find at a general convention, the spirit of suspicion and hostility to Carr-Burdette College— as "Christian College" was finally named, and, at important committee meetings, it would be plainly declared that the college was a private enterprise and did not belong to the church.

But we will never get our college up at this rate. Let us pass on to the winter of 1893, which takes O. A. Carr once more to Kentucky. Who would ever have thought that the Kentucky boy of May's Lick, chalking his problems on his father's barn-door, would, at a later day, be going up and down his native State, selling college lots, and looking out for prospective pupils of his own? These pupils are for next year. The day for laying the corner-stone of the college, is to dawn while Mr. Carr is far away from Sherman.

On December 26th, Mrs. Carr writes to him: "I hope you will have a happy time with your kindred. I am very lonely without you; but it must be thus, until those twenty lots are sold. Necessity is a stern tyrant. But we have borne thus far, and we can bear a little longer. How happy we'll be, when we can be at home together all the time! The corner-stone will be laid New Year's Day at 3 p. m. I am dispatching you tonight to have your message in your own hand writing, to be read on the occasion, and it will be deposited in the bowl of the corner-stone. It is too bad you can't be here. This sacrifice should make a heart-appealing chapter in my book. Have your speech here without fail, in your own hand writing. Your message in your letter to me is beautiful, and I'll read that if necessary, but there are other things in that letter I don't want to go into the corner-stone. Suppose you send a dispatch, for fear your speech will not come in time. Do this at once. I send this to Maysville, and a copy to Carmel. A merry Christmas to all! How I wish I were with you!"

As to the "book" referred to, that, of course, is the "History of Carr-Burdette College;" the book which Mrs. Carr intends to write—after the college is built, of course; a book which will tell of almost superhuman struggles, of cruel sacrifices and, thank God! of words of love and cheer, and of final peace "in our home, where we shall live together." But the book was never written. Here and there among groups of old letters we find a document superscribed "Important," or, "For the Book"—and we know Mrs. Carr wrote that, with her mind upon some future day, when she would have time—time in her old age, the heat of battle dying away, and the calm of memory softening the past—a time that never came, else *this* book would have had no being.

January 10, 1894, Mr. Carr to Mrs. Carr: "I go to hold a meeting at Vanceburg, Kentucky. I am sorry I could not be at Sherman when the corner-stone was laid. Of course, it was laid right side up, with care; and as my wife is to see to it, I'm sure it will be well done. But it is too bad that I have to be away, causing you to work yourself down, and get sick. I am devoutly thankful to Sister Hildebrand for her care of you. Tell her she shall have her reward, by and by! I suppose the corner-stone was laid on the 7th—" sickness having made New Year's Day impossible. "I do hope you will excuse me for not sending a message worthy of the occasion. I wonder what you did with my poetry? If you planted it in the rock, I will have to get up something else for your Book. Look here! What did you think of that poetry? Perhaps there has been another delay of corner-stone ceremonies,—pshaw! if I could get into the spirit of it, I could write something, but I am so unsettled and so put out from not doing anything, that I can scarcely write a letter, to say nothing of writing what is to be left as a monument!"

The following, from Mr. Carr, January 24th, is a fitting trumpet-note with which to close the discords and harmonies of the college-overture: "I received a paper to-day—Picture of college is fine. Hurrah! Your address is grand—Just the thing! You are doing fine work."

CHAPTER XVIII.

That was, without a doubt, the proudest day in Mrs. Carr's life when she faced the expectant multitude, on the day of the corner-stone ceremonies, and told in simple words, the story of her striving and achievement. It was, in truth, the day most significant in her history.

She could cast her eyes over that plowed field, and in fancy see rising before her, the outlines of the college which she had designed as her monument. The money was all raised; never was Carr-Burdette to rest under the shadow of mortgage, or suspend payments.

Fresh in the minds of her audience were many instances of plans for the selling of lots to erect college buildings,—plans that had resulted in forced sales, spasmodic flickerings of uncertain life, and humiliating defeat. She and her husband had accomplished what well-organized boards and influential committees with fleet financial agents, had not been able to consummate. They had accomplished this, not because Texas felt a great educational want,—a vacuum in the intellectual thermometer,—but in spite of the fact that many Texans believed they had schools a-plenty. This they had accomplished, although misunderstood and misrepresented by different factions; although it was persistently denied that the property belonged to the church; and although the State papers, on more than one occasion, refused to print an advertisement of the enterprise.

Mrs. Carr did not rehearse these difficulties, save in general and mild terms. A record of her sad experiences was placed by her own hand in the dark recess of the corner-stone; but we, who are unable to hide our record in so sacred a receptacle, must be content to lay it before the public eye, with all good-will, and, we trust, all fairness. In her address, that January day of 1894, Mrs. Carr said:

"To sell 250 lots at $200 each and to collect the money, was the work to be accomplished in order to secure the college—a work that demanded enormous courage and indomitable will power and persistence. We struck out the word "fail," and all its derivatives from our vocabulary, and addressed ourselves to the task. We traveled in five different States; and, amid the distraction of the most intense political excitement and under the pressure of the severest financial crisis the country has ever experienced since 1873, we completed the sale of the lots after nearly two long years of labor, worry and anxiety inexpressible. The way has been long and hard, but you have been kind to us and God has been with us. The corner-stone of our life-work is laid to-day; we behold the consummation of our heart's desire, and we feel generous towards all and profoundly grateful to our Heavenly Father for the many and devoted friends that He has given us to cheer us by their kind words and deeds when our burden seemed ofttimes greater than we could bear. The sacrifice that we have made and the trials and humiliations that we have endured are too sacred to be told, even in this paper that shall be hid in the silence and darkness of the corner-stone, whose peace the cyclonic onrush of the Twentieth Century may never disturb. They are known only to our own hearts and to God. But we count them all joy and would endure tenfold more if need be, because we believe that for the Christian girls who shall be educated here from generation to generation there shall work out a far more exceeding and eternal weight of glory. We are building, not for ourselves, but for coming generations of girls. This thought has been from the beginning our inspiration and our strength; and it is useless to say that to donate this college to the Church of Christ in Texas for the education of the daughters of the South is the supremest happiness of our united lives. It is the child of our adoption, and to its interests we consecrate the best energies of our remaining years. Of all the glad New Years this is to me the gladdest. The only thing that disturbs the fitness and happiness of the hour is the unavoidable absence in Kentucky of my husband, who has labored so long and so faithfully under circumstances the most painful to "humor his wife (as he expresses it) in helping her to bring to a successful issue the pet scheme of her life." But a gladder time is yet before us—the Jubilee Opening next September, 1894, of the completed college—when it shall be lighted by the faces of happy girls, and when Mr. Carr will participate in person as well as in spirit, and nothing will be lacking to perfect our joy in the crowning work of our lives. And best of all, the years of blessed work that shall follow! Oh, I pray that our Heavenly Father may give us health and strength, and length of days, and that the fruits of our labors may be abundant; so

'That when our summons comes to join The innumerable caravan that moves To that mysterious realm where each shall take His chamber in the silent halls of death, We go, not like the quarry-slave at night, Scourged to his dungeon; but, sustained and soothed By an unfaltering trust, approach our grave Like one who wraps the drapery of his couch About him and lies down to pleasant dreams.'"

But was the work now ended? It was only about to begin; all else had been preparation. But how different to work in uncertainty, and to work in confidence!

There were the catalogues to be thought of, and notices in the papers to be judiciously given out, and furniture to be bought, and trees, and shrubbery, and pianos, and charts, and all things else needful to college life. Above all, there is the building itself to be erected.

And, of course, many who have subscribed for lots do not want to pay for them, when paytime comes due,—and are indignant at being held to their bond, and say bitter things, and spread unkind rumors. And some have to be excused from paying interest, else they will pay nothing; and some move away, one knows not whither!

"Mrs. O. A. Carr is in the city," says a daily paper. "Carr-Burdette Christian College at Sherman will open in September. The college has been donated to the Christian churches in the State, but will be open to all denominations. Mr. and Mrs. Carr are doing much for the educational interests of Texas, and their philanthropic devotion to this interest sets an example which we hope will be emulated."

"The College is Built at Last."—Carr-Burdette.

Mrs. Carr clips the foregoing and sends it to the *Gospel Advocate*, hoping they will reproduce all, or a part, of the "local".

"My dear Sister," says the *Gospel Advocate*—it is in August of the cornerstone year, "it is our settled policy not to advertise one school more than another. We do not see any reason why we should advertise the Carr-Burdette College any more than the Add Rann College. There are a number of good schools controlled by the brethren, to whom we have never given free advertisement. Yours truly and fraternally—" Very fraternally, without doubt. So Mrs. Carr may be in our city as often as she pleases, and she and her husband do all they can, for a dozen colleges, but we mustn't mention the fact; such is our policy!

John A. Brooks, pastor of the Christian church at Memphis, writes to Mr. and Mrs. Carr: "I am pleased to see that you are about to open a female school in Sherman. I know your education and character are such as to commend you to the public as most competent teachers. Most heartily I wish you both a successful voyage on the sea of life."

This from Palestine, Texas, July 13th, to Mrs. Carr, is a voice from the camp of misconception: "I have read your letter with much interest. I accord to you the purest and best motives in your work, and believe you to be a noble woman. But it is reported, on good authority, that you and Brother Carr are not in sympathy with our work in Texas, the United States and abroad. I shall not enter the lists against you and your work, however—I shall attend to my own business, which will keep me busy enough * * * Fraternally yours—"

That word "Fraternally," which we find closing so many bitter and discourteous letters, seems to be used as a parting blow. They all write "Fraternally"—that stereotyped phrase of a stereotyped brotherhood! But the present biographer feels indeed fraternally toward these indignant and suspicious and mistaken letter-writers, and shall prove it by reproducing none of their letters.

For these writers who were so warmly "fraternal" did not understand, and seemingly would not understand, that the Carrs had deeded the college and the extensive grounds to the Church; that the Carrs furnished the buildings throughout, at their own expense, to present them to the Church fully and beautifully equipped; that the Carrs had insured, and would keep insured, the buildings, not for themselves, but for the Church; that they did not, and never would, receive a penny of money-contributions from anyone; and that this Carr-Burdette College, this monument to Mrs. Carr, was given to the Church as the most priceless gift in her possession, to the cause dearest to her heart.

In the meantime, college-work did not wholly absorb the life of this busy woman. Here comes a letter from the Christian Woman's Board of Missions in Missouri; the state-secretary, at this time, is Mrs. Elizabeth Bantz. Mrs. Bantz writes:

"This year marks the twenty-fifth year of the C. W. B. M. in Missouri— 1894. My board has authorized me to issue an historical sketch of the work. We are publishing the faces of many of those who served us officially. We want your picture for this book. Please, my dear sister, send me a half-tone cut, as soon as possible."

Mrs. A. B. Jones of Liberty, Mo., seconds the request: "I have been asked to write an historical sketch of our C. W. B. M. for a book which our state secretary is preparing for our 25th anniversary. We want our state officers from the time of our organization. Will you kindly send a photo, or cut, to Mrs. Bantz at St. Louis? I would be so glad to have a picture of yourself and Brother Carr. Both of you are lovingly remembered by us."

Now that the college is built at last, and Mr. and Mrs. Carr have assumed its management, the story of their lives enters the peaceful channel of daily service together.

A few events of distinction stand out from among the minor affairs of fourteen years. The incessant work in the school room, the canvassing tours during vacations,—involving lectures with the stereopticon,—the correspondence with new pupils, old pupils and prospective pupils, the worrying over misunderstandings and misrepresentations; the struggle against prejudice, and jealousy; the sweet companionship with each other, and with congenial friends—all this is the story of daily living, that does not belong to the world of books.

Let the reader imagine the interlinked events of these fourteen years—the fourteen years that followed the accomplishment of Mrs. Carr's life-work. The honors bestowed upon her and her girls at the Confederate Reunion at New Orleans, and at the World's Fair at St. Louis, may be found fully described in the great daily papers of those days. The mass of printed programs that lie before me tell of brilliant success before the footlights—and hint at long hours of nerve-racking rehearsals. And here are confessions of school-girls who have done wrong, and who ask to be forgiven; and other letters which wound cruelly and do not ask for pardon. But shall we not forgive all? And how can we forgive, if we do not forget?

Upon my table lies documents from disobedient pupils of Carr-Burdette College, ungrateful pupils, narrow-minded pupils, and parents naturally championing the cause of their daughters—in which, all these stand self-accused. Here is one who has discovered how unjust were charges she had made against the Carrs—but not until she had spread those reports to willing ears. And here is one who asks with tears that she may be forgiven; but who laments that the harm she has done can never be overcome.

But what of it all, now! I should not mention these things if it were not for this: that the evil reports live in some minds and, no doubt, are handed down to strangers. Here are the refutations to several such reports, but we push them aside. Can falsehood wound beyond the grave?

Nor would we expose anyone to shame by bringing her name upon the printed page, with quotations of her own rash words. There is no punishment for a malicious nature so terrible as the vengeance of its own malice which reacts upon itself, dwarfing, embittering, deadening the higher capabilities of the soul that harbors it. He who took the snake to his warm hearth to nourish it to life, is not he who suffers from the ingratitude of a friend, but rather he who admits hate to warm it in his own bosom; for it wounds him, first of all.

Fourteen years of labor in the work Mrs. Carr loved best, amid surroundings best adapted to call forth one's greatest capabilities, and then—the last journey. The school year of 1907-8 had opened prosperously. September passed, and in the warmth of its haze, and in the tender blue of its Texan sky, there was no hint that its sister-month would bring the chill of death.

It was on the thirty-first of October that there came the summons of which she had spoken in her dedicatory speech. Not, indeed, as a quarry slave, scourged to his dungeon, did she go to meet that call, but rather as one who had followed her Lord across the seas, who had dwelt with him in many lands, and who was now to abide with Him forever.

He who was left behind, dwells in the lofty halls her wisdom and her love fashioned out of brick and stone. The great work of her life is continued by President O. A. Carr, and when one visits that "College Beautiful," that "College Home," tapestries and statuary, pictures and mosaics, engravings and flowers—all seem instinct with the presence of Mrs. Carr.

One passes through spacious reception-rooms and ample halls, into parlors of refined and exquisite workmanship. Yonder is the winding stairway, with its "Cosy Nook" behind the ferns. Here is the library with its cheerful hearth. Nothing is to be seen to suggest Latin and Geometry! It is, first of all, a home for young ladies.

But when we are shown the mystic way that leads to schoolrooms, we find them stript, as it were, for service. Here is little or no adornment. They are placed before us in stern reality—desk and blackboard and floor—with no pretense that knowledge walks on velvet carpets. In this wing, we find ourselves indeed in a school; and we feel instinctively that if we do not immediately fall to, at some difficult textbook, we have no business here, and should be sent home to our parents.

And that is just what Mrs. Carr would have done for us. Education had always for her, meant something serious, something life-long, something to become an integral part of one's character. First, Carr-Burdette College is to be a *home* in which young ladies are to be taught conduct and hygiene; but it is a *College* Home, where study is not play, any more than play is study. We cannot determine where we feel Mrs. Carr's influence stronger—whether in these unadorned schoolrooms, or in the luxurious parlors. Taken together, they typify the extremes of her character. She sought to build in every soul that came under her moulding touch, the firm foundation of eternal truth; and upon this foundation to erect a structure traced with all the beauty of eternal love.

"He Who was Left Behind."
THE END

APPENDIX.

By O. A. Carr.

(Page 31.)

Our mother made our clothes from the same piece, which, for many years, was her own weaving; and our resemblance was such in childhood that many thought we were twins. For sixteen years we were together day and night—in the field, in the school-room, in the home. "Bud and Ol.," our familiar names, were pronounced together, and the presence of one suggested the other. Our separation came when I said good-by to go to Kentucky University, and then to the other side of the earth. I can even now recall my feelings when I would go into Fitzroy Gardens, Melbourne, Australia, where, alone, I would read Owen's letters over and over. Though himself not a preacher, he came as near as any one I ever knew to an identification of his life with the lives of those who preach the word.

After my return from Australia it was our happiness to go together to a church composed of many whom I baptized when I began preaching forty-five years ago, some of them our relatives. The building was within a mile of where we were born, and near the site of the first school-house we ever entered. There were the boys and girls with whom we played in childhood, heads of families now. Such an audience was an inspiration to me, and especially the presence of "Bud." I ever felt that I could preach better when he was hearing. We went over the familiar roads planning a meeting to be held when the weather would permit, and I thought this happiness would be mine, but alas! there came the telegram: "Bud is very sick, come at once." We all came to him, except one brother who was far away. There were the chairs my mother used, my father's desk, the little chair in which I sat in earliest childhood, and the pictures on the wall of those whom my brother loved. There, amid all to remind me of early days, I took my seat beside him with the sad duty on me to report to the physician his pulse and fever day and night. What was revealed by his tearful eyes fixed upon us can never be put in a book; but when the physician told him he must die, he simply said "I am ready."

With the exception of a short sojourn in Missouri and Illinois Owen spent his life in Kentucky, at May's Lick, also at Lexington, Maysville and Mt. Carmel. The call for a young man who neither blasphemed nor drank secured for him his first business engagement at Lexington. He was engaged in Maysville many years, and he spent his earnings in helping our afflicted parents; and from the needy he never turned away. After the death of father and mother, Owen made his home with his sister, Mary E. Goddard, near Mt. Carmel, whence he was called to go up higher, Thursday, January 14, 1902.

Owen Carr was a Christian. His life was very quiet, but useful. His faith was simple, his convictions were strong and he was true to them. To maintain what he held to be truth I believe he would have laid down his life. Yes, he did this in effect, toiling for the good of others, bearing heavy burdens of suffering, fulfilling his mission to the family, in the community, in the church. How can I speak his praise? Does he know, now, how we all loved him? No words could ever tell it.

A companion wrote: "Though our association was not long at any one time, yet he was so transparent and companionable that in a short time I knew Owen Carr well. He was one of the few men in the world that I really loved ardently; and I have his obituary on the 'Treasure page' of my little scrap book. He was the divinest and sweetest impersonation of unostentatious unselfishness and of transparent honesty and integrity that I ever knew among men.

J. H. M."

IN MEMORY OF THE NOBLE.
(Page 46.)

"Not of the blood," though they were Englishmen: "nor of the will of the flesh nor of the will of man", and yet the Myalls, Eneas, Jonas, George and Edward, stand in memory as NOBLE MEN. In the days of their activity, their motto seemed to be: "We will do more than any others". Of these four men two—Jonas at May's Lick, and Edward, at Maysville, Kentucky—still live, and they are my witnesses. Eneas and Jonas Myall were blacksmiths; and they shod one hundred mules in a day, at a time when mules were driven overland to market! Energy, perseverance, generosity characterized these men—each in his own way.—Remembrance of them has been with me and has been presented to the young men in many lands and on both sides of the earth.

Of Eneas Myall Longfellow's words in "THE VILLAGE BLACKSMITH" are true in almost every line.

If money was to be raised for benevolent purposes Eneas Myall was the one to secure it; for he headed the list with a liberal offering, and while others did the talking, he did the work. He was more eloquent in deed than they were in speech: hence May's Lick church was in the lead of all churches in that part of the country in expenditures at home and abroad.

As a deacon in the church he was well nigh perfection. I have never seen a better.

His constancy made him great in usefulness. For more than sixty years he led the songs in the May's Lick church. For a period of twenty years he was never known to be absent from the meeting on Lord's day morning and night and the Wednesday night prayer meeting except on one occasion, when he went to Paris to see his sick brother. His best singing was done, as it seems, on occasions when the boy, his protege, was in the pulpit. Such singing is seldom heard now-a-days as was heard when these men, Ed., George, Jonas and Eneas Myall sang together with Eneas to lead. There was only one occasion, as I remember, when Eneas Myall could not sing, and that was the morning when my father came forward to confess his faith in Jesus. He wept for joy; but could not talk—could not sing. The circumstances seemed to me to magnify his sincerity; for it was just at the close of the war. Eneas Myall was of strong prejudice, and he was opposed to my father politically, but the welcome he extended seemed to say: we differ out yonder in the world where political troubles are, and war rages; but here, in the church, there is peace, and we have fellowship. When I took my father down into the water to bury him with Christ in baptism, Eneas Myall had recovered himself so as to sing:

"How happy are they, who their Savior obey."

It is not strange that a man possessed of such firmness, such perseverance and such energy should become wealthy. His earnings increased: He sowed with an unsparing hand, and he reaped bountifully. Wealth did not make him proud nor dry up the fountain of his generosity. He seemed never so happy as when he was dividing what he possessed with his friends. When he and his good wife, "aunt Sallie" would spread the banquet, and he would gather all the preachers he could find and those who loved such company to his house, and around the table where he presided, what a feast for body and soul was there! What preacher who has ever been at May's Lick does not remember Eneas Myall and his family? He has gone; and shall we ever see his like again? Before him across the silent river had passed his faithful wife and the elders of the May's Lick church, as nearly models, as mortals could be expected to be, of what the Scriptures say of bishops, elders, pastors. What a church that was! over which Aaron Mitchell, Waller Small and Benjamin James presided, and taught by precept and example and led and protected, in those days when Walter Scott did the preaching and Eneas Myall led in song!

MY SHEEP.

(Page 272.)

"A sheep can never become a goat!" True of the woolly quadruped but this fact is no reply to my sermon; for the Savior was not talking about animals. He meant people when he said "My sheep hear my voice and follow me". That is what sheep (animals) do; hence people who hear his voice and follow him he calls his sheep; and says "they shall never perish". Who? His sheep; that is, people who hear his voice and follow him. If they should cease to hear his voice and follow they would cease to be his sheep and the Savior did not say of such, "they shall never perish."

But were they his sheep before they heard his voice.

They might have been called "sheep" on account of some other resemblance, such as proneness to wander away, need of guidance, of protection; but for these reasons it would not be true of them that "they shall never perish". It is certain that they would perish; hence the Great Good Shepherd came and called them home, saved and protected them.

If you say they were his sheep because he died for them—"laid down his life for the sheep", I answer: He called them his sheep before he laid down his life for them; and when he died it was not for them alone but "he died for all".

The truth is that the characteristic of sheep, to hear and follow, is possessed by all mankind; and whose sheep they are depends upon whose voice they hear and whom they follow. They are not the Savior's sheep unless they hear HIS voice and follow HIM. When persons do turn away from other voices and give heed to HIS they become HIS sheep. Would you say, this is not true, and give as a reason, "a GOAT can never become a SHEEP?" As well say this as to say "a sheep can never become a goat" as a proof that a believer may not, can not, cease to be a believer.

The one expression is fate fixed as fatally as is the other; and neither of them contains any Scripture idea.

The TRIAL was unique. The purpose was to determine whether I should be permitted to use their baptistry; and this depended on whether I was sound on what they called "the design of the ordinance." There were the officers of the Baptist Church to hear and a lawyer to ask questions. He put them in such a way that each question could be answered by simply quoting the Scripture; and that was happy; it was right, too, whether he intended it or not: "What do you believe baptism is for—what purpose has it?" Answer. "Repent and be baptized—in the name of Jesus the Christ FOR the remission of sins, and you shall receive the gift of the Holy Spirit." Acts 2:38.

"Do you regard it as a saving ordinance?" Answer—"He that believeth and is baptized shall be saved." Mark 16:15-16.

"Yes, we believe that: of course, we believe the Scriptures, but what do YOU THINK? Do you think a person cannot be saved without baptism?" Answer—"I think just what the Savior says: 'He that believeth and is baptized shall be saved.' It is not my privilege to THINK anything except what the Savior said, and what his Apostles preached and practiced. Aside from this I have no ability to think; for I have nothing to think about." "Well, our Savior says: 'he that believeth not shall be damned' and he does not say he that believeth not and is not baptized shall be damned." "Does not this show that baptism is not necessary to salvation, that it is not a saving ordinance?" Answer—"Baptism is not named in that clause, hence, we cannot think what that clause says and have baptism in mind at all; since it is not there. The way to be saved, Jesus says, is: 'he that believeth and is baptized shall be saved;' but the way to be damned, he says, is, 'he that believeth not shall be damned.' I think just what the Savior says on the subject of DAMNATION; and I think just what he says on the subject of SALVATION."

Then Brother Jones, a Baptist, addressed the meeting in substance thus: "Brethren, I have heard every sermon our young brother has preached in Hobart, and I have found no fault with it. He says just what the Scriptures say, and surely you cannot refuse that. You heard the sermon on, 'What must I do to be saved'"? Then Brother Jones gave an outline of that sermon—the first I had ever heard that I understood—heard it from W. T. Moore at May's Lick, Ky., and from him I learned how to preach it. Thereupon a good man of the company of Baptists arose and said: "I would rather give up my life than countenance FREE-GRACE preaching." I did not want him to give up his life, and so the interview ended with my resolution not to use the baptistry; I would use the public baths instead.

MRS. CARR AND A LITTLE BOY—THIRTY-FIVE YEARS AGO.

(Page 198.)

A letter to be read between the lines. "Melbourne, Australia, September 5, 1909."

"Dear Brother Carr:

"Father wishes me to express to you how very sorry he was to hear of Mrs. Carr's death, and how deeply he was moved by the touching references to and description of her beautiful life and character. She, indeed, was a wonderful woman, and must be sorely missed by many. It must be a terrible blank in your home and we deeply feel for you. Father felt it very much and very often spoke of her. Indeed, I felt it too. My mind goes back to my school days when my sister, Eliza (now gone many years) and I attended Mrs. Carr's school in Melbourne. I was then but a little fellow—about eleven years of age—(I am now forty-five and have three children.) It was a school for young ladies, but four of us boys were allowed to go—George Thomson, Willie Robinson, Willie Church and myself—and many a heart ache, I think, we boys gave Mrs. Carr. I can remember that Mrs. Carr put me in a room by myself for fighting Willie Church. I was in terrible disgrace that day; and I remember you came into the room and asked me what I had been doing. I told you I had been fighting Willie Church; for which you gave me to understand how naughty it was to fight. Then, I think, you were sorry for me, and said: 'Never mind Nat., we will have some fun,' which we did; and in the midst of it all Mrs. Carr came in and we both got in for it. The poor dear lady was doing what she thought best for me, and instead of punishment I was having a good time, with you. However, she was always very, very kind. I do not know that during my young life anyone so impressed me as the dear soul that has gone from us all; and I see by the book you sent us that I am not alone in this respect.

"The Church at Lygon Street is still to the fore. What delight it would give us all in Melbourne if you could manage to pay us a visit! Would it be possible for you to do so? You know the distance now is not so great as when you were here. The trip would do you good; and you could stay at my house (and we would have some fun.) The fine, grand steamers now running out to Australia should tempt you, and what a pleasure it would give us all to know that you were coming—won't you come?

NAT. HADDOW."

"AVOID ALL OFFENSE."
(Page 186.)

The admonition, so impressive then, and needed always, caused the revision of many a manuscript from that time on. "That which offends will never convince." But then, when one's position is assailed, the very assault is considered an offense: such is human nature. Few are sufficiently civilized to discuss religious differences and at the same time "avoid all offense;" for each one holds his religious position as sacred, whereas, it is sacred only when it is true, when it is divine.

The Rev. James Ballantyne, a prominent preacher in Melbourne, had issued a tract. It was no offense for him so to do: it was right—even noble from to correct them; and you will be grateful after awhile for having given heed to many things that you do not like now. You will say in your hearts: 'I see now that Mrs. Carr was right, and I am glad she said[11] NO to many of my wishes and warned me against so many little things that tempted me.' I would deny you nothing you want except those things that I think will injure you. I am sleepless at night, thinking of you, planning for your good, how I can best discharge the weighty responsibility that is on me."

She was happiest when she knew she was pleasing us, would join in our merry-making, and laugh aloud at our pranks. To reward us was her delight. What happy talks she made when she bestowed medals and honors! Talks, sparkling with wit and glowing with love and enthusiasm, on that last night of the session before we all went home. She is on the rostrum, the medals in their cases are on the stand; she takes them up, displays them to the audience, one by one, and talks about each, its meaning, what it is for, talks to the audience about the girl who is to receive it and who could ever equal her grace of diction and whole-souled sympathy? How she kept the audience in suspense, in excitement; how she amused all by her wit, and then, with tearful joy, pinned the medal on the girl whom she called to the rostrum to receive it. Holding up the house-keeper's medal, she would say to the audience: "This medal I esteem the best of all; the best house-keeper is to be the most honored. To be neat, to be orderly, to show ability to keep a home, to mind the little things that make for neatness, to sweep in the corners, to be tasteful—all this is to be lovely in conduct; and, remember, that all honors of every kind bestowed by Carr-Burdette College have this meaning namely, every medal, every diploma is hedged about by conduct."

TO MATTIE'S MEMORY.

[From a letter written by O. A. Carr.]

"Carr-Burdette College, Sherman, Texas, is the monument to the memory of my dear departed wife. She gave the last thirteen years of her life to the college. I feel that she literally sacrificed her life in the accomplishment of her high purpose; for I know she toiled beyond her strength, forgetful of self. She conceived of building the college as a Home and School for young women, and of how the funds[12] were to be secured. She planned the building, which was erected under her immediate supervision, and there is not an idea in it that is not hers. She devised and toiled to within a few days of her death, and expended all earnings on the college, that she might attain her ideal.

According to her heart's desire that the college should never suspend its work, and that her purposes may be carried out as nearly as possible, I, with the assistance of able and devoted teachers, continue the struggle. I can not do the work my dear wife did; nor do I think that any one else could do what she has been doing all these years; but an honest effort will be made to accomplish her purpose—that Carr-Burdette College may continue to be her IDEAL, as it is now her MONUMENT.

Saturday, October 26, 1907, on her return from shopping with some of the students, I offered to assist Mattie with the writing. She said: "I am not able to think now; I must rest." The next day she was unable to rise. The physician pronounced the trouble lagrippe, and he assured me, even at noon, Thursday, that she would recover. Alas! at 7:30 p. m. the same day, death came. There was no symptom of suffering. She seemed to be sleeping.

The loving hands of students and teachers and kind friends arranged all for the funeral—the first public assembly held in the college over which she did not preside and direct in detail. Her lifeless body lay in her own beautiful college parlor, where the funeral was conducted by Brother J. H. Fuller and Brother A. O. Riall assisted by Brother R. D. Smith, and Dr. Clyce, President of Austin College. Mattie told me years ago that she wished Brother Graham, with whom she was associated at Hamilton College, and Brother McGarvey, to preach her funeral; but Brother Graham had gone where there are no funerals, and Brother McGarvey could not be here. The students in a line of march descended the stairway, preceded by a young girl in white, who bore their beautiful floral offering. They stood on either side of the casket and sang (1) "Some Day", (2) "Going Home", (3) "My Savior First of All", (4) "I Am Only Waiting Here", (5) "Sweet By and By."

One who knew Mattie well wrote me years ago, saying, "I know of no one who can show a more valid claim than[13] yourself to have a living commentary on the last chapter of Proverbs". That chapter was read from the twelfth verse to the conclusion, by Brother Smith, and Brother Fuller chose as the text for his beautiful, hopeful discourse, "The gift of God is eternal life, through our Lord Jesus the Christ".

For nearly forty years Mattie and I have toiled together. She took responsibility, financial and domestic from me, and bore it herself. I trusted to her judgment, and felt that all was well when she approved. And now, at night, I sit alone where we used to sit together. I look around to see her, but see only her empty chair."

Mattie's Grave.

FOOTNOTES:

[1] That "drill in Rhetoric, in English pure and undefiled" when she analyzed and parsed every sentence of the Manuscript read to the class Mrs. Carr often spoke of, and of John Smith who, in his last days, abode at Daughters' College to furnish material for his biography. She was always proud of the fact that John Augustus Williams taught her English.

[2] See appendix.

[3] See appendix.

[4] "These boys," Garrett S. Wall (now Judge Wall, of Maysville, Ky.), Jacob Riley, Anthony Latham and O. A. Carr, all from May's Lick, had lively discussion on the way. "Which church is right?" was the awkward way the talk went on: Garrett explained Jacob's Theological puzzles: Oliver presented the points in that first sermon he ever heard that he understood, and to him the Scripture statements were plain: Anthony, true son of "Calvin", dwelt on the "decrees". These boys were going to be taught, and Anthony seemed willing that the "Spirit should guide him into all truth" provided it did not make a Campbellite of him; for he knew that was wrong religion. The count stood—three against one, and in boy fashion it was claimed that if "what is to be will be" Anthony ought to be satisfied.

O. A. C.

[5] When first I saw the following lines, I called Mattie to hear me read them to her. I thought of her "CHILDREN," the girls she had taught. We were seated in her private parlor; and her attention was fixed from the first stanza: "Shedding sunshine of love on my face." The reading ended, she threw herself on the bed and wept aloud. Her feelings, when fully aroused, were paroxysms of joy or grief; and now the two alternated as memory of her first school at Lancaster, and of the girls on the other side of the earth,

at Melbourne, mingled with all her life of love for "THE CHILDREN." She made notes when she read Milton, Spencer, Mrs. Browning, Longfellow, Tennison, but this little poem was literally bathed in her tears.

O. A. C.

When the lessons and tasks are all ended And the school for the day is dismissed, And the little ones gather around me, To bid me good night and be kissed; Oh, the little white arms that encircle My neck in a tender embrace! On, the smiles that are halos of heaven Shedding sunshine of love on my face!

And when they are gone I sit dreaming Of my childhood—too lovely to last; Of love that my heart will remember When it wakes to the pulse of the past, Ere the world and its wickedness made me, A partner of sorrow and of sin When the glory of God was about me, And the glory of gladness within.

Oh, my heart grows weak as a woman's And the fountains of feeling will flow, When I think of the paths steep and stony, Where the feet of the dear ones must go; Of the mountains of sin hanging o'er them, Of the tempest of fate blowing wild; Oh, there's nothing on earth half so holy As the innocent heart of a child.

They are idols of hearts and of households, They are angels of God in disguise; His sunlight still sleeps in their tresses, His glory still beams in their eyes; Oh, those truants from home and from heaven, They have made me more manly and mild— And I know how Jesus could liken The kingdom of God to a child.

I ask not a life for the dear ones, All radiant, as others have done; But that life may have just enough shadow To temper the glare of the sun; I would pray God to guard them from evil, But my prayer would bound back to myself. Ah! a seraph may pray for a sinner, But a sinner must pray for himself.

The twig is so easily bended I have banished the rule and the rod; I have taught them the goodness of knowledge They have taught me the goodness of God: My heart is a dungeon of darkness, Where I shut them for breaking a rule; My frown is sufficient correction; My love is the law of the school.

I shall leave the old home in the Autumn, To traverse its threshold no more; Ah! how shall I sigh for the dear ones, That met me each morn at the door; I shall miss the goodnights and the kisses. And the gush of their innocent glee, The group on the green and the flowers That are brought every morning to me.

I shall miss them at morn and at eve, The song in the school and the street; I shall miss the low hum of their voices, And the tramp of their delicate feet— When the lessons and tasks are all ended, And death says: "The school is dismissed" May the little ones gather around me To bid me good night and be kissed.

[6] I must have preached "big sermons" in these days; for Brother Benjamin Coleman saw to it that I received $25.00 each time I went to Macedonia. No thanks to him and the church, their contribution was to help me through College.

O. A. C.

[7] Just then, it seemed that every one on the ship "cared": That drunken, card-playing priest proposed to say "mass for the poor boy's soul"; but Captain Myles said: "None of your foolishness here". I could not escape the thought that he would have "read mass", if it had been in the Prayer-book, whether foolishness or not; for the ship's Captain is ordained to read the church service, or to appoint some one to read it. That desire to do something, springing from a feeling of helplessness and grief seems natural to mortals and cries out most pitilessly when faith is absent. I doubt not it was as sincere as any prayer ever uttered when Luther wanted to "say mass for the soul" of his mother. I had seen the poor boy cuffed about deck, driven to his hard task, beaten with a broom, and had remonstrated in vain. Between the priest with his rollicking ditties, gambling and drunkenness and the boy there was a great gulf fixed on that ship. "No association with second-class passengers" was the edict; and was not the priest first-class? and the boy, what was he? He had hidden himself among the boxes in the ship's hold at Liverpool to be taken any where, perhaps, out of the world, and so it was. That boy, that scene, what led to it and what followed, Mrs. Carr never forgot—"A neglected one, a prodigal, it may have been, but still a human; he needed something other than sacerdotal robes to show him that you are the servants of the Most High." Yes, she "cared" and so do I, even to this day.

O. A. C.

[8] Martin Zelius, happy man! About the time Eneas Myall was seeking work and found it at May's Lick, Kentucky, Martin Zelius stood in the streets of Melbourne, wondering to what he should turn his hand. He turned his eye and saw across the street a flaming placard: "Evangelist from

America, H. S. Earl, will preach in St. George's Hall," etc. "No where to go," he thought to himself, "I will go hear that man." He was charmed with what he heard, and soon became obedient to the faith. He entered upon a business life in which his success was marvelous: everything he touched seemed to turn to gold. Whole-souled, enthusiastic, he stood before the church and asked the privilege of sending from his own earnings the money to pay the expenses of the evangelists from America. One night, when he had come from church he learned that a brother was aggrieved at him: he hired a "cab", drove across the city to that Brother's home, called him from his bed out to talk with him alone, and broached the matter in such a way that the Brother said: "O, it was a trifle, I should not have mentioned; I am ashamed of myself because I did. Is it possible that you have come all this distance to talk about that?" "Why, yes," said Martin Zelius, "our Savior said, 'if thou bring thy gift to the altar and there remember that thy Brother hath aught against thee, leave there thy gift; go be reconciled to thy Brother, and then come and offer thy gift.' I could not pray to-night until I came to see you, and know what I had done to offend you." "Well, I always thought a great deal of you, but more now than ever." Forgiven and happy he goes home, at peace with all the world.

His wife, fit companion for such a man, of meek and quiet spirit, entered into fullest sympathy with Mrs. Carr, understood her, knew her and loved her. She entreated Mrs. Carr to visit her daughter in California and arrangements were made to do so, to start in two weeks (in November, 1907); but in five days she had gone to the eternal home.

O. A. C.

[9] See appendix.

[10] Alexander T. Magarey and Vaney J. Magarey were sons of Thomas Magarey, M. P., of South Australia. They made their home with us while attending the University of Melbourne. Two more congenial spirits I never met; nor better students. Then, too, they were Christians from very love of the Savior, and delighted in the truths of the Gospel. They were very intelligent in the Scriptures. After my return from Australia Alex. visited me in Kentucky. It was my delight to take him among my kindred; for he and his brother seemed to me like one of my own family, and to present him to the Brethren as a specimen of what sort could be found in Australia. The memory of him, his father, brother and the Magarey family is very precious. Alex. would have me take him to see the mother of Brother Be. sley who went to Australia, came home an invalid and died of consumption: he must weep with that mother and see the grave of that young man: he must see those—teachers and preachers—of whom he had read; he wanted to take them all by the hand, and such a hand grasp as he

gave was remembered. We were sitting together in the Main Street Church in Louisville during the State Meeting in 1880, when T. P. Haley asked if any knew of rich men's sons who are preachers of the Gospel. Only two were known—T. M. Arnold of Covington, Kentucky, and Alex. Magarey. On one occasion his horse, which no one drove but him, took us in a buggy from his father's home to a church near Adelaide where Alex. preached. The people there were poor, and he would minister to them— "preach the gospel to the poor". He taught them to give. A woman who had no money had gathered the wild flowers—her offering—better than gold to him. He took them home and pressed them, possibly had them as long as he lived.

The name "Magarey" always honored in the Campbell Home, is it strange that when Alex. came to the United States the next time it was for the express purpose of bearing to his Australian home a bride—niece of Alexander Campbell?

These young men (A. T. and S. J. Magarey) were my ideals of what young Christians ought to be and do: they were so congenial to me—my companions even playmates, sympathized with me so fully, helped me in my work, that when their earthly life ended it seemed that a part of my own life had gone with them.

O. A. C.

[11] Philip Santo—a prince among men—a generous, sympathetic soul "Come to see us", was his message to me, "Jeff." (T. J. Gore) "wants to see you—I will take no excuse". Of course, I had to go. When we had enjoyed his home for a while he sent "Jeff." and me to the seaside—to Port Elliot, the farthest limit of land toward the South. Up on the immense cliff at the hotel we feasted the body and rested, while we looked far out over the Southern ocean toward the South Pole. At night the tide would lash the waves up in sprays to the very top of this cliff: in the afternoon we strolled the beach, gathering shells, and leaving our little (?) footprints to be washed away at even. Every year T. J. Gore visits Port Elliot with his family for a season; and a picture of it hangs on the wall at Carr-Burdette College.

Philip Santo, happy man, was always planning, preparing something for the good of the Church. He would sit in his Library at night and read until absorbed in some happy thought he would say: "Jeff., what does this Scripture mean?" and then he would be silent until next Lord's day morning when "Jeff." would be delighted with the lesson, and the exhortation Philip Santo would give at the church. Those who heard him speak in the House of Parliament were glad to hear him in the Church; for in the honesty of his soul he ministered in each place. When I bade him good-by he insisted that I take fifty dollars; for, said he, "I do not permit the preachers to come to see me at their own expense".

He visited us in Hobart City, Tasmania. He entered the store of his old time friend, with a cordial greeting. "How do you prosper"? The friend, a hypercalvinist, he who heard O. A. Carr gladly, read Milligan's Scheme of redemption and pronounced it the best book, next to his Bible, he had ever seen, "but who drew back when he heard a sermon on 'My Sheep'—"Very well indeed," he said, "until the preacher (Carr) began to preach Campbellism". "What is that you said he preached", said Santo. "What is Campbellism?" "Oh, I don't know; but that is what they said he preached". Then he enveloped himself in a mist of dreary theology, and proceeded into the darkness of the decrees of foreknowledge and "fixed the fate" of all, as he thought. Whereupon Santo remarked: "Do you think that any man of ordinary sense can understand what you have been saying?" Our friend was a good man, and he could bear it, when Philip Santo said it; but he went into the other room to cool off; but soon returned to indulge in reminiscences. He read in a few days the announcement that "The Hon. Philip Santo, from Adelaide, would preach the next Lord's day in O. A. Carr's place". Then it was revealed that he had given himself away together with his cause; but he continued to maintain stoutly that a "sheep could never become a goat". On leaving us he said: "I want to give you this: you may need some pocket change"—and placed $50.00 in my hand. Thus he moved around among the churches—distributing to the necessity of saints like he was "given to hospitality" in his home. His heart's desire was to visit his brethren in America. His active business life forbade a lingering while here. He telegraphed to me to meet him in St. Louis. Feeling that we must have him in our home at Columbia, my answer was to tell him how he could come, and be sure to come; but he must set sail from California at a fixed date and could not. We missed the joy of his presence. How I would love now to have the opportunity to do his bidding; but he has gone from the earthly life.

O. A. C.

[12] By association with him and his family in his own home I learned to love Thomas Magarey, and henceforth to think of him very much as his sons thought, and to feel that he was a father to us all to correct and to help us. He could not offend me if he would by any strange position he might take, or any thing he might say; nor would he intentionally do so. He was born to be heard, to say what should be in the affairs of men. Right or wrong in what he claimed as truth, he was a genuine man.

O. A. C.

[13] See appendix.

[14] See appendix, "My Sheep."

[15] See appendix.

[16] A letter from Mrs. Carr to one of her pupils she taught in Melbourne. The letter was discovered recently with "the little wild flower gathered on the plains of Sharon" pinned to it: the letter had never been mailed: written thirty-three years ago, it shows how Mrs. Carr talked to her girls. Possibly she wondered why "Maria" did not answer her letter, and here is the letter found in a pigeon hole at the College. Mr. Carr sends it on to Maria with apology.

"Fulton, Mo., U.S.A., January 8th, 1877"

"My Dear Maria:

I received a letter from Maggie a few days since in which she stated that you had written to me, but receiving no answer, feel discouraged to write again. Be assured your letter never reached me, or it would have been answered. I often think of my dear girls in Australia, and especially of you and Maggie, because I loved you best of all my pupils in Melbourne; for my association with you was longest and most intimate, and because your mothers were friends that never failed me amid the little annoyances and trials that life is so surely heir to. I cannot tell you how much I long to see you all once more. I cannot imagine how you think for a moment that I forget you. I wrote you from Jerusalem. I wrote to you from Rome, and I sent you a French Journal from Paris. I would love to visit you in your happy home that Maggie so graphically described and to see that beautiful boy upon whom she lavished so many praises. Vaney a husband and father, and my little Maria a wife and mother! Well, I am truly glad it is so, and pray that your lives may be happy and useful. After all, Maria, the sweetest thing in life is the privilege of BEING USEFUL—the privilege of WORK. What greater blessing, beyond redemption, can a woman ask than the privilege of serving her husband and her generation. We are now stationed in a very pretty little city in Missouri and our work is pleasant. Mr. Carr preaches for the Church here, and I have charge of Floral Hill College. My school is prospering and I am very happy in my work. Tell Miss Ashley I wish she were here to work with me. However, we may have the happiness of working together in Australia. Every winter I pine for the hot winds—yes—THE HOT WINDS—of Australia. My health has been poor during the winters ever since our return to America. We may meet you all again. How are Brother and Sister Magarey and family? Remember us very kindly to them all, also to Brother and Sister Santo and family, especially to ETTIE. We had a short, but pleasant intercourse with Alex. (Magarey) during his visit to America. Extend our congratulations to him and his bride, and our best wishes for their happiness and usefulness." [Alex. had come to the United States to marry Miss Campbell of Bethany, Va..—niece of Alex. Campbell—O. A. C.] "The snow is falling drearily and the snow birds are hopping about cheerily, as though the snow was the greatest boon that God ever bestowed upon his creatures. It is not 'The Rainy Day,' but the spirit of Longfellow is about me. By the way, during my tour East last summer, I called upon the grand old poet, and had a happy talk with him in his own historic drawing room. As you doubtless know, the Longfellow Mansion was at one time during the Revolution the headquarters of General Washington. Longfellow is one of the few glorious poetic spirits that have withstood the corrupting influence of the world's applause. When I visited the Centennial Exposition I availed myself of the privilege of visiting many places of historic interest in the East. This is the only tour that I ever made through the Eastern States EXPRESSLY for information, and I need not tell you that I enjoyed it intensely and feel greatly benefited thereby. When I see you, you shall have all particulars. Now, Maria, you must not fail to answer without delay. [What grief it gave Mrs. Carr that she did not have a letter from Maria—because this letter was not posted!] Write me a 'chatty' letter. Tell me how you like housekeeping, if baby ever has the colic, if Vaney kisses him over a dozen times a day, etc., etc. Give my love to your mother and tell her I would love to receive one more pledge of her friendship in the form of a letter for the sake of 'Auld Lang Syne.' Or if she is the busy housewife of yore, she can press Willie into service. Remember us very kindly to our friend, the Scotchman, your father and Mr. Jacques. "I enclose a little wild flower that I gathered in the Plain of Sharon. I collected many curios in my travels and arranged them into a Museum during Christmas holidays. The first day of January it was opened with nice entertainment to my young ladies, and CHRISTENED FLORAL HILL MUSEUM. My girls acquitted themselves splendidly.

"Write soon and believe me, affectionately yours,"

"I will write to Maggie soon."

MRS. CARR."

[17] Now, 1910, he and his good wife are in a most efficient ministry in Pittsburg, Pa. O. A. C.

[18] Their names are in those "Envelopes" at the College inscribed "for my book" and Mrs. Carr intended to honor them thus; memory of them and incidents she often recalled; and she praised them always.

Milton Keynes UK
Ingram Content Group UK Ltd.
UKHW020829231024
450026UK00004B/473

9 789362 926562